MENTOR'S GUIDE **Capstone** Curriculum

Module 6

Theology and Ethics

God *the* Father

Prolegomena:

THE DOCTRINE OF GOD *and*
THE ADVANCE OF THE KINGDOM

God as the Creator:

THE PROVIDENCE OF GOD

The Triune God:

THE GREATNESS OF GOD

God as Father:

THE GOODNESS OF GOD

This curriculum is the result of thousands of hours of work by The Urban Ministry Institute (TUMI) and should not be reproduced without their express permission. TUMI supports all who wish to use these materials for the advance of God's Kingdom, and affordable licensing to reproduce them is available. Please confirm with your instructor that this book is properly licensed. For more information on TUMI and our licensing program, visit *www.tumi.org* and *www.tumi.org/license*.

Capstone Module 6: God the Father Mentor's Guide

ISBN: 978-1-62932-026-7

© 2005, 2011, 2013, 2015. The Urban Ministry Institute. All Rights Reserved.
First edition 2005, Second edition 2011, Third edition 2013, Fourth edition 2015.

Copying, redistribution and/or sale of these materials, or any unauthorized transmission, except as may be expressly permitted by the 1976 Copyright Act or in writing from the publisher is prohibited. Requests for permission should be addressed in writing to: The Urban Ministry Institute, 3701 E. 13th Street, Wichita, KS 67208.

The Urban Ministry Institute is a ministry of World Impact, Inc.

All Scripture quotations, unless otherwise noted, are from The Holy Bible, English Standard Version, copyright © 2001 by Crossway Bible, a division of Good News Publishers. Used by permission. All Rights Reserved.

Contents

Course Overview
3   About the Instructor
5   Introduction to the Module
7   Course Requirements

13   **Lesson 1**
Prolegomena: The Doctrine of God and the Advance of the Kingdom

43   **Lesson 2**
God as the Creator: The Providence of God

73   **Lesson 3**
The Triune God: The Greatness of God

109   **Lesson 4**
God as Father: The Goodness of God

145   Appendices

257   **Mentoring the Capstone Curriculum**

265   Lesson 1 Mentor's Notes
273   Lesson 2 Mentor's Notes
281   Lesson 3 Mentor's Notes
289   Lesson 4 Mentor's Notes

About the Instructor

Rev. Dr. Don L. Davis is the Executive Director of The Urban Ministry Institute and a Senior Vice President of World Impact. He attended Wheaton College and Wheaton Graduate School, and graduated summa cum laude in both his B.A. (1988) and M.A. (1989) degrees, in Biblical Studies and Systematic Theology, respectively. He earned his Ph.D. in Religion (Theology and Ethics) from the University of Iowa School of Religion.

As the Institute's Executive Director and World Impact's Senior Vice President, he oversees the training of urban missionaries, church planters, and city pastors, and facilitates training opportunities for urban Christian workers in evangelism, church growth, and pioneer missions. He also leads the Institute's extensive distance learning programs and facilitates leadership development efforts for organizations and denominations like Prison Fellowship, the Evangelical Free Church of America, and the Church of God in Christ.

A recipient of numerous teaching and academic awards, Dr. Davis has served as professor and faculty at a number of fine academic institutions, having lectured and taught courses in religion, theology, philosophy, and biblical studies at schools such as Wheaton College, St. Ambrose University, the Houston Graduate School of Theology, the University of Iowa School of Religion, the Robert E. Webber Institute of Worship Studies. He has authored a number of books, curricula, and study materials to equip urban leaders, including *The Capstone Curriculum*, TUMI's premiere sixteen-module distance education seminary instruction, *Sacred Roots: A Primer on Retrieving the Great Tradition*, which focuses on how urban churches can be renewed through a rediscovery of the historic orthodox faith, and *Black and Human: Rediscovering King as a Resource for Black Theology and Ethics*. Dr. Davis has participated in academic lectureships such as the Staley Lecture series, renewal conferences like the Promise Keepers rallies, and theological consortiums like the University of Virginia Lived Theology Project Series. He received the Distinguished Alumni Fellow Award from the University of Iowa College of Liberal Arts and Sciences in 2009. Dr. Davis is also a member of the Society of Biblical Literature, and the American Academy of Religion.

Introduction to the Module

Greetings, dearest friends, in the strong name of Jesus Christ!

The study of the person of our God, the Father Almighty, is one of the most important and richest of all studies in the Word of God. It affects every part of our discipleship, worship, and ministry; truly, as our Lord Jesus said, "And this is eternal life, that they know you the only true God, and Jesus Christ whom you have sent," (John 17.3).

In our first lesson, *Prolegomena: The Doctrine of God and the Advance of the Kingdom,* we will briefly explore the first things, the prolegomena, which undergirds a study of theology, looking at the necessity of God revealing himself to us. We will study the concepts of *general and special revelation*, and carefully explore the importance of studying the doctrine of God in terms of God's *immanence*, i.e., his present and active involvement in creation, as well as his *transcendence*, God's infinite nature and unknowableness.

In our second lesson, *God as the Creator: The Providence of God*, we will examine God's supreme authority and providence over all creation and history. God works all things according to his will. The Father Almighty is sovereign over all, the source of all life, and the Sustainer of all through his Son, Jesus Christ. We will also explore how God's providence is expressed in his preservation and governance of all things, and see how a solid, biblical understanding of God's providence resolves major modern errors in philosophy and theology, namely, pantheism, deism, fatalism, and chance.

We take a slightly different turn in our third lesson, *The Triune God: The Greatness of God.* We will look at the biblical evidence for the Trinity, God's triune personhood. The Scriptures teach that there is only one God, and yet this same God reveals himself as God the Father, Son, and Holy Spirit. The members of the Trinity are one, diverse and equal, the one true God, Father, Son, and Holy Spirit. After examining the Trinity, we will then briefly examine the attributes of God's *greatness*: his spirituality, his life, his personality, his infinite character, and his unchanging essence.

Finally, in lesson four we turn our attention to *God as Father: The Goodness of God.* Here we will discover God's marvelous goodness demonstrated in his moral attributes of his perfect moral purity, absolute integrity, and unbounded love. And, we close our module with a look at the *goodness and severity of God*, exploring the relationship between God's goodness and severity, his love and justice.

Truly, our God the Father Almighty is the one, true, and glorious God of heaven. Knowing him better will equip us to represent him with honor as his servants. May God bless you as you explore the untold riches of Scripture regarding our great and mighty God!

- Rev. Dr. Don L. Davis

Course Requirements

Required Books and Materials

- Bible (for the purposes of this course, your Bible should be a translation [ex. NIV, NASB, RSV, KJV, NKJV, etc.], and not a paraphrase [ex. The Living Bible, The Message]).

- Each Capstone module has assigned textbooks which are read and discussed throughout the course. We encourage you to read, reflect upon, and respond to these with your professors, mentors, and fellow learners. Because of the fluid availability of the texts (e.g., books going out of print), we maintain our *official* Capstone Required Textbook list on our website. Please visit *www.tumi.org/books* to obtain the current listing of this module's texts.

- Paper and pen for taking notes and completing in-class assignments.

Suggested Readings

- Hemphill, Ken. *The Names of God*. Nashville: Broadman and Holman Publishers, 2001.

- Pink, A. W. *The Attributes of God*. Grand Rapids: Baker Book House, 1991.

- Stone, Nathan. *The Names of God*. Chicago: Moody Press, 1944.

Summary of Grade Categories and Weights

Attendance & Class Participation.	30%	90 pts
Quizzes	10%	30 pts
Memory Verses	15%	45 pts
Exegetical Project	15%	45 pts
Ministry Project.	10%	30 pts
Readings and Homework Assignments.	10%	30 pts
Final Exam	10%	30 pts
Total:	100%	300 pts

Course Requirements

Grade Requirements

Attendance at each class session is a course requirement. Absences will affect your grade. If an absence cannot be avoided, please let the Mentor know in advance. If you miss a class it is your responsibility to find out the assignments you missed, and to talk with the Mentor about turning in late work. Much of the learning associated with this course takes place through discussion. Therefore, your active involvement will be sought and expected in every class session.

Attendance and Class Participation

Every class will begin with a short quiz over the basic ideas from the last lesson. The best way to prepare for the quiz is to review the Student Workbook material and class notes taken during the last lesson.

Quizzes

The memorized Word is a central priority for your life and ministry as a believer and leader in the Church of Jesus Christ. There are relatively few verses, but they are significant in their content. Each class session you will be expected to recite (orally or in writing) the assigned verses to your Mentor.

Memory Verses

The Scriptures are God's potent instrument to equip the man or woman of God for every work of ministry he calls them to (2 Tim. 3.16-17). In order to complete the requirements for this course you must select a passage and do an inductive Bible study (i.e., an exegetical study) upon it. The study will have to be five pages in length (double-spaced, typed or neatly hand written) and deal with one of the various aspects of the person and work of God the Father highlighted in this course. Our desire and hope is that you will be deeply convinced of Scripture's ability to change and

Exegetical Project

Ministry Project

practically affect your life, and the lives of those to whom you minister. As you go through the course, be open to finding an extended passage (roughly 4-9 verses) on a subject you would like to study more intensely. The details of the project are covered on pages 10-11, and will be discussed in the introductory session of this course.

Our expectation is that all students will apply their learning practically in their lives and in their ministry responsibilities. The student will be responsible for developing a ministry project that combines principles learned with practical ministry. The details of this project are covered on page 12, and will be discussed in the introductory session of the course.

Class and Homework Assignments

Classwork and homework of various types may be given during class by your Mentor or be written in your Student Workbook. If you have any question about what is required by these or when they are due, please ask your Mentor.

Readings

It is important that the student read the assigned readings from the text and from the Scriptures in order to be prepared for class discussion. Please turn in the "Reading Completion Sheet" from your Student Workbook on a weekly basis. There will be an option to receive extra credit for extended readings.

Take-Home Final Exam

At the end of the course, your Mentor will give you a final exam (closed book) to be completed at home. You will be asked a question that helps you reflect on what you have learned in the course and how it affects the way you think about or practice ministry. Your Mentor will give you due dates and other information when the Final Exam is handed out.

Grading

The following grades will be given in this class at the end of the session, and placed on each student's record:

A - Superior work	D - Passing work
B - Excellent work	F - Unsatisfactory work
C - Satisfactory work	I - Incomplete

Letter grades with appropriate pluses and minuses will be given for each final grade, and grade points for your grade will be factored into your overall grade point average. Unexcused late work or failure to turn in assignments will affect your grade, so please plan ahead, and communicate conflicts with your instructor.

Exegetical Project

This assignment represents a key part of your participation in the *God the Father* module of study. In order to fulfill this requirement, you must *select a passage of Scripture*, and do *an inductive study* (*exegesis*) on the text. You may choose any one of the following Scripture texts:

- ☐ Acts 17.24-31
- ☐ Romans 9.13-18
- ☐ Psalms 103.9-18
- ☐ Psalms 104.24-30
- ☐ Isaiah 40.22-26
- ☐ Daniel 4.34-37
- ☐ Matthew 6.25-33

Purpose

The purpose of this project is to give you an opportunity to do a detailed study of a major passage on the subject of God's providence, his preservation and governance over all creation, and what this means for our lives today. Perhaps nothing is more important for a Christian leader than their ability to make plain the meaning of Scripture, and relate it to the real life concerns of people today. The aim is for you to not only make clear the meaning of the passage, but also relate the meaning of the passage directly to your own personal walk of discipleship, and to those whom God has called you to minister to in and through your church or ministry.

Outline and Composition

This is a Bible study project, and, in order to do *exegesis*, you must be committed to understand the meaning of the passage in its own setting. Once you know what it meant, you can then draw out principles that apply to all of us, and then relate those principles to life. A simple three step process can guide you in your personal study of the Bible passage:

1. What was *God saying to the people in the text's original situation*?

2. What principle(s) does *the text teach that is true for all people everywhere*, including today?

3. What is *the Holy Spirit asking me to do with this principle here, today*, in my life and ministry?

Once you have answered these questions in your personal study, you are then ready to write out your insights for your *paper assignment*.

Here is a *sample outline* for your paper:

1. List out what you believe is *the main theme or idea* of the text you selected.

2. *Summarize the meaning* of the passage (you may do this in two or three paragraphs, or, if you prefer, by writing a short verse-by-verse commentary on the passage).

3. *Outline one to three key principles or insights* this text provides on God the Father.

4. Tell how one, some, or all of the principles may relate to *one or more* of the following:

    a. Your personal spirituality and walk with Christ

    b. Your life and ministry in your local church

    c. Situations or challenges in your community and general society

As an aid or guide, please feel free to read the course texts and/or commentaries, and integrate insights from them into your work. Make sure that you give credit to whom credit is due if you borrow or build upon someone else's insights. Use in-the-text references, footnotes, or endnotes. Any way you choose to cite your references will be acceptable, as long as you 1) use only one way consistently throughout your paper, and 2) indicate where you are using someone else's ideas, and are giving them credit for it. (For more information, see *Documenting Your Work: A Guide to Help You Give Credit Where Credit Is Due* in the Appendix.)

Make certain that your exegetical project, when turned in meets the following standards:

- It is legibly written or typed.
- It is a study of one of the passages above.
- It is turned in on time (not late).
- It is 5 pages in length.
- It follows the outline given above, clearly laid out for the reader to follow.
- It shows how the passage relates to life and ministry today.

Do not let these instructions intimidate you; this is a Bible study project! All you need to show in this paper is that you *studied* the passage, *summarized* its meaning, *drew out* a few key principles from it, and *related* them to your own life and ministry.

Grading

The exegetical project is worth 45 points, and represents 15% of your overall grade, so make certain that you make your project an excellent and informative study of the Word.

Ministry Project

Christian leadership is not merely knowing what the Bible says; it involves the ability to use the Word of God in such a way that others are edified and equipped for ministry. God's Word is living and active, and penetrates to the very heart of our lives and innermost thoughts (Heb. 4.12). James the Apostle emphasizes the need to be doers of the Word of God, not hearers only, deceiving ourselves. We are exhorted to apply the Word, to obey it. Neglecting this discipline, he suggests, is analogous to a person viewing our natural face in a mirror and then forgetting who we are, and are meant to be. In every case, the doer of the Word of God will be blessed in what he or she does (James 1.22-25).

Our sincere desire is that you will apply your learning practically, correlating your learning with real experiences and needs in your personal life, and in your ministry in and through your church.

Theology Essay: Letter to a Friend. Ministering the Word often involves not merely delivering a sermon or teaching a formal Bible class, but telling a friend, family member, or co-worker why you believe what you believe. The purpose of this essay is to help you increase your skill in speaking informally about important theological topics.

Think of a person you know or an imaginary person who wrestles with issues surrounding the person of God and coming to faith in Jesus. Write a letter to this person, offering reasons why faith in God is important and makes good sense. Each letter will be graded on the following criteria:

- Legibly written or typed, presented on time
- Two to four pages in length
- Written in common, everyday conversational language
- Clearly given reasons made with scriptural support
- Solid invitation to believe in God through Christ

Your essay should follow the form of a traditional letter that you would write to a friend. Begin your letter with a short paragraph about the person to whom this letter is written. Offer a few details about this person: their age, where they live, what they know about the Bible (if anything), their current or previous openness, etc. Feel free to imagine any kind of person and their situation to address. In the body of your letter, present the case to your friend for their placing their faith in God. Give them reasons, and back up the reasons with Scripture. If necessary, think about what objections they might have and answer them. Be persuasive! Again, this is a personal letter, not a formal academic paper.

The Ministry Project is worth 30 points and represents 10% of your overall grade, so make certain to share your insights with confidence and make your summary clear.

Purpose

Planning and Summary

Grading

Prolegomena
The Doctrine of God and the Advance of the Kingdom

page 265　1

Lesson Objectives

page 265　2

Welcome in the strong name of Jesus Christ! After your reading, study, discussion, and application of the materials in this lesson, you will be able to:

- Recite the first things, the *prolegomena*, associated with the formal study of the doctrine of God the Father, or *theology proper*.

page 265　3

- Give reasons why is it critically important for God to reveal himself to us *before* we can know him.

- Highlight the truths connected to *general revelation*, the means by which God reveals himself to all people everywhere, and *special revelation* where God reveals himself to particular human beings at particular times and places.

- Show how *the Nicene Creed* provides a clear statement of the *greatness* of the one true God, the God and Father of our Lord Jesus Christ.

- Give evidence of God's *immanence* (i.e., God's present and active involvement in creation) and his *transcendence* (God's infinite nature and unknowableness).

- Provide an explanation of the meaning of the *attributes of God*, their problem and purpose, as well as their nature and classification.

Devotion

No Excuses Allowed

page 266　4

Rom. 1.18-20 - For the wrath of God is revealed from heaven against all ungodliness and unrighteousness of men, who by their unrighteousness suppress the truth. [19] For what can be known about God is plain to them, because God has shown it to them. [20] For his invisible attributes, namely, his eternal power and divine nature, have been clearly perceived, ever since the creation of the world, in the things that have been made. So they are without excuse.

The Nicene Creed begins with a clear statement of the greatness of the one true God, the God and Father of our Lord Jesus Christ. It begins with the phrase "We believe in one God, the Father Almighty, Maker of heaven and earth and of all things visible and invisible." This is an affirmation of a truth that is asserted everywhere in Scripture: God's existence is seen plainly in the splendor of his universe and creation. While our society is fond of talking about *whether* or not God exists, that is, if there really is a God in heaven, the Bible engages in no such debate. On the contrary, God's wrath is revealed from heaven against all ungodliness and unrighteousness of men because what can be known of God is denied by them. God's *invisible attributes*, those qualities which human beings cannot see with the naked eye, his eternal power and divine nature, are *clearly perceived* according to Paul *ever since the creation of the world*. The things that our great God has made, the sun and moon, the stars in their glory, and the earth in its magnificence, all show that not only is God real, but he also is a being of omnipotence (all power) and glory.

How can anyone behold birds on the wing, hear a newborn baby's cry, see a herd of cattle grazing on a spectacular green carpet meadow under a bright, shining sky and say that there is no God? How can anyone feel the crisp wind of a winter's night on their face, see the moon hanging in sleepy elegance on a pitch black spring night, or see a horse in full stride and really believe that there is no intelligent mind behind the glorious beauty of the earth?

Dear friend, the most persuasive argument for the existence of God is not doctrinal, it is physical.

> *Ps. 19.1-3 - "The heavens declare the glory of God, and the sky above proclaims his handiwork. [2] Day to day pours out speech, and night to night reveals knowledge. [3] There is no speech, nor are there words, whose voice is not heard."*

The clear word of Scripture is moving: the heavens declare the glory of God, and the sky above proclaims his handiwork. Enough is spoken in God's creation that any reasonable person must admit that there is a divine being behind this glory. The problem of the atheist and the skeptic is not that there is insufficient evidence, but that their own hearts are hard. There's proof enough to repent; the skeptic is therefore without excuse for not coming to Messiah.

After reciting and/or singing the Nicene Creed (located in the Appendix), pray the following prayers:

> *O God, your immensity fills the earth and the whole universe, but the universe itself cannot contain you, much less the earth, and still less the world of my thoughts.*
>
> ~ Yves Raguin, SJ. Appleton, George, ed. **The Oxford Book of Prayer**. Oxford; New York: Oxford University Press, 1988. p. 4

Nicene Creed and Prayer

Almighty God who created all things in time and space and made man in your own image: Lead us to recognize your hand in all you have created and always to praise you for your wisdom and love; through Jesus Christ our Lord who with you and the Holy Spirit reigns supreme over all things now and for ever.

~ Church of the Province of South Africa. **Minister's Book for Use With the Holy Eucharist and Morning and Evening Prayer.** Braamfontein: Publishing Department of the Church of the Province of South Africa. p. 12

Quiz	No quiz this lesson
Scripture Memorization Review	No Scripture memorization this lesson
Assignments Due	No assignments due this lesson

"There Is Only One God - Allah."

page 267 5

Encountering a member of the *Nation of Islam* (the Louis Farrakhan-headed group of the Black Muslims) on the street selling papers, you pause a moment to engage in conversation. As the subject turns to the person of God and who God is, the young, bright-eyed follower of Islam shouts "There is no God but Allah. He alone created the heavens and earth." How would you respond to his assertion?

"Where Was He Then?"

In a Sunday School class speaking of the suffering of the Jewish people when they were taken into captivity by the nations of Assyria and Babylon, one of the teens asks the question, "We always talk about God being present with us, and loving us and everything, but if God was present with his people and cared for them, then why did he allow his own people to be hurt and mistreated like that? Where was he then?" As teacher of the class, how would you answer this student's important question?

"I Just Don't Know."

A young mother who recently lost one of her young children to leukemia has been suffering from depression. As much as she has tried, she simply can't seem to overcome the temptation to think that God doesn't exist, or, if he does, he just can't be loving. Why would he allow their darling little Martha to suffer for so long, and die so young. Sharing with you her heart, she says, "When I pray, when I read my Bible, when I look into the night sky, I feel so alone. I know what the preacher and the counselor I go to say, but neither of them have helped me understand why, if God loves us, would this happen. Is God real? Is God loving? I just don't know." How would you respond to this dear young sister's plea for understanding?

Prolegomena: The Doctrine of God and the Advance of the Kingdom

Segment 1: Does God Exist, and Does He Reveal Himself?

Rev. Dr. Don L. Davis

In this segment we will explore God's sovereign purpose to reveal himself to humankind through general and special revelation.

Our objective for this segment, *Does God Exist, and Does He Reveal Himself?* is to enable you to see that:

- A Prolegomena, the study of "first things," of theology proper (the study of God), suggests that God must reveal himself to us if we are ever to know God. No one can know God without him revealing himself to us.

- God has revealed himself to humankind in two connected ways, through both general and special revelation.

- Through general revelation God reveals himself to all people everywhere, and through special revelation God reveals himself to particular human beings at particular times and places.

Summary of Segment 1

page 267 6

Video Segment 1 Outline

John 17.3
"And this is eternal life, that they know you the only true God, and Jesus Christ whom you have sent."

I. **Prolegomena (pronounced PRAW-ley-gaw-men-uh): Groundwork for a Study about God**

Theology means "the study of God."

(*"theos"* = God, *"logos"* = the study of, word)

A. Christianity assumes that God exists and that apart from revealing himself, God is unknowable.

1. God as he is in himself is unknowable, 1 Tim. 6.13-16.

    a. Only God can reveal himself to us; no human being can initiate a relationship with God.

        (1) Exod. 33.20

        (2) John 1.18

        (3) John 6.46

    b. Only God can interpret accurately the meaning of his revelation of himself to us.

        (1) John 1.18

        (2) Matt. 11.27

2. God has chosen to reveal himself through his works of creation and redemption in history (in creation, in redemption, in Scripture, and Jesus).

    a. Through creation

        (1) Ps. 19.1-3

        (2) Jer. 10.11-12

b. Through history, Acts 14.15-17

3. God has given humankind the capacities to know of his existence, Rom. 1.18-20.

4. Knowledge of God demands a new relationship with him through Jesus Christ, not merely the intellectual study of concepts and ideas about him.

   a. 1 John 5.20

   b. 2 Cor. 4.6

B. Implications for our study of God

1. *Reason and study* are insufficient to discover God and his person; reason requires the illumination of the Spirit to know God.

2. We must be *born again* (regenerated) to know God through Jesus Christ.

   a. Intellectual preparation and scientific methods alone will always be limited in theological study.

   b. To study God well, you must know God personally.

3. Theology is *reflection about revelation*; it is human thinking about God's person and revelation.

   a. We should be alert to how *our culture* influences our thinking about God.

   b. We ought not trust our own judgments about God *unaided by the Holy Spirit*.

   c. Many theologies exist because *no theology explains God fully*.

   d. *Humility* is the cardinal virtue for theological study.

4. Credible theology issues *from Scripture and Church*: theology is the Church reflecting on God's revelation anchored in Scripture.

5. Theology may consult other disciplines but must never follow them absolutely; *God alone can reveal himself to us by his Spirit through the Scriptures*.

II. The Sovereign God Makes Himself Known to Us: General and Special Revelation

General revelation: *"God's communication of himself to all persons at all times in all places."*

Special revelation: *"God's particular communications and manifestations of himself to particular persons at particular times, communications and manifestations which are available now only by consulting certain sacred writings [i.e., the Bible]."*

~ Millard Erickson, **Introducing Christian Doctrine**, 2nd Ed. Grand Rapids: Baker Book House, 2001. p. 42

A. *General revelation*: God revealing himself to all beings everywhere through creation, human history, and in the inner capacities of human beings

1. God has revealed himself *through creation and nature*.

    a. Biblical evidence

        (1) Isa. 40.25-26

        (2) Rom. 1.18-20

        (3) Acts 14.15-17

        (4) Acts 17.24-31

    b. Philosophical arguments for a natural theology: Thomas Aquinas

        (1) *Cosmological* proof: God as the first uncaused Cause

        (2) *Teleological* proof: God is the author of the orderliness and purposefulness of the universe.

        (3) *Anthropological* argument: The moral order of things demands that God exists and will judge our actions.

        (4) *Ontological* argument (Anselm): God is the greatest of all conceivable beings.

2. God has revealed himself in *human history*.

    a. The preservation of God's special people, Israel

    b. God's redemptive work in human history: the Jesus of history, Acts 2.22-23

        (1) *Historie*: actual human history

(2) *Heilsgeschicte*: God's historical work in the nation of Israel leading to the person of Jesus Christ

3. God has revealed himself in *human beings themselves*.

   a. Reason, Isa. 1.18

   b. Moral judgments: conscience, Rom. 2.15

   c. Religious nature: all human cultures carry some notion of the divine.
      (1) Ps. 10.4
      (2) Ps. 73.3

B. *Special revelation*: God revealing himself to particular human beings at particular times and places

   1. Special revelation is *personal* (God is revealing himself to us).

      a. I am that I am, Exod. 3.14-15.

      b. The God of Abraham, Isaac, and Jacob
         (1) Exod. 3.6
         (2) Exod. 4.5

2. Special revelation is *anthropic* (anthropology = "*anthropos*," human, "*logos*," study of): God uses human language and forms to communicate with us.

   a. In the realm of human language and experience, 1 Cor. 2.12-13

   b. In the person of Jesus Christ

      (1) John 1.14

      (2) John 1.18

      (3) Luke 10.22

3. Special revelation is *analogical*. (God uses analogies to model for us who he is and what our relationship with him is like.)

   a. An analogy = inviting us to understand one thing by its comparison with another thing: as A is to B, so C is to D.

      (1) John 10.9

      (2) John 10.14-15

   b. God selects the components to compare, and suggests the connection for our understanding.

   c. He communicates to the whole person, not merely in concepts or ideas alone (e.g., Jesus is the Lion of Judah).

4. Special revelation is *concrete*.

a. Through *historical events* (e.g., the call of Abraham), Gen. 12.1-3

b. Through *divine speech*, e.g., Heb. 1.1-2

c. Through *the Incarnation of Jesus Christ*, 1 John 1.1-3

Conclusion

» God must reveal himself to us if we are to know him.

» God reveals himself to us in two special modes or ways: through *general revelation*, God reveals himself to all people everywhere, and through *special revelation*, God reveals himself to particular human beings at particular times and places.

Segue 1

Student Questions and Response

page 268 📖 *8*

Please take as much time as you have available to answer these and other questions that the video may have raised for you. The necessity of God revealing himself to us, and the nature of general and special revelation are at the heart of our study of God the Father. Be clear and concise in your answers, and where possible, support with Scripture!

1. What is the meaning of the term "prolegomena?" Why is it important to get your assumptions clear first *before* you engage in a formal study of the person and work of God?

2. Why is it simply not possible for someone to know God on their own terms and by their own strength?

3. What role does reason and study play in the study of God? Why are they not sufficient, in and of themselves, to help anyone come to a full knowledge of God?

4. What is the role of the Holy Spirit in helping us know God?

5. What is *general revelation*? In what specific ways has God revealed himself to all human beings everywhere? Is this knowledge of God enough to save? Explain your answer.

6. What is *special revelation*? What are the characteristics of special revelation? What is the most clear and powerful way God has ever revealed himself to humankind?

7. Why is it necessary for God alone to reveal himself to us, whether it be through general or special revelation? What, then, should always be our attitude in the study of God?

Prolegomena: The Doctrine of God and the Advance of the Kingdom

Segment 2: Can God Be Known to Us?

Rev. Dr. Don L. Davis

As a God who created the heavens and the earth, the Father is both *present and active everywhere within the universe* (i.e., God is *immanent*), as well as *infinitely beyond all creation and all beings* (i.e., God is *transcendent*). In theology, we study the *attributes of God*, those qualities which describe the various traits of God's eternal greatness and goodness.

Summary of Segment 2

page 269 📖 9

Our objective for this segment, *Can God Be Known to Us?* is to enable you to see that:

- God, as Creator and Maker of all things, has a unique relationship to his universe which can be described in terms of his *immanence* and his *transcendence*.

- God's *immanence* refers to his present and active involvement in all his creation.

- On the other hand, God's *transcendence* refers to God's infinite nature and unknowableness.

- The *attributes* of God refer to the traits of the entire Godhead, Father, Son, and Holy Spirit.

- We may classify God's attributes in terms of God's *greatness* and *goodness*.

- God's attributes of *greatness* are spirituality, life, personality, infinity, and constancy.

- God's attributes of *goodness* include his moral purity, integrity, and love.

Video Segment 2 Outline

The Nicene Creed, which serves as the theological foundation of our Capstone curriculum, begins with a clear statement of the greatness of the one true God, the God and Father of our Lord Jesus Christ. It begins with the phrase "We believe in one God, the Father Almighty, Maker of heaven and earth and of all things visible and invisible." This statement emphasizes both the transcendence of God as well as his immanence.

I. **The Immanence and Transcendence of God**

  A. Definitions: this pair of emphases have to do with God's relationship to his creation as Maker of heaven and earth, and of all things visible and invisible.

   1. The *immanence* of God = God is present and active everywhere within the universe.

   2. The *transcendence* of God = God's person is infinitely beyond creation and the power of any being other than himself to understand himself.

  B. The *immanence* of God

   1. God is present and active within creation.

      a. Jer. 23.23-24

      b. Ps. 135.5-7

   2. God is present and active within the human race.

  a. Ps. 139.1-10

  b. Dan. 4.35

 3. Implications of God's immanence

  a. God can use both generally accessible and universal means to work his will in the world.

  b. God is free to use anything and anyone to accomplish his will.

  c. All of God's creation reveals his glory and handiwork.

  d. Creation offers humankind (at one level) true knowledge of God.

  e. Points of contact exist between and among all peoples because God is the Maker of all things.

C. The *transcendence* of God

 1. God is above and beyond all the things that he has created: they exist by him and for his glory alone.

  a. 1 Kings 8.27

  b. 2 Chron. 6.18

c. Neh. 9.6

d. Isa. 66.1

2. God cannot be known through the efforts and activities of human beings; his glory and nature are infinitely beyond the scope of human understanding and experience.

   a. Deut. 10.14

   b. Ps. 113.4-6

3. Implications of God's transcendence

   a. Human life is not nor has it ever been the highest form of being in the universe.

   b. God cannot be limited to or captured by the concepts that theology or any other discipline creates of him.

   c. God alone is bringing all things back under his reign for our salvation and ultimately for his glory.

   d. God is a *sui generis* being (i.e., in a class by himself). No other being will ever attain to his fully glory.

   e. God is to be feared above all else and all things.

f. We should expect God to go beyond us and our thoughts in all things.

II. The Challenge We Face in Studying the Person of God: the Problem and Purpose in Studying the Attributes of God

A. The unity of God and the attributes of God

1. Definition of God's attributes = "those qualities of God which constitute what he is. They are the very characteristics of his nature." Erickson, *Introducing Christian Doctrine*, p. 89.

2. The nature of the one triune God is integrated and whole.

   a. God's nature (for the sake of study only) can be separated for analysis and worship.

   b. God himself, however, is *an integrated being who exercises every characteristic in perfect harmony with all others* in unity with his total will and being in every act.

3. Problem: can we truly understand God's *whole* character by analyzing his *specific* characteristics?

   a. God is one.

   (1) Deut. 6.4

   (2) Deut. 4.35

   (3) Isa. 42.8

(4) Isa. 44.6

(5) Isa. 44.8

(6) Jer. 10.10

b. God's attributes are all connected.

c. No one can do an anatomy of God's person.

d. We tend to become "reductive" in our analysis of God (we emphasize one characteristic to the exclusion or understatement of others).

4. Ways to overcome the problem

a. Be *careful* in your judgments.

b. Be *aware* of the tendency to be reductive.

c. Be *humble* in statements about God.

B. The purpose of the study of the attributes of God

1. To meditate on the perfections of God for confidence and conviction, Ps. 40.4-5

2. To think God's thoughts after him in regards to his mighty character, John 14.26

3. To learn of the glory of God revealed in creation and in Jesus Christ

   a. John 17.3

   b. Matt. 11.25-27

4. To make God known to others, Ps. 71.17-19

III. The Structure of the Study of God: the Nature and Classification of the Attributes of God

A. The *nature* of the attributes of God

1. Attributes reflect the traits of *the entire Godhead*.

   a. They are not the same as *properties*, that is, those functions which relate to the distinct members of the Trinity.

   b. They are not the same as the *activities or acts* of the members, which are more specific characteristics of each particular member of the Trinity.

2. Attributes are *permanent qualities*, intrinsic to God.

3. Attributes speak of *the very essence of who God is*.

The heaviest obligation lying upon the Christian Church today is to purify and elevate her concept of God until it is once more worthy of him–and of her. In all her prayers and labors this should have first place. We do the greatest service to the next generation of Christians by passing on to them undimmed and undiminished that noble concept of God which we receive from our Hebrew and Christian fathers of generations past. This will prove of greater value to them than anything that art or science can devise.
~ A.W. Tozer. *The Knowledge of the Holy.* New York: Harper San Francisco, 1961. p. 4.

B. The *classification* of the attributes of God

1. The *greatness* of God (those traits associated with splendor of God, God in Godself, usually called in theological works "*natural attributes*")

    a. Spirituality

    b. Life

    c. Personality

    d. Infinity

    e. Constancy

2. The *goodness* of God (those traits associated with God's relationship with his creation, including humankind, usually called in theological works "*moral attributes*")

    a. Moral purity

    b. Integrity

    c. Love

Conclusion

» As Maker and Creator of all things, God relates to his universe as One who is both *immanent* and *transcendent*.

» As One who is *immanent* within creation, God is both present and actively involved in the universe.

» As One who is *transcendent* above creation, God is infinite and cannot be known without enabling us to see and know him.

» The *attributes of God* refer to the qualities of God's *greatness* and *goodness*.

Segue 2

Student Questions and Response

The following questions were designed to help you review the material in the second video segment. As the Nicene Creed suggests, only one God exists, the Father Almighty, Maker of heaven and earth and of all things visible and invisible. As one who is both present and active in, yet also beyond his creation, we must understand his attributes in light of his greatness and goodness. As you reflect on the questions below, seek to be simple and direct in your answers, and where possible, support with Scripture!

1. The Nicene Creed suggests that the Father Almighty is the Maker of heaven and earth, of all things visible and invisible. Why do you think this is the first and foundational truth to all discussion and study about God? Explain your answer.

2. What is the nature of God's *immanence*? In what ways does God show us that he is present and active in his involvement in the affairs of creation and humankind?

3. Why is a knowledge of God's immanence so important for us as students of theology? What might be some implications of this doctrine for missions, for winning people who have no knowledge of God in Jesus Christ?

4. What is the nature of God's *transcendence*? Why must we assert that God cannot be known as he is in and of himself without the aid of the Holy Spirit?

5. What are the implications for understanding God as one who is transcendent above all things? How does this doctrine undergird all valid worship and service to God?

6. What is an *attribute of God*? Why is it important to always remember the unity of God when studying his individual attributes? What are the errors we must avoid as we seek to understand God's qualities one by one, separate from all the rest?

7. How do theologians classify the attributes of God? What qualities are associated with God's *greatness*, and which are associated with his *goodness*?

CONNECTION

Summary of Key Concepts

page 270  10

This lesson focuses upon those critical, first truths that must be understood for a solid, biblical study of the doctrine of God. It is important to establish the "big picture" of one's study before we dig into the weighty matters of God's person and works. Knowing the assumptions behind our study, we will be guided into the truth of the doctrine of God. At every step we must guard against pride and arrogance, thinking that we can understand the person of God unaided by the Holy Spirit, apart from his illumination of the Scriptures. Below are some of the key ideas we covered in our study of lesson one.

- A *prolegomena*, a study of the "first things" of the doctrine of God, is critical for a valid, biblical study of the doctrine of God the Father, or *theology proper*.

- Because of the nature of God and our finite character, we must affirm that God must reveal himself to us *before* we can know him.

- Knowing that God is beyond our own reason and reflection, we must be humble and careful in all our reflections and assertions about God and his person. God must reveal himself to us if we are to know him personally.

- As Maker of all things, God has revealed himself to us in two special modes. In *general revelation*, God reveals himself to all people everywhere, and in *special revelation*, God reveals himself to particular human beings at particular times and places.

- The *Nicene Creed* provides a clear statement of the greatness of the one true God, the God and Father of our Lord Jesus Christ.

- In his relationship to his created universe, God is both *immanent* and *transcendent*.

- God's *immanence* refers to his present and active involvement in all his creation.

- God's *transcendence* refers to the truth that God is infinite and therefore cannot be contained within creation or known without his sovereign choice to reveal himself to others.

- The *attributes of God* refer to the traits of the entire Godhead, Father, Son, and Holy Spirit, and may be classified in terms of his *greatness* and his *goodness*.

- The attributes associated with God's *greatness* include his spirituality, life, personality, infinity, and constancy.

- The attributes associated with God's *goodness* include his moral purity, integrity, and love.

Student Application and Implications

page 270 11

Now is the time for you to discuss with your fellow students your questions about this introductory lesson on the doctrine of God. What particular questions do you have in light of the material you have just studied? Maybe some of the questions below might help you form your own, more specific and critical questions.

* What difference does it make to assert that God the Father Almighty is the Maker of heaven and earth, of all things visible and invisible, and not some impersonal force? Why do you think the bishops of the Church began the Creed with this affirmation?

* Why must we assert wholeheartedly that no one can know God without God initiating the encounter? If this is so, how can God hold anyone to blame for not coming to him and knowing him, if God must begin the relationship?

* What happens when someone emphasizes general revelation over the importance of special revelation? On the other hand, what happens when someone emphasizes special revelation without understanding God's role in general revelation?

* What might it mean to say that God is immanent in the affairs of a community wracked by crime and gang violence? If God is immanent in such situations, how do we recognize his presence among us?

* How do you assert the transcendence of God above the chaos of many urban communities without also saying that God has abandoned the city? How can God be both immanent and transcendent in the affairs of our urban neighborhoods today?

* How should the doctrine of God's immanence and transcendence affect us as we minister in our churches in the city? How should they affect our understanding of worship? Of ministry to the hurting? Of dealing with tough situations in the community? Of our own lives and ministries?

* How can a person really get the most from studying the attributes of God without focusing on one thing to the exclusion of others? What qualities are associated with God's greatness, and which are associated with his goodness?

* Does your own life and ministry reflect that you understand that God is the unity of all his wonderful attributes, or do you focus on one of his qualities more than the rest? How might you overcome this normal tendency in doctrinal study?

CASE STUDIES

What about All Those People?

In a conversation with one of your friends whom you are sharing the Lord with, they highlight a particular problem that they can't seem to shake in their thinking about the Lord and salvation. Troubled that there are hundreds of millions of people who have yet to hear of God's saving work in Jesus, your friend shares that he thinks the Christian faith is terribly unfair. "Okay, I'll grant you that God has revealed himself in the beauty of creation–it is mighty wonderful. But I have a problem still; if general revelation is not enough to lead a person to believe on Christ, then what is to happen to all of those millions of people who haven't heard about Christ yet? Are they doomed to die, lost forever? If you need a special revelation to know about Jesus, then what about all those people?" How would you answer the question of your friend?

An Absentee God

With a high rise in violent crime in the community, your church is hosting a block wide prayer meeting for the members of the community. Having organized prayer walks and prayer vigils, your congregation is deeply aware of the spiritual forces which underlie the kinds of violence and cruelty taking place in the neighborhood right now. During one of the prayer sessions, a community resident who it not a part of your church stands up and says, "I don't go to this church, and honestly, I don't go to any church because God seems to not care for us as he does for others. Why does our neighborhood always have to be terrorized and miserable? He seems to care far more for people who live in the rich suburbs than us down here. He just seems absent a lot down here!" The entire prayer meeting is quieted, and turn to you for an answer to the heart cry of this frustrated neighbor. What words of explanation and comfort would you give in the prayer meeting to this observation?

The Lord Who Is My Pal

A struggle has been brewing for a long time among the members of your local church because of the new emphasis in "intimate praise and worship." Fed up by the old, stodgy nature of the hymn singing and liturgy of the past, the new worship leader has been infusing in the order of service new songs of praise and worship, many which speak of God in very intimate, personal terms. Some of the older parishioners object, feeling that the new music and emphasis does make God seem more personal, but all fear of God as the *Wholly Other* than us is gone. They fear that the awe of God has been replaced with the Lord who is my Cosmic Pal. Who's right and who's wrong here? Can both be right and wrong at the same time–how? If you were the leader of this church, how might you help both sides understand how God's immanence and transcendence enrich our experience of worship to God?

A *prolegomena*, a study of the "first things" of the doctrine of God, humbly affirms that God must reveal himself to us before we can know him. God has revealed himself to us in two special modes. In *general revelation*, God reveals himself to all people everywhere, and in *special revelation*, God reveals himself to particular human beings at particular times and places. In his relationship to his created universe, God is both *immanent* and *transcendent*. God's *immanence* refers to his present and active involvement in all his creation, while God's *transcendence* refers to the truth that God is infinite and therefore cannot be contained within creation

Restatement of the Lesson's Thesis

or known without his sovereign choice to reveal himself to others. The *attributes of God* refer to the traits of the entire Godhead, Father, Son, and Holy Spirit, and may be classified in terms of his *greatness* and his *goodness*. The attributes of his greatness include his spirituality, life, personality, infinity, and constancy, while those of his goodness include his moral purity, integrity, and love.

Resources and Bibliographies

If you are interested in pursuing some of the ideas of *Prolegomena: The Doctrine of God and the Advance of the Kingdom*, you might want to give these books a try:

Evans, William. *The Great Doctrines of the Bible*. Chicago: Moody Press, 1976.

Schaeffer, Francis A. *The God Who is There*. Chicago: InterVarsity Press, 1968.

Stone, Nathan J. *Names of God*. Chicago: Moody Press, 1993.

Ministry Connections

Now is the time for you to think practically about the meaning of these truths for your own personal life and ministry. Concentrate on your own life situation today, and think about the way in which the Holy Spirit might want you to relate these truths regarding the nature and being of God to what you are doing right now. James' promise in James 1.22-25 is that the special blessing comes to those who are not merely hearers of the Word of God but doers of it. Think about what in particular the Holy Spirit is suggesting to you to concentrate upon this week in regards to God's general and special revelation, his immanence and transcendence, and the meaning of these great truths for what God is calling you to do today?

What particular person, event, or situation comes to mind for your own consideration and application when you think about these truths on the doctrine of God?

Is there an area in your life and ministry that calls for your present application of these truths now? If so, what does God want you to do in regards to these areas?

Are you ministering to someone who especially needs to understand and apply the teaching of the Word of God to these areas in their life? How will you introduce the teaching to them? When is the best time or circumstance to share your insights with them?

The heart of this lesson is that God is both present and active as well as infinite and transcendent. He reveals himself to all people through his glorious creation, and yet, he personally reveals his own heart and person to all who repent and believe in Messiah Jesus. Seek the Lord for his strength and wisdom to live true to what you know and believe about God, and ask for his aid in helping you communicate with greater clarity and boldness the truth concerning God's glorious attributes and person. Solicit support from your leaders and Mentor in any area that God may be speaking to you, and ask God for the filling of the Spirit so you can promptly obey all that God is asking you to do as a result of his teaching to your heart and mind this week.

Counseling and Prayer

ASSIGNMENTS

Psalm 19.1-3

Scripture Memory

To prepare for class, please visit *www.tumi.org/books* to find next week's reading assignment, or ask your mentor.

Reading Assignment

Dear student, remember that *you will be quizzed on the content (the video content)* of this lesson next week. Please be sure to you spend plenty of time this next week reviewing your notes, especially those which focus on the key concepts and main ideas of the lesson. Also, please read the assigned pages listed above, and summarize each reading with no more than a paragraph or two for each. Make it your aim in this summary to give your best understanding of what you think *the main point* was in each reading. Do not be overly concerned about providing lots of detailed summary; simply write out what you consider to be *the main point discussed in that section of the book*. Please bring these summaries to class next week. (Please see the *Reading Completion Sheet* at the end of this lesson.)

Other Assignments

page 271  *13*

Looking Forward to the Next Lesson

In our next lesson, we will move our attention to understand God's supreme authority and providence over all creation and history. We will see that the Father is Sovereign over all, the Source of all, and the Sustainer of all through his Son, Jesus Christ. We will also explore God's preservation of all things, and his governance over all creation, with his promise to restore all creation back to its original glory at Christ's return.

This curriculum is the result of thousands of hours of work by The Urban Ministry Institute (TUMI) and should not be reproduced without their express permission. TUMI supports all who wish to use these materials for the advance of God's Kingdom, and affordable licensing to reproduce them is available. Please confirm with your instructor that this book is properly licensed. For more information on TUMI and our licensing program, visit *www.tumi.org* and *www.tumi.org/license*.

Capstone Curriculum

Module 6: God the Father
Reading Completion Sheet

Name _____

Date _____

For each assigned reading, write a brief summary (one or two paragraphs) of the author's main point. (For additional readings, use the back of this sheet.)

Reading 1

Title and Author: _____ Pages _____

Reading 2

Title and Author: _____ Pages _____

LESSON 2

God as the Creator
The Providence of God

page 273

Lesson Objectives

Welcome in the strong name of Jesus Christ! After your reading, study, discussion, and application of the materials in this lesson, you will be able to:

- Explain how God's supreme authority and providence is shown over all creation and history.

- Show how "providence" means that "God works out his sovereign will in the universe whereby all events are disposed by him to fulfill his purposes for himself and his creation for good."

- Use the Scriptures to show how the Father is Sovereign over all, the Source of all, and the Sustainer of all through his Son, Jesus Christ. All things are disposed to sync up with his will for himself, so he can receive glory for all things.

- Demonstrate how God's special work of providence is revealed in his preservation and governance of all things.

- Make clear how many of the errors associated with modern philosophy and religion come from misunderstanding the providence of God over creation and history.

- Show an understanding of the key elements of preservation and governance, along with God's intent to restore creation at Christ's return.

- Provide a brief explanation of how the providence of God resolves some of the modern errors of philosophy and theology, namely, pantheism, deism, fatalism, and chance.

Devotion

Truly One of a Kind

page 274

1 Tim. 6.13-16 - I charge you in the presence of God, who gives life to all things, and of Christ Jesus, who in his testimony before Pontius Pilate made the good confession, [14] to keep the commandment unstained and free from reproach until the appearing of our Lord Jesus Christ, [15] which he will display at the proper time—he who is the blessed and only Sovereign, the King of kings and Lord of lords, [16] who alone has immortality, who dwells in unapproachable light, whom no one has ever seen or can see. To him be honor and eternal dominion. Amen.

The term *sui generis* (pronounced SUE-ee gin-air-us) is a Latin phrase meaning, "one of a kind" or "one of a class of things." It is shorthand for meaning "the only one of its kind." This is a wonderful way to describe the infinitely lovely God and Father of our Lord Jesus Christ.

One of the most important truths for the man or woman of God is the concept of God as a God of sovereign providence, a being who works all things according to the pleasure of his own will. This truth, that the God and Father of our Lord Jesus is a God of sovereign purpose, lies at the center of all other doctrines and commands of Scripture. As the true God, the Maker and Creator of all things, Yahweh can do what he wills with whomever he desires for whatever reasons are acceptable to him. Regardless of how terrible the situation appears, how drastic the need is, how tragic the circumstances look, he is the God of Abraham, the God of our Lord Jesus, the same One who raises the dead and transforms all of life to conform to his own high will and purpose. The unqualified testimony of the Bible is that the God of Scripture did not create the universe and then walk away from it, for it to unravel in any way it wishes. Although he has permitted evil to exist for a time, he set in motion from the beginning a plan to redeem his creation through his Son Messiah Jesus. Now that his Son has accomplished his redemption, he has determined at a time of his own choosing a moment, a season in which all things will be brought back under his sovereign rule forever. Furthermore, he has determined to accomplish all of this through the One who is the blessed and only Sovereign, King Jesus, the Lord of lords and King of kings. As Paul suggests to Timothy in our text above, only our Sovereign Lord Jesus dwells in that light of his Father, the true God, the only one who has immortality, who dwells in the unapproachable, blinding light of pure divine spirit, whom no human being has seen or can see.

Our God is the true God, the sovereign Maker of the universe, who is working all things according to his own wisdom and power. His will can be resisted but never overwhelmed or thwarted. He created all things, sustains all, and will consummate all for his own sake. He preserves all things, governs all things, and will lead all things to his own appointed end, and nothing and no one can stop him from accomplishing his purpose. He is God!

Because this great God is our God, we ought to give him his due, as Paul says, "to him be honor and eternal dominion, Amen!" Only worship and unconditional surrender to God are worthy gifts to a God so majestic and high. Let us make this our aim; to align ourselves with the high, exalted purpose of this great God, and to give him the glory and praise he so truly deserves. Our God is truly One of a Kind.

Nicene Creed and Prayer

After reciting and/or singing the Nicene Creed (located in the Appendix), pray the following prayer:

> *Lead us, O God, from the sight of the lovely things of the world to the thought of thee their Creator; and grant that delighting in the beautiful things of thy creation we may delight in thee, the first author of beauty and the Sovereign Lord of all thy works, blessed for evermore.*
>
> ~ Appleton, George, ed. **The Oxford Book of Prayer**. Oxford; New York: Oxford University Press, 1988. p. 62.

> *Lord of all power and might, the author and giver of all good things: Graft in our hearts the love of your Name; increase in us true religion; nourish us with all goodness; and bring forth in us the fruit of good works; through Jesus Christ our Lord, who lives and reigns with you and the Holy Spirit, one God, for ever and ever. Amen.*
>
> ~ The Episcopal Church. **The Book of Common Prayer and Administrations of the Sacraments and Other Rites and Ceremonies of the Church, Together with the Psalter or Psalms of David** New York: The Church Hymnal Corporation, 1979. p. 233.

Quiz
page 275

Put away your notes, gather up your thoughts and reflections, and take the quiz for Lesson 1, *Prolegomena: The Doctrine of God and the Advance of the Kingdom*.

Scripture Memorization Review

Review with a partner, write out and/or recite the text for last class session's assigned memory verse: Psalm 19.1-3.

Assignments Due

Turn in your summary of the reading assignment for last week, that is, your brief response and explanation of the main points that the authors were seeking to make in the assigned reading (Reading Completion Sheet).

He Doesn't Know or Doesn't Care

Over lunch break, in a remark about a horrible terrorist bomb that recently went off and hurt many innocent bystanders, one of your coworkers seeks to put you on the spot. Knowing you to be a Christian he says, "How can you say that God exists when all of this bad stuff is happening to people who are totally innocent? It just don't make any sense. You see, if God knows about this kinda stuff, he ought to stop it, right? If he knows about it and doesn't do anything, then well, how can God care about people at all? You see, it just doesn't make sense that these things keep happening without God doing somethin' about it!" If all eyes turned toward you and asked you to explain how this all works, what would you say?

The Thrill Is Gone

In talking with one of the young fellows in the neighborhood, you are stunned to find out that he believes that there is no overarching purpose for life, no single reason or purpose behind all things. He says that all that he has known in this life has been sorrow and tragedy; things have never worked out for him in anything, he's always been last, always been without, never been happy. He cannot even conceive of times being different from this since his experience is mirrored in the lives of those at home, and his entire extended family. For him, he says, the thrill of life is like the B.B. King song; *The Thrill Is Gone*. How do we engage in a conversation with this brother on his level without giving in to his despair about life?

God Is Everything and Everywhere

In one of her classes at the local junior college, one of your young adults in the Sunday School class says she does not know what to make of her teacher who believes that God is a part of the entire universe. The instructor said in class, "God is everywhere and in everything. We don't need organized religion because everything is sacred, for everything is God." How might the college student answer her teacher's claims about God being all of creation?

page 275 4

CONTENT **God as the Creator: The Providence of God**

Segment 1: Nicene Affirmation of God the Father Almighty

Rev. Dr. Don L. Davis

Summary of Segment 1

God the Father Almighty, Maker of heaven and earth, is sovereign over all that he has made, is the source of all life everywhere, and sustains all things by his work through Jesus Christ. All that God does he does in order that his name might be exalted and glorified throughout all heaven and earth.

Our objective for this segment, *Nicene Affirmation of God the Father Almighty* is to enable you to see that:

- The God and Father of our Lord Jesus, the Father Almighty, is the supreme authority and providential ruler over all creation and history.

- The fact that God is a God of "providence" means that he "works out his sovereign will in the universe whereby all events are disposed by him to fulfill his purposes for himself and his creation for good."

- As Lord and Maker, we will see that the Father is Sovereign over all, the Source of all, and the Sustainer of all through his Son, Jesus Christ.

- God directs and moves all things in such a way as to line up everything with his will for himself, all done for his glory and honor.

Video Segment 1 Outline

I. God the Father Almighty Is Sovereign Over All.

A. He is sovereign over all creation, 1 Tim. 6.15-16.

1. The Father made the heavens and earth, Ps. 33.6.

2. Creation belongs to God, Ps. 115.16.

3. God interacts and engages his creation for his own purposes.

   a. God does what he wants everywhere, Ps. 135.5-6.

   b. God is incomparable in his providential actions, Isa. 40.22-26.

4. God is sovereign in all the affairs and activities of all the angelic beings within the universe.

B. He is sovereign over the purpose and events history.

1. The purpose of God's heart will be accomplished.

   a. Ps. 33.11

   b. Ps. 115.3

   c. Isa. 46.10

   d. Dan. 4.35

2. God is providential in the outworking of human history, Acts 14.15-17.

3. God is the determiner of the history of specific nations and peoples, Acts 17.26-28.

C. He is sovereign over the purpose and plan of salvation.

1. In his choice of his people, Israel, Deut. 10.14-15

2. God delighted in Abraham and his offspring.

    a. Deut. 4.37

    b. Deut. 7.7-8

3. Mercy is rooted in God's sovereign choice, not in human will, Rom. 9.13-18.

D. He is sovereign over the final judgment and destiny.

1. The final judgment is connected to God's own sovereign act of committal, 2 Thess. 1.5-10.

2. Glorification is the inheritance of God's chosen company.

    a. It is the pleasure of God to give the Kingdom to the redeemed, Luke 12.32.

    b. Believers are made joint heirs with Christ, Rom. 8.16-17.

    c. God has chosen the poor as heirs of the Kingdom, James 2.5.

d. God's call to his people involves an inheritance from him, 1 Pet. 1.4-5.

II. God the Father Almighty Is the Source of All.

A. He has life in and of himself, Exod. 3.14.

1. The Father is self-existent (i.e., his providence is rooted in his own nature, not dependent on anything external to himself), John 5.26.

2. He needs nothing from anyone, Acts 17.25.

3. He is immortal (containing never-ending life within himself).

    a. 1 Tim. 1.17

    b. 1 Tim. 6.16

4. God's gift of life pours from his own mighty nature.

    a. Ps. 36.9

    b. Ps. 90.2

B. He is the source of all goodness.

1. He is good to everything he has made, Ps. 145.9.

2. God provides life and health to all things, Ps. 145.15-16.

3. All humankind benefits from God's bounty, Ps. 36.5-7.

III. God the Father Almighty Is the Sustainer of All Things.

A. He sustains all created things and beings.

1. God fills all creatures and beings with good things, Ps. 104.24-30.

2. God's providential mercies sustain and touch all the things he has made.

    a. All the universe feels God's providential care, Ps. 145.9.

    b. Every living thing owes its life to God, Ps. 145.15-16.

    c. Jesus taught God's providential provision for all things, Luke 12.24-28.

3. God is even good to those who neither know him nor love him, Luke 6.35.

B. God does his act of sustaining through the mediation of Jesus Christ.

1. God created the universe through Jesus Christ.

    a. God created all things through the Word, John 1.3.

    b. All things find their origins and purpose in Christ's creative power, Col. 1.15-16.

    c. Heb. 1.2

2. God continues to sustain all things through Christ.

    a. All things hold together in him, Col. 1.17.

    b. We exist through God's operations through Christ, 1 Cor. 8.6.

C. All of God's works of creation and upholding are done in order that his name might be exalted and glorified.

    1. 1 Chron. 29.11

    2. Ps. 57.11

    3. Ps. 72.18-19

    4. Rev. 4.11

5. Eph. 3.20-21

Conclusion

> 1 Tim. 1.17
> *To the King of ages, immortal, invisible, the only God, be honor and glory forever and ever. Amen.*

» God the Father Almighty possesses supreme authority and providence over all creation and history.

» God's "providence" refers to the truth that God works out his sovereign will in the universe whereby all events are disposed by him to fulfill his purposes for himself and his creation for good.

» The Father Almighty is the sovereign Lord over all, the life-giving source of all, and the all powerful Sustainer of all through his Son, Jesus Christ.

Segue 1

Student Questions and Response

page 275 📖 5

Please take some time now to answer these and other questions that the video teaching produced in your mind. This segment specifically asserts the "Godhood" of God, that is, the idea that the God and Father of our Lord Jesus is the sovereign Lord of all things, creating, sustaining, and supplying for the needs of all things under creation. Such a lofty truth is bound to generate some curiosities, or raise questions for clarification. As usual, be clear and concise in your answers, and where possible, support with Scripture!

1. How does God's ownership of the world and the universe as their Maker make it easy for us to understand him as sovereign over all things?

2. If creation belongs to God, and if he made all the heavens and the earth, then why doesn't everything happen just as God desires all the time?

3. What does it mean that God interacts with creation for his own purposes? Does that mean that God purposes the earthquakes, hurricanes, and tornadoes that take the lives of hundreds of people each year?

4. With all the war and destruction in human history, how can we say that God is working all things according to his will in the earth?

5. What does the term "providence" mean? How does this concept make plain God's relationship with his created universe?

6. According to the Scriptures, why is God able to be the source and provider of all things? How can God sustain all things and yet not lose any strength or show any weakness in his own person?

7. What role does our Lord Jesus play in God's ongoing sustaining of all things? What role did Jesus play in the actual creation of all the universe?

8. What is the single and uncontested purpose of all things in creation? How do we know that the universe will in fact fulfill this high purpose?

God as the Creator: The Providence of God

Segment 2: Implications of the Nicene Affirmation

Rev. Dr. Don L. Davis

God expresses his sovereign providence through his preservation and governance of all things. Saying that God *preserves all things* suggests that all things exist and hold together by virtue of God's sovereign care and provision. Correspondingly, in saying that God *governs all things* we are asserting that God possesses and exercises his authority within his universe, doing with his creation whatever he purposes.

Our objective for this segment, *Implications of the Nicene Affirmation*, is to enable you to see that:

- God's special work of providence is revealed in his preservation and governance of all things.

- "Preservation" refers to the fact that all things exist and hold together by virtue of God's sovereign care and provision.

- Regardless of theories given about the origins of the universe, no one and nothing can claim any kind of independence from God as the source of all being.

- "Governance" refers to the truth that God is sovereign over the entire universe, possessing all authority to do with creation whatever he purposes.

Summary of Segment 2

- God will restore his creation from its exposure to evil at Christ's glorious return.

- Accurately teaching on the providence of God resolves some of the modern errors of philosophy and theology, namely, pantheism, deism, fatalism, and chance.

Video Segment 2 Outline

The Nicene Creed regarding the person of God the Father: "We believe in one God, the Father Almighty, Maker of heaven and earth and of all things visible and invisible."

I. **God's Special Work of Providence Is Revealed in His Preservation of All Things.**

   A. Definition of God's preservation of all things in the universe

   1. *Preservation* = all things exist and hold together by virtue of God's sovereign care and provision. Nothing could or will survive without God's personal provision for its life and sustenance.

   2. Nothing and no one has life in and of themselves, Ps. 104.27-32.

   3. All things function purely on the basis of God's permissive will alone.

      a. Nothing could survive without God's ongoing care, Job 34.14-15.

      b. Human life is not self-sustaining, Ps. 146.4.

      c. When death occurs for beings upon the earth, their substance returns to the earth, and the life of the thing returns to God, Eccles. 12.7.

d. God alone gives life and breath to everything, Acts 17.25.

4. No one and nothing can claim any kind of independence from God as source of all being.

   a. God disposes of life here on earth, Job 12.10.

   b. God alone is the origin of our creation and our breath, Job 33.4.

   c. God made the worlds and preserves the life of all beings upon the earth, Isa. 42.5.

   d. In God alone do we have our movement and our existence, Acts 17.28.

B. Implications of God's preservation of all things in the universe

   1. What about the *evolution debate*? Does a belief in evolution science deny one's faith that the Father Almighty is the Maker of the heavens and the earth?

      a. The Bible's central aim is not to give scientific explanations that will satisfy atheistic skeptics, but *to clearly reveal the Father Almighty as the source and Sustainer of all things*.

      b. The writers of the Bible had different aims than 21st-century debates about origins, but this does not mean we should ignore their teachings about the universe.

The unqualified teaching of Scripture is that God the Father Almighty, the Maker of the heavens and the earth, of all things visible and invisible is a sovereign God whose providential care touches all his works and creatures. Nothing has life outside of him, nothing can sustain itself apart from his care, and no one can keep their life or existence one nano-second longer than he determines. He is the Lord of life, and preserves the life of all things according to his good will.

(1) The Father Almighty is the Maker of heaven and earth.

(2) God is not to be equated with the worlds he made.

(3) All life finds its being and existence in God.

(4) Without God's providential care, nothing would survive or continue; all things find their source and life in God.

2. Precisely how long did it take God to create the universe - a week or billions of years?

a. Because the Bible does not go into great specific detail on the "science" of creation, we can assume that the Lord's primary aim was not scientific clarification of the "*how*" of the creation. (The focus is obviously upon the "*who*" not on a detailed scientific explanation of the "*how*".)

b. We must embrace *the integrity of the biblical headship of Adam* (which is everywhere affirmed in Scripture, as well as by the Lord Jesus himself).

c. The future of the universe does not rest on the latest scientific theory about its origins but in *the providential plan of God the Father Almighty!*

II. God's Special Work of Providence Is Further Revealed in His Governance Over all Things.

A. Definition of God's governance over the universe

1. *Governance* = God is the Sovereign of the universe, possessing supreme authority to dispose his creation however he wills, Ps. 47.2.

2. God rules over all; the universe and the disposal of history are in his hands, 2 Chron. 20.6

3. It is in God's hand to turn all human affairs to his purpose, to make great and give strength.

   a. God is the Lord of the Kingdom, 1 Chron. 29.11-12.

   b. He is exalted above the nations, Ps. 47.8.

   c. God's dominion is eternal and touches all the inhabitants of the heavens and the earth, Dan. 4.34-35.

4. All things exist solely for his glory.

   a. His creation and preservation of Israel
      (1) Isa. 43.7
      (2) Isa. 43.21
      (3) Rom. 11.36
      (4) Rev. 4.11

5. All creation groans awaiting the release of the glorious freedom of the children of God, Rom. 8.18-23.

6. The present creation will be remade under God's direction, 2 Pet. 3.5-13.

B. Implications of God's governance over the universe

1. Is God the author of *evil and sin*?

   a. *No!* The chaos and destruction of the world has been caused by the rebellion of the devil and humankind in their opposition to God's kingdom reign (God is not the author of sin, cf. James).

   b. The trouble and cruelty of the world finds its source in the lust, greed, and pride of the world system, and those within it, 1 John 2.15-17.

   c. Things meant for evil God can use for the good of his own purpose.

      (1) The enslavement of Joseph, Gen. 50.20

      (2) The death of Jesus, Acts 2.23

2. If God is not the author of evil and sin, *why has or does he permit it?*

   a. God's providential will goes beyond our understanding of what is permitted and/or disallowed. As a sovereign God, he is working all things according to his will.

      (1) All things find their source, sustenance, and end in God, Rom. 11.36.

      (2) All things have been made for God's glory, Prov. 16.4.

b. His timing and methods have given some room for evil to exist until he determines its final end.

   (1) The Lord sets boundaries on the suffering of evil, 2 Pet. 2.9.

   (2) God employs evil to show forth his power, Rom. 9.22-24.

3. Since God is in charge of all things, *how can human beings truly be responsible for their actions?*

   a. Every person will bear their own burden for their choices, Rom. 9.19-21.

   b. God completes what is appointed for people based on their choice or rejection of his will.

      (1) God's purpose is not the reason people suffer, Gal. 6.7-8.

      (2) You reap in kind, Job 4.8.

      (3) The reward for our decisions is sure and certain, Prov. 11.18.

      (4) Sow the breeze and reap the tornado, Hos. 8.7.

      (5) Sow righteousness and you will reap the reward in kind, Hos. 10.12.

      (6) Everyone will receive according to their works, Rom. 2.6-10.

III. Key Lessons in the Doctrine of God the Father Almighty as Preserver and Governor of All Things

The Doctrine of the providence of God refutes modern errors of philosophy and theology.

A. *Error one:* God is a part of creation, and his identity is *not separate from creation*.

   1. He is separate from the substance of the universe (he is not a part of the created order).

   2. He is separate from the being and personality of all other beings (he reveals himself to human beings; he is not a part of their inner workings or makeup).

   3. God is the creator *ex nihilo* ("out of nothing") of the universe.

      a. This refutes *panentheism* (that God dwells alongside and interrelated in some fundamental way to all material things).

      b. This refutes *pantheism* (that God is directly associated with or arising from the matter of the universe).

B. *Error two:* God is *detached from the present workings of the universe*.

   1. God did not create the world and leave it to operate on its own (like a machine).

   2. God is personally involved in every moment of human affairs and upholds the created order for his own purposes.

   3. This refutes *deism* (that God created the heavens and earth and then left it to its own devices and directions).

C. *Error three: Fatalism* and *chance* are at the heart of the created order or human history.

1. God the Father Almighty is in charge of the universe.

2. God's higher purpose runs alongside and within every happening both in nature and human affairs.

3. God's divine concern touches all of life in this present age, and will ensure a new heavens and earth at the return of Jesus Christ.

4. Truly all things work together for good for those who are called according to the high purpose of God.

D. *Error four:* What there is now is all there has been or will be (this is *determinism*).

1. Creation and history are moving toward God's great consummation: God will create a new heavens and earth.

   a. God will create the heavens and earth anew, Isa. 65.17.

   b. John beheld this in his apocalyptic vision of the end, Rev. 21.1.

2. Living for this current world system is futile and shortsighted. We look for our real home, the New Jerusalem of God.

> **Isa. 40.6-8**
> *A voice says, "Cry!" And I said, "What shall I cry?" All flesh is grass, and all its beauty is like the flower of the field. The grass withers, the flower fades when the breath of the Lord blows on it; surely the people are grass. The grass withers, the flower fades, but the word of our God will stand forever.*

a. This present world system is doomed, 1 John 2.16-17.

b. Our citizenship is in heaven, Phil. 3.20.

c. We await the reward of Christ himself, 2 Tim. 4.8.

Conclusion

» God's special work of providence is revealed in his preservation and governance of all things.

» Our God not only made all things, but preserves them in his power and governs them in his wisdom, all for his glory.

Segue 2

Student Questions and Response

page 276 📖 6

Answer the following questions which will help you rethink the content and implications of the material you viewed in the second video segment. Undoubtedly, seeking to understand the relationship of God as sovereign Lord of the universe to the world system filled with all kinds of evil, distraction, chaos, and cruelty demands our best thinking and prayers. Seek to be thorough and plain in your answers to the following questions, and always, as usual, back up your claims by an appeal to the Scriptures!

1. What is the meaning of the theological term "God's preservation?" Why is it simply not possible to assert that anything in the universe can sustain itself by its own purpose and energy?

2. Can anything in all creation claim to be independent of God and his power? Explain your answer.

3. What implication does the doctrine of God's preservation have upon the evolution debate? What must we claim as believers about creation in the midst of such discussions and disagreements?

4. What is the definition of the doctrinal phrase "God's governance?" What is the relationship of God to the affairs of human beings and the nations?

5. What is the single purpose of all things in the universe? What is God's intent for creation at the Second Coming of Jesus Christ?

6. Is God the author of evil and tragedy in the world? If God is not the author of evil, then why does he permit it?

7. How can human beings be responsible for their actions if God is truly the governor of all things in heaven and earth? What is the nature of God's purpose to human free will?

8. How does the doctrine of God's preservation and governance answer the error of *pantheism*? How does it answer *deistic claims* that God is not present and active in the affairs of creation? How does the fact that God preserves and governs all things answer the errors of *fatalism* and *determinism*?

Summary of Key Concepts

This lesson highlights God as the God of providence, the sovereign Lord who is the source and Sustainer of all things, preserving and governing all things in his wisdom. All things exist by virtue of his will as Maker of all, and all things will bring glory to his name, which is the single unifying intention behind all life everywhere.

- That God possesses supreme authority and providence is shown over all creation and history.

- The "providence of God" refers to the fact that "God works out his sovereign will in the universe whereby all events are disposed by him to fulfill his purposes for himself and his creation for good."

- The Scriptures teach that the Father Almighty is Sovereign over all, the Source of all, and the Sustainer of all through his Son, Jesus Christ. All things are disposed to sync up with his will for himself, so he can receive glory for all things.

- God expresses his sovereign providence over all through his preservation and governance of all things.

- "Preservation" refers to the fact that all things exist and hold together by virtue of God's sovereign care and provision, and "governance" refers to the truth that God is sovereign over the entire universe, possessing all authority to do with creation whatever he purposes.

- As he who sustains all things through Jesus Christ, God will display a new heavens and earth at the restoration of all things at the Second Coming of Christ.

- Regardless of theories given regarding the origins of the universe, no one and nothing can claim any kind of independence from God as the source of all being.

- An accurate understanding of the providence of God resolves some of the modern errors of philosophy and theology, namely, *pantheism*, *deism*, *fatalism*, and *chance*.

Student Application and Implications

The idea of the providence of God has direct and important implications for all that you will ever do in ministry for the Lord. This is now your opportunity to take your group discussion into issues and areas that grow directly out of your own interests, questions, and situations. In order to minister effectively to others, you must be able to draw out principles and relate the truths of Scripture to your own life first. What particular questions come to your mind and spirit after having studied the present truths regarding God's providence, preservation, and governance? The questions below are meant to "jump start" your own more specific and critical questions.

* We know that the Lord does not "play favorites" (cf. James 2.1), but it seems like, from first glance, that the inner cities take a large part of the misery and cruelty of life. How do we explain this in light of God's governance over all things?

* Many people blame the poor for their hard times and misery. How are we to understand their struggle in light of the teaching of God's providence?

* Why didn't God simply put an end to all sin and the curse at the death of Jesus? Why does he give any latitude at all to the devil and his work in the world?

* How do we assert with all our hearts that although God is in control of all things, he is not the author of the death, destruction, and cruelty that makes up the world today?

* How are we to respond to evil and sin in light of the knowledge we have that God is neither the author of it, nor the one who desires for it to occur?

* How can we so understand the doctrine of God's providence that we use these powerful truths to counsel and comfort those who are enduring trial and tribulation in their lives?

Evolution, Creation, or What?

After youth group, one of the students, Shirley, asks if she can talk to you about a school project she is working on. As a part of her high school chemistry essay, she has chosen to write a paper on the evolution debate. She is not certain if she should reveal in the paper that she is a Christian herself, or if she should merely list the different arguments that are swirling around this discussion. In researching it, she has come to believe that perhaps parts of evolution may not be so far from the truth, but her conscience is bound to her faith that God Almighty alone is the Creator of the heavens and the earth. She is hurt and confused when she hears her teacher suggest that creationism is not science but fanciful imagination, but wants not to burn bridges as she shares her faith as a follower of Jesus. She is confused about what should be the best strategy for her paper. How would you advise Shirley in her project–what approach should she take, and how should she handle her work?

page 277 7

Holocaust a Punishment

While browsing the shelf in a local bookstore, you come across a book which makes the argument that the Holocaust (the extermination of six million Jews by the Third Reich from 1939-1945) was an actual punishment upon them for having crucified the Messiah. The author claims to be a historian, although he suggests that his analysis is largely theological (he also claims to be a Christian). What are we to make of this book? How are we to take analysis like this which looks at events in history and then suggests that God intended for the events to take place to fulfill *a divine purpose.* (For instance, many believed in the early part of the 19th century, that slavery was predestined for African Americans since, according to their argument, they were included in Noah's cursing of Ham for his indiscretion after the flood [cf. Gen. 9.24-25]).

A White Man's God

Many people believe today that the Christian faith is a religious tradition that has been shaped and determined by European culture, that was created by Whites for white people. It is not hard to see how they could get such a notion: the Christian tradition is associated with European cultures, with most of the liturgies, artistic expressions, and written sources springing from European roots, and God is always associated with nations of the West, more than the "South" and the "East." As a matter of fact, many wind up rejecting Christianity because they confuse faith in the Father Almighty with endorsement of Euro-American culture and lifestyle.

If you encountered someone who made the claim that the God of Christianity appears to favor the White peoples of this world, and ignores the cries of the colored peoples of history, how would you counter this? Do the doctrines of God's providence, preservation, and governance shed any light on our problem today to show that the God and Father of our Lord Jesus Christ is not a White man's God?

Restatement of the Lesson's Thesis

page 278 8

God the Father Almighty is the God of providence, the sovereign Lord who is the source and Sustainer of all things, preserving and governing all things in his wisdom. All things exist by virtue of his will as Maker of all, and all things will bring glory to his name, which is the single unifying intention behind all life everywhere. The "providence of God" refers to the fact that "God works out his sovereign will in the universe whereby all events are disposed by him to fulfill his purposes for himself and his creation for good." "Preservation" refers to the fact that all things exist and hold together by virtue of God's sovereign care and provision, and "governance" refers to the truth that God is sovereign over the entire universe, possessing all authority to do with creation whatever he purposes, and will restore all creation at Christ's return. Regardless of theories given regarding the origins of the universe, no one and nothing can claim any kind of independence from God as the source of all being. An accurate understanding of the providence of God resolves some of the modern errors of philosophy and theology, namely, pantheism, deism, fatalism, and chance.

Resources and Bibliographies

If you are interested in pursuing some of the ideas of *God as the Creator: The Providence of God*, you might want to give these books a try:

Hocking, David. *Who God Is*. Dallas: Word Publishing, 1984.

Packer, J. I. *Evangelism and the Sovereignty of God*. Downers Grove, IL: InterVarsity Press, 1991.

Pink, A. W. *The Sovereignty of God*. Grand Rapids: Baker Book House, 1984.

Ministry Connections

The providence of God has multiple kinds of implications for every phase of our lives and ministries. This is your opportunity again in the lesson to zero in on a particular point or issue that the Holy Spirit may want you to delve into for your own ministry. Of all the issues covered above, what is the one thing that the Holy Spirit impresses upon your heart and mind for your own life and ministry? What particular truth concerning God's providence, preservation, and/or governance resonates deepest with your own burdens and needs today. Reviewing this material is critical for your own in-depth application of the truth. Take the time to seek the Lord and isolate the issue or truths that seem to stay on your mind regarding the nature of God's providential working in the world.

Counseling and Prayer

page 278 9

While we know that we cannot possibly understand all the many intricacies of the providence of God, we do know that our own hearts are filled and encouraged as we reflect upon the sovereignty of God for our lives. All of Scripture makes plain that God the Father Almighty is the Maker of the heavens and the earth and therefore the entire universe belongs to him, and he is working all things together for the good of those who are called according to his purpose (Rom. 8.28). Without a doubt, you have issues and concerns that need to be brought before the Lord, the God of providence and governance, the God who preserves and directs. Take some time to lift up your heart desires to the Lord, on behalf of your own life, your loved ones, and those whom you serve in ministry. Remember that your instructor is available to intercede with and for you in these and other matters related to your life and ministry.

ASSIGNMENTS

Scripture Memory

1 Chronicles 29.11-12

Reading Assignment

To prepare for class, please visit *www.tumi.org/books* to find next week's reading assignment, or ask your mentor.

Other Assignments

Take careful note of all the assignments which are due for our next session above, and make certain that you again write a brief summary for each of your reading portions. Bring your listing of the main points to class next week (please see the "Reading Completion Sheet" at the end of this lesson).

Also, now is the time for you to think about the ministry project that will be due before the end of the module, as well which particular passage of Scripture you will select to do your exegetical project. Make sure that you neither procrastinate nor delay in determining either your ministry or exegetical project. The more you are aware of your ministry project, and the sooner you select your study passage, the more time you will have to prepare, and the better your work will be!

Looking Forward to the Next Lesson

In our next lesson we will study together one of the great mysteries of the doctrine of God, the doctrine of the Trinity, or God's triune nature. We will learn that the Bible teaches us that there is only one God, and yet this same God reveals himself as God the Father, Son, and Holy Spirit. The Scriptures declare that the one true God possesses a trinitarian nature, and that the members of the Trinity are one, diverse, and equal, the one true God, Father, Son, and Holy Spirit. We will also explore the glorious greatness of our God in his spirituality, his life, his personality, his infinite character, and his unchanging essence.

Capstone Curriculum

Module 6: God the Father
Reading Completion Sheet

Name _____

Date _____

For each assigned reading, write a brief summary (one or two paragraphs) of the author's main point. (For additional readings, use the back of this sheet.)

Reading 1

Title and Author: _____ Pages _____

Reading 2

Title and Author: _____ Pages _____

The Triune God
The Greatness of God

LESSON 3

page 281

Lesson Objectives

Welcome in the strong name of Jesus Christ! After your reading, study, discussion, and application of the materials in this lesson, you will be able to:

- Show from Scripture a general outline of the Bible's teaching about the doctrine of the *Trinity*, God's triune personhood.

- Explain that the Bible teaches us both that there is only one God, and yet this same God reveals himself as God the Father, Son, and Holy Spirit.

- Demonstrate from the Scriptures how God is spoken of as one God yet also as *plural*, that is, more than one person, which speaks of the Father, the Son, and the Holy Spirit as being persons within the Godhead.

- Recite some of the major historical understandings of the Trinity.

- Recognize the meaning of God's trinitarian nature, affirming that the members of the Trinity are one, diverse, and equal, the one true God, Father, Son, and Holy Spirit.

- Show an understanding of the various aspects of the Father's greatness, i.e., his spirituality, his life, his personality, his infinite character, and his unchanging essence.

Devotion

page 282

The Blessed Trinity

2 Cor. 13.14 - The grace of the Lord Jesus Christ and the love of God and the fellowship of the Holy Spirit be with you all.

It ought to never surprise us that God is beyond our comprehension, that mystery, wonder, and awe are associated with an infinite spirit being who spoke and twirled millions of galaxies on nothing and flung them into the blackness of space. Modern people cannot stand mystery; science and knowledge must (it is asserted) pull back the curtains of every false wizard pulling cords and speaking into megaphones like the false wizard in the Wizard of Oz. Everything can be explained by appeal to logic, evidence, and reliable processes of truth seeking. Our cultures today have no patience nor confidence in any faith that does not first make itself valid at the bar of the explainable and the testable.

The religion of the Jehovah's Witnesses is a perfect example. Everything in the Bible that cannot be immediately understood is changed to conform to their plumb line of reason and logic. For instance, since they cannot understand completely God as a tri-unity, they reject the scriptural teaching on the Trinity even though the Bible clearly asserts the divinity of the Father, the Son, and the Holy Spirit. In their theology, Jesus becomes the archangel Michael and the Holy Spirit becomes an "active force," like electricity. If you want to look full face at a religion stripped of all mystery and wonder you'll find it in the teachings of the Witnesses.

Regardless of what our intellects might scream at us, the simple word of the Apostles and prophets should be our ground and foundation. We are to baptize in the name (singular) of the Father, Son, and Holy Spirit, and at the baptism of Jesus, the Holy Spirit rests upon him as a dove, and the Father's voice declares that he is well pleased with our Lord (Matt. 3.17). This text in 2 Corinthians speaks of the grace of Jesus, the love of God and the communion of the Spirit (2 Cor. 13.14). All of the members are referred to as God, and all of them share the same attributes of greatness. Yet, the Bible states that there is only *one God*, not *three*. The Trinity is the result of biblical affirmation, not our own logic.

Should it surprise us that our God is beyond our thought, that God as he is in himself cannot be known or comprehended? Let us kneel before the Lord our Maker, asserting with joyful heart the very word of our Lord in Matthew 11:

> *Matt. 11.27 - All things have been handed over to me by my Father, and no one knows the Son except the Father, and no one knows the Father except the Son and anyone to whom the Son chooses to reveal him.*

Let's affirm the truth of Scripture and give praise and honor to the God of heaven, Father, Son, and Holy Spirit.

Nicene Creed and Prayer

After reciting and/or singing the Nicene Creed (located in the Appendix), pray the following prayers:

> *O God, you are infinite, eternal and unchangeable, glorious in holiness, full of love and compassion, abundant in grace and truth. Your works everywhere praise you, and your glory is revealed in Jesus Christ our Savior. Therefore we praise you, blessed and holy Trinity, one God, forever and ever. Amen.*
>
> ~ Presbyterian Church (U.S.A.) and Cumberland Presbyterian Church, The Theology and Worship Ministry Unit. **Book of Common Worship**. Louisville, KY.: Westminster/John Knox Press, 1993. p. 51

O Father, my hope; O Son, my refuge; O Holy Spirit, my protection. Holy Trinity, glory to Thee.

~ Compline, Eastern Orthodox, St. Joannikios
Appleton, George, ed. **The Oxford Book of Prayer**.
Oxford/New York: Oxford University Press, 1988. p. 183

Quiz

Put away your notes, gather up your thoughts and reflections, and take the quiz for Lesson 2, *God as the Creator: The Providence of God*.

Scripture Memorization Review

Review with a partner, write out and/or recite the text for last class session's assigned memory verse: 1 Chronicles 29.11-12.

Assignments Due

Turn in your summary of the reading assignment for last week, that is, your brief response and explanation of the main points that the authors were seeking to make in the assigned reading (Reading Completion Sheet).

page 284 *3*

A Faith that Doesn't Make Sense?

One of your church members, Mrs. Jackson, was visited by a Jehovah's Witness the other day, and the conversation has haunted her ever since. For over an hour Mrs. Jackson listened carefully to the clean, simple, and appealing logic of the Witnesses who visited her home. She felt completely overwhelmed as these visitors ran down their laundry list of errors they say that the organized Church believes. Rejecting a host of doctrines as simple falsehoods and historical blunders, the Witnesses argued passionately against the personality of the Holy Spirit, the doctrine of the Trinity, the deity of Christ, the existence of hell, salvation by grace, and on and on. Frustrated, the member asked the Witnesses, "You guys seem to have everything figured out; you don't seem to believe anything that does not line up with your reason." "That's right," shot back the head person of the Witness team, "for why do you want a faith that doesn't make sense to you?" That phrase has been with your member since it was spoken. How would you answer the question of the Witness: must everything in the Bible make "sense" to us before we believe its testimony? Are we or are we not obliged to believe whatever the Bible asserts, even if it goes beyond our knowledge and logic?

And Greatly to Be Praised

Arguing that God is worthy of our best and most excellent worship, the music minister at your church is making a pitch for a dramatic increase in the budget for sound, music, and the worship band. Having been deeply impacted by the pastor's preaching series on the *attributes of God*, he realized, he says, that he has been giving God *wounded sacrifices*, reserving the best resources and monies for his own personal needs and desires. With great passion and clarity, he articulated that if God is infinitely great, he is greatly to be praised! "The most important way," he suggests, "we can really show this great God that we love him is to give him our very best, and that means immediately!" If you were a member in the business meeting, what would you suggest about your music minister's understanding of the greatness of God, and his views that this should immediately influence the way in which we conduct business, spend money, and offer worship?

Much Ado about Nothing

On his return from seminary, Bill is upset because none of the people in his church seem as concerned about the things he has been learning as he is. After many semesters of wrestling with the great doctrines of the faith, he is anxious to share his answers to all their doctrinal questions, but they appear to have none. As a matter of fact, they find the discussions of doctrine and such "quite boring; it's much ado about nothing" as one deacon said. What is the relationship between the need to know and defend what the Bible asserts about God and his Kingdom and the simple faith of most people in the pew who simply cling to the Bible as God's Word? What advice do you have for Bill?

CONTENT

The Triune God: The Greatness of God

Segment 1: God's Greatness (Natural Attributes)

Rev. Dr. Don L. Davis

Summary of Segment 1

The Word of God plainly asserts that there is only one God (the *Shema*, Deut. 6.4), and yet also affirms the deity of God the Father, the Son, and Holy Spirit. The doctrine of the Trinity is the product of accepting the Bible's teaching on *God's oneness*, while at the same time, affirming what it says regarding the *divine nature* of the persons of the Father, the Son, and the Holy Spirit.

Our objective for this segment, *God's Greatness,* is to enable you to see that:

- The doctrine of the Trinity refers to the Bible's teaching about God's triune personhood.

- The Scriptures assert that God is one, and that there is none other than the one God, and yet they also assert that the one God reveals himself as God the Father, Son, and Holy Spirit.

- Each member of the Trinity (Father, Son, and Holy Spirit) possess the attributes and do the work of God, are called God, and exercise authority as God.

- The Bible affirms both God's oneness and God's plurality (that the Godhead is more than one person), with the persons Father, Son, and Holy Spirit addressed together as being persons within the Godhead.

- The Church has attempted to draft understandings of the Bible's teachings on the Trinity, with varying degrees of acceptance among believers.

- We must assert God's trinitarian nature, affirming that the members of the Trinity, though God in three persons, are in fact one, diverse, and equal, together comprising the one true God, Father, Son, and Holy Spirit.

I. The Lord God Is a Triune God.

Video Segment 1
Outline

A. The logic and biblical necessity of the Trinity

1. Trinitarian doctrine arises from an attempt to take the Bible seriously on its teaching about the nature of God.

2. The essence of the trinitarian argument: the Scriptures mandate a triune understanding of God.

   a. First, the Bible asserts that there is only one God.

   b. Yet, the Bible also speaks of three different persons within this Godhead who share the same authority, substance, and essence.

   c. God, therefore, must be a triune God.

3. Basic implications

   a. The Trinity, while the word is not in Scripture, is essentially a biblical teaching, or rather, an attempt to take the Bible seriously.

   b. The Trinity is incomprehensible (beyond our ability to understand).

   c. The Trinity should inspire awe, humility, and worship.

B. God is one God.

1. The Decalogue, Exod. 20.1-6

    a. The Lord God is the one true God. No other gods are to receive his worship and due.

    b. All other gods are idols. Only the Lord made the heavens and delivered his people.

    c. God is jealous; he will not share his glory with other deities or idols.

2. The *Shema*, Deut. 6.4-5

    a. Asserts the divinity of Yahweh God as the only God

    b. Asserts the unity and singleness of Yahweh

3. Jesus' affirmation of the unity and oneness of God, Mark 12.29-30

C. God exists in three Persons.

1. The Father is spoken of and referred to as God.

    a. Eph. 1.17

b. John 10.29

c. John 20.17

d. Rom. 15.6

e. 2 Cor. 1.3

f. 2 Cor. 11.31

g. Phil. 2.11

2. The Son is spoken of and referred to as God.

   a. Phil. 2.5-11

   b. John 1.1-18

   c. Heb. 1.1-12

   d. John 8.58

3. The Holy Spirit is spoken of and referred to as God.

   a. Acts 5.3-4

b. John 16.8-11

c. 1 Cor. 12.4-11

d. Matt. 28.19

e. 2 Cor. 13.14

4. Yet, there are not three Gods, but one blessed God, Father, Son, and Holy Spirit.

D. Biblical evidence for viewing God as one God in three persons

1. All the different members of the Trinity share the same attributes.

a. Eternal

(1) Rom. 16.26

(2) Rev. 22.12

(3) Heb. 9.14

b. Holy

(1) Rev. 4.8

(2) Rev. 15.4

(3) Acts 3.14

c. True

   (1) John 7.28

   (2) John 17.3

   (3) Rev. 3.7

d. Omnipresent

   (1) Jer. 23.24

   (2) Eph. 1.23

   (3) Ps. 139.7

e. Omnipotent

   (1) Gen. 17.1 with Rev. 1.8

   (2) Rom. 15.19

   (3) Jer. 32.17

f. Omniscient

   (1) Acts 15.18

   (2) John 21.17

   (3) 1 Cor. 2.10-11

g. Creator

   (1) Gen. 1.1 with Col. 1.16

   (2) Job 33.4

   (3) Ps. 148.5 with John 1.3

   (4) Job 26.13

h. Source of eternal life

   (1) Rom. 6.23

   (2) John 10.28

   (3) Gal. 6.8

i. Raising Christ from the dead

   (1) 1 Cor. 6.14 with John 2.19

   (2) 1 Pet. 3.18

2. Old Testament witness as to God's oneness

   a. Deut. 6.4

   b. 2 Kings 19.15

   c. 2 Kings 19.19

   d. Ps. 86.10

   e. Isa. 43.10

   f. Isa. 44.6

3. Old Testament witness as to God's plurality

a. The plural form of the noun for God: *Elohim* (cf. Gen. 1.26 with Isa. 6.8)

b. The self-mention of God at the creation of the *imago Dei* in humankind, Gen. 1.27 with 2.24

4. Trinitarian formulae (plural names of the Lord as triune in the New Testament)

    a. The baptism of Jesus, Matt. 3.16-17

    b. The Great Commission, Matt. 28.19

    c. The Corinthian benediction, 2 Cor. 13.14

5. Jesus' claim of oneness with the Father

    a. John asserts that Jesus is the Word, being with God, who is God, and giving revelation of God, John 1.1-18.

    b. Jesus and the Father are one, John 10.30.

    c. The one who sees Jesus has seen the Father, John 14.9.

    d. The Father and Jesus shared a fundamental glory before his self-emptying for our salvation, cf. John 17.21 with Phil. 2.6-8.

II. Views of the Trinity from History

A. *The Economic View:* the three persons are involved in various dimensions through both creation and redemption.

1. Hippolytus and Tertullian (early fathers of the Church)

2. This view made no attempt to explore the relations among the three members of the Trinity.

3. Focused on creation and redemption: Son and Spirit are not the Father, but are connected to God in his eternal being

B. *Dynamic Monarchianism:* God coming in power upon the person Jesus

1. Developed in the late 2nd and 3rd centuries, originated by Theodotus

2. God was present in the life of the man, Jesus of Nazareth.

   a. God was a working force upon, in, or through Jesus, but no real presence within Jesus.

   b. Before his baptism, Jesus was simply an ordinary man (although a remarkably virtuous one), cf. Matt. 3.16-17.

   c. At the baptism, the Spirit descended on Jesus, and God's power flowed through him from that point onward.

3. This view never became popular in the Church.

C. *Modalistic Monarchianism:* One God manifesting himself in three forms

1. There is one Godhead, which may be designated as Father, Son, or Spirit.

2. These terms do not stand for real distinctions of different members or personalities within the Godhead.

3. These terms refer to the one God working at different times in different modes.

4. Father, Son, and Spirit are the same person acting in three different modes (one person with three different names, activities, or roles).

5. This view cannot explain fully what the Bible actually teaches about the Father, Son, and Holy Spirit.

D. *The Orthodox Formulation* (The Council of Constantinople [381] and the view of Athanasius [293-373] and the "Cappadocian fathers" [Basil, Gregory of Nazianzus, and Gregory of Nyssa])

1. God has one *essence* or *substance* (*ousia*) which exists in *three persons* (*hypostases*).

2. God has a *common essence*, but exists in *three separate persons*.

3. The Cappadocian focus

   a. Individual *hypostases* is the *ousia* of the one God.

   b. Each member has characteristics or properties *unique to him* (e.g., individual people within universal humanity).

4. The orthodox view is *monotheistic*, not *tri-theistic* (i.e., belief that the Trinity teaches three separate Gods).

III. We believe in God: The Threefold Affirmation of Nicea (325)

A. The Nicene Creed confesses each member of the one Godhead.

   1. We believe in *God the Father Almighty* – the Father is God.

   2. We believe in *Jesus Christ the Lord* – the Son is God.

   3. We believe in *the Holy Spirit* – the Spirit is God.

B. The need to affirm the true nature of *the one God*, Father, Son, and Holy Spirit

   1. Affirm the *unity* of God.

2. Affirm the *diversity* of the members within the Trinity.

3. Affirm the *equality* of the members (in glory, substance, and majesty).

Conclusion

» The Word of God teaches that there is only one God, and yet this same God reveals himself as God the Father, Son, and Holy Spirit.

» Furthermore, the Scriptures teach not only that God is one God, but also speaks of God in three persons, as the Father, the Son, and the Holy Spirit.

Please take as much time as you have available to answer these and other questions that the video brought out. The biblical teaching on the Trinity is neither easy nor quick to comprehend and understand. What must be understood, however, is that the Trinity is an attempt to accept with full authority and honesty the *scriptural testimony* of God's unity as one God, and yet the divinity of the Father, the Son, and the Holy Spirit. Rehearse the key concepts on this important teaching, and make sure that you are able to defend any claims you make with the Scriptures themselves (Acts 17.11).

1. What is the meaning of the "doctrine of the *Trinity*?" To what of the Bible's teaching does this term refer?

2. Summarize how the Scriptures assert both God is one, while at the same time, affirming the divinity of the Father, Son, and Holy Spirit.

3. Give examples of some of the biblical evidence for asserting that each member of the Trinity (Father, Son, and Holy Spirit) are God, (i.e., show from the Bible how the various members possess the attributes of God, do the work of God, are called God, and exercise authority as God).

4. In what sense can we affirm both God's oneness, and God's plurality?

5. What is the meaning and relationship of God's persons and God's single essence? How has the Church attempted to understand the Bible's teachings on the Trinity (list an example).

Segue 1

Student Questions and Response

page 285 4

6. Why is it absolutely necessary never to state the idea of Trinity as meaning three gods? Why has the Church been so careful to distinguish between the single Godhood of God while affirming the *three persons of God*?

7. How do the creeds help us to understand how something is not doctrinally true about the Trinity? Can you deny either of these ideas and still have an acceptable view of the Trinity: the unity of God, the *differences* between the Father, Son, and the Holy Spirit, and the *equality* of the members?

The Triune God: The Greatness of God

Segment 2: God's Triune Glory: The Trinity

Rev. Dr. Don L. Davis

Summary of Segment 2

God the Father Almighty, often referred to as the first person of the Trinity, possesses attributes which speak powerfully and definitively as to his greatness. In every way, God the Father is spirit, possesses life in himself, has authentic personality, is infinite in his divine nature and character, and his essence never changes.

Our objective for this segment, *God's Triune Glory: The Trinity,* is to enable you to see that:

- God the Father Almighty is God, and possesses the divine attributes of greatness in his person.

- The Father Almighty is a spirit, not composed of matter or a physical nature.

- God the Father Almighty also is and has life, he has always been and is indestructible and immortal.

- God the Father Almighty is a person, he is self-conscious, capable of knowing, feeling, and choosing, and able to relate to other beings and creation.

- God the Father Almighty is infinite: in regards to space he is omnipresent, in regards to time he is eternal, in regards to knowledge he is omniscient, and in regards to power, he is omnipotent.

- God the Father Almighty is finally unchanging and constant: he will never not be, he has always been what he ever will be, and he will not alter in any of his perfections, glories, or excellencies.

I. God the Father Almighty Is a Spirit.

Video Segment 2 Outline

A. Aspects of God's spirituality

1. God is a spirit (he is not composed of matter, nor possesses a physical nature).

    a. John 4.24

    b. 1 Tim. 1.17

    c. 1 Tim. 6.15-16

2. God is invisible.

    a. John 1.18

    b. John 6.46

    c. Col. 1.15

3. God is not limited to any particular geographical location or place.

   a. Jer. 23.23-24

   b. Amos 9.2-3

B. Implications of God's spirituality

1. God possesses no limitations applicable to physical nature and being.

2. God does not need to dwell in an edifice, or live in shrines built by people, Acts 17.24-25.

3. Mention of "seeing God" or the physical features of God (e.g., hands, feet, eyes, etc.) are *anthropomorphisms* (expressing truths about God through comparisons with human features)

4. Appearances of God in the Old Testament should be understood as theophanies (appearances of the Son of God in the Old Testament era, [e.g., Genesis 18]).

II. God the Father Almighty Is Life.

A. Aspects of God's life

1. God is alive (he has always been and will always be indestructible).

a. Deut. 5.26

b. Ps. 42.2

c. Isa. 37.17

d. Jer. 10.10

e. Dan. 6.26

2. God is eternal (beyond the realm of time itself but able to engage it as he sees fit).

　a. Deut. 33.27

　b. Rom. 16.26

　c. 1 Tim. 1.17

3. God is self-existent; he has life in and of himself.

　a. John 5.26

　b. Exod. 3.14

c. Ps. 36.9

d. Ps. 90.2

B. Implications of God's life

1. God derives nothing externally for his own being.

2. God is dependent on nothing (i.e., he needs nothing outside of himself), Acts 17.24-25.

3. Although God is independent of external necessities, he is neither isolated, aloof, nor disinterested in creation and human affairs.

III. God the Father Almighty Is a Person.

A. Aspects of God's personhood

1. God is self-conscious (he has a will, is capable of knowing, feeling, and choosing).

a. Exod. 3.14

b. Exod. 6.3

c. Isa. 44.6

d. Rev. 1.8

2. God is relational (he can understand and relate to other persons and social beings).

   a. Deut. 7.6-9

   b. 1 John 4.7-9

B. Implications of God's personality

   1. Relationship is intrinsic to the nature of God the Father, John 17.25.

   2. God is not an object or a force (like a meteor or electricity); to be made in God's image is to be both personal and relational (cf. Gen. 1.26-27).

   3. God is an end in himself; we relate to him not for what we get out of him but because of who he is.

   4. Eternal life is not merely an ethic or a religion, but a new relationship with God through Jesus Christ, John 17.3.

IV. God the Father Almighty Is Infinite.

A. Aspects of God's infinitude

   1. In regards to space (omnipresent)

a. Questions of location do not apply to God, Jer. 23.23-24.

b. There is no place where God cannot be found to be, Ps. 139.7-12.

2. In regards to time (eternal)

a. His nature is eternal, Isa. 40.28.

b. God has always been and will always be (i.e., he is the Alpha and the Omega).

(1) Rev. 1.8

(2) Ps. 90.1-2

(3) Jude 1.25

c. Time has no holding power on his consciousness or person, 2 Pet. 3.8.

3. In regards to knowledge (omniscient)

a. His understanding of all things has no limits, Ps. 147.5.

b. All things are naked and open to his comprehension and understanding.

(1) Isa. 40.28

(2) Heb. 4.13

c. He has access to all information about all things, as well as all possible things, but is himself subject to no one's scrutiny, Rom. 11.33

4. In regards to power (omnipotent)

   a. His name *El Shaddai* speaks to his almighty power.

      (1) Gen. 17.1

      (2) Gen. 28.3

      (3) Gen. 35.11

      (4) Exod. 6.3

      (5) Rev. 19.6

   b. Nothing is too hard for God to accomplish or complete.

      (1) Gen. 18.14

      (2) Num. 11.23

      (3) Ps. 115.3

      (4) Jer. 32.17

      (5) Dan. 4.35

      (6) Matt. 19.26

   c. God can do beyond what any of us can conceive (within his own will), Eph. 3.20.

B. Implications of God's infinitude

1. God is unlimited in his person, and therefore is free to do anything he wills within his own purpose and will.

2. God is not constrained by time and space; he is above and beyond those categories, yet able to understand them and use them for his purposes.

3. God sees all things in proper perspective, having all access to all information about all things simultaneously in perfect understanding.

4. God is free, because of his infinite power, wisdom, and nature, to accomplish any and everything according to the good pleasure of his own will.

V. God the Father Almighty Is Unchanging (Constant).

A. Aspects of God's constancy

1. God will never not be; he will endure beyond all and over all, Ps. 102.26-27.

2. The Lord does not change; who he is, is what he has always been and shall ever be.

    a. Mal. 3.6

    b. Num. 23.19

c. 1 Sam. 15.29

d. Heb. 6.18

e. Rev. 22.13

3. God does not alter his Word, nor does his character shift and vary.

   a. James 1.17

   b. Rom. 11.29

B. Implications of God's constancy

   1. God neither increases nor decreases in any attribute or characteristic.

   2. God's Word is absolutely reliable and credible; he cannot lie and will always be faithful to his promises and covenants.

   3. God's being as constant should not be equated with the Greek notion of immobility (God the Father Almighty is not a static force but a loving Father who acts and reacts in relationship to his people).

   4. While God does not change, what of the biblical statements about God changing his mind?

a. Some are *anthropomorphisms*.

b. God can work out phases of his plans which may appear as changes of mind to us (e.g., the offer of salvation to the Gentiles).

c. God responds to human changes (e.g., the repentance of Nineveh in Jonah).

Conclusion

» God the Father Almighty is glorious in his divine greatness.

» His attributes associated with his greatness include his spirituality, his life, his personality, his infinite character, and his unchanging essence.

Segue 2

Student Questions and Response

page 286 📖 5

Now is your time again to review the critical concepts associated with the material in the second video segment. The greatness of God the Father Almighty is not possible to comprehend, and the intent of this segment was to provide you with a general outline of the "natural attributes" associated with the greatness of God, his incomparable glory and majesty. As you answer the following questions, make sure that you are thorough in your answers, seeking to understand the underlying assumptions which are connected to each one. Strive to be clear in your responses to the questions, making sure that you use the Word of God to support and validate your conclusions.

1. What is the meaning of the term *greatness* as it relates to the person of God the Father Almighty? What precisely do the divine attributes of *greatness* suggest about the nature of the Father's character and person?

2. What does Scripture teach regarding the spiritual nature of the Father Almighty? As a spirit, what then do we know regarding God's nature that is not true of any other being? How is the nature of God as spirit different or similar to that of the angels?

3. What is the definition of the attribute of God as possessing *life*? What does it mean to say that God the Father Almighty is "immortal?" In what way can we say that the life of God, having no beginning nor end, is "indestructible?"

4. List some of the elements included in the understanding that God the Father Almighty is a person? In what ways is God's personality different from our own? What does the personality of God suggest about his ability to relate to other self-conscious beings?

5. In what ways can we say that the nature of God the Father Almighty is infinite? What does God's infinitude *applied to space* tell us about him? What about his infinitude applied to time? What about his infinitude in regards to knowledge? What about his infinitude in regards to power?

6. What does it mean to suggest that God the Father Almighty is unchanging and constant? Does God *change his mind* in any sense at all? If so, how so? Why is it important to assert the unchanging nature of God in regards to his covenant promise? In regards to his love for humankind? In regards to his purpose to redeem?

7. In what way can we so understand the attributes of God's greatness together that we can comprehend them *in light of one another*? Can you suggest a way in which we can understand these mighty and glorious attributes *together* rather than *separately*?

Summary of Key Concepts

This lesson concentrates on both the triune nature of the Trinity as well as the attributes of greatness of God the Father Almighty. The doctrine of the Trinity affirms Scripture's claims that God is both one and yet exists as three distinct persons, all who are referred to as God, and share the glory of the divine nature. God the Father, the first person of the Trinity, possesses attributes which speak powerfully and definitively as to his greatness. As God the Father is spirit, he possesses life in himself, has authentic personality, is infinite in his divine nature and character, and possesses an essence that never changes.

- The doctrine of the *Trinity* refers to the Bible's teaching about God's triune personhood.

- The Scriptures assert that God is one, and that there is none other than the one God, and yet they also assert that the one God reveals himself as God the Father, Son, and Holy Spirit.

- Each member of the Trinity (Father, Son, and Holy Spirit) possess the attributes and do the work of God, are called God, and exercise authority as God.

- The Bible affirms both God's oneness, and God's plurality (that the Godhead is *more than one person*), with the persons Father, Son, and Holy Spirit addressed together as being persons within the Godhead.

- The doctrine of the Trinity asserts that God exists in three persons, and that all the members share the same essence, are distinct in their personalities and work, and yet are co-equal in glory, together comprising the one true God, Father, Son, and Holy Spirit.

- God the Father Almighty is God, and displays all of the divine attributes of greatness.

- God the Father Almighty is a spirit, not composed of matter or a physical nature.

- God the Father Almighty is and has life, he has always been and is indestructible and immortal.

- God the Father Almighty is a person, he is self-conscious, capable of knowing, feeling, and choosing, and able to relate to other beings and creation.

- God the Father Almighty is infinite: in regards to space he is *omnipresent*, in regards to time he is *eternal*, in regards to knowledge he is *omniscient*, and in regards to power, he is *omnipotent*.

- God the Father Almighty is finally unchanging and constant: he will never not be, he has always been what he ever will be, and he will not alter in any of his perfections, glories, or excellencies.

Student Application and Implications

Now is the time for you to discuss with your fellow students your own tough questions about the Trinity and the divine attributes of the Father's greatness. Undoubtedly you have some questions that have come to mind as you have listened, studied, prayed, and reflected on these great topics of the Word of God. Take a moment to gather up your own particular questions on these and related subjects, and share them with your fellow learners. Interact together on the issues and concerns that have now surfaced in your study of the materials. Perhaps questions below might point you in some different directions.

* Can a person be a Christian and deny the doctrine of the *Trinity*? Is it as important as the doctrine of salvation by grace through faith, or can a person have a different view of God than the Trinity and still be considered "orthodox?"

* Since the word "Trinity" is not itself in the Bible, how can theology make it out to be an "essential doctrine" of the faith?

* Can one believe something about God like what the Jehovah's Witnesses believe (God the Father alone is God; Jesus is the second greatest being made by God and the Spirit is God's power for service) and still be considered biblical? Why or why not?

* How can you so understand the greatness of God that it affects all that you do: your worship, your conduct and character, and your ministry? How do you translate this high truth into a radical lifestyle for God?

* So many look at God as one who wants to meet their needs, and not as the triune and sovereign God of the universe. How do you make the switch *from seeing God as one who lives for me to the God for which all things exist*?

* What are practical ways to help growing believers desire and learn the "deeper truths" of the Word of God regarding God's attributes, character, and name?

* The attributes of God's greatness (i.e., his spirituality, life, person, infinitude, and constancy) speak of a being far beyond our comprehension. How does our faith in Jesus Christ make the Father more accessible to us (cf. John 1.18; John 14.7-9)?

"It Don't Seem Relevant"

During a series on the attributes of God in the Pastor's mid-week Bible study, a young, hungry new believer raises her hand and makes a comment about the study. "Pastor," she says nearly apologetically, "I know that this may be important in a seminary kind of setting, but honestly, I am struggling to see why we ought to be studying all of these funny words and things about God. Why do we have to understand what Christians believed long ago about the nature of God, or use any other words like *ousios* or *homousia* or any of the fifty dollar terms. I just want to know about Jesus, really I don't care much for doctrine anyway. Can you tell me why on earth I, as a new Christian, should be interested in all of this stuff–to me, it just don't seem to matter much, it just don't seem relevant to anything I do." As pastor, how would you respond to the genuine question being raised by this dear sister in Christ?

One God, in Three Modes

A popular televangelist/preacher has recently come out with a view of the Trinity that has many eyebrows raising in the Christian community. Rather than affirm the traditional Christian view of the Trinity as one God who manifests himself in three distinct persons (Father, Son, and Holy Spirit), this popular teacher believes that there is one God who actually displays himself in three modes depending on the situation. In other words, while he affirms that God is one, he denies that the persons of the Trinity are distinct persons. There is only one God who manifests himself in three different modes. Why is this view unacceptable according to the Word of God? Would you count this view to be heresy? Why or why not?

"A Little too Friendly"

So many of the praise and worship songs today highlight the intimacy and personal relationship that the believer now has with God. Many of the songs speak of God as friend, confidant, even as lover, with a strong emphasis on the *personal dimension* of our relationship with God. Yet, it is clear that with the absence of solid doctrinal teaching in many of our churches, and with hymns being sung less and less in most fellowships, many believers have no orientation to the attributes of the *greatness* of God the Father Almighty. In a real sense, the God of many churches is only large enough to meet the needs of our hearts, not tackle the problems of the world, let alone redeem a universe out of control. As one has characterized this state: "the God of many churches is a good pal, but doesn't seem to be the great God and our Savior, the God and Father of our Lord Jesus Christ. We seem to be just a little too friendly with him who is a consuming fire."

Imagine that the Lord has called you to be a minister of music and worship in a church. List out eight different emphases or things you could do to help believers in your church gain a greater, richer, and more biblical appreciation for the *greatness* of God in your worship and life together.

The doctrine of the Trinity is a biblical doctrine which asserts that God's nature is a tri-unity of three persons who share the same essence as God. The Bible claims that God is one God (Deut. 6.4), and yet this one God exists in three distinct yet co-equal, co-eternal persons, each of whom is referred to as God in Scripture, and are said to share the glory of the divine nature. The Holy Trinity (i.e., God the Father, the Son, and the Holy Spirit) is the name given to affirm Scripture's own assertion of the unity, diversity, and equality of the members of the one Godhead. God the Father Almighty, the first person of the Trinity, possesses attributes which speak powerfully and definitively as to his greatness. As God, the Father is spirit, possesses life in himself, has authentic personality, is infinite in his divine nature and character, and his essence never changes.

Restatement of the Lesson's Thesis

If you are interested in pursuing some of the ideas on the nature of the Trinity and the greatness of God the Father Almighty, you might want to give these books a try (be warned, these are not easy readings!):

Resources and Bibliographies

> Charnock, Stephen. *The Existence and Attributes of God*. Grand Rapids: Baker Book House, 1996.
>
> O'Collins, Gerald, S. J. *The Tripersonal God: Understanding and Interpreting the Trinity*. Mahwah, NJ: Paulist Press, 1999.
>
> White, James R. *The Forgotten Trinity: Recovering the Heart of Christian Belief*. Bloomington, MN: Bethany House Publishing, 1998.

Ministry Connections

The doctrine of the Trinity and the greatness of God the Father are not merely theological themes to be studied and filed away. On the contrary, these are the great truths of the faith, and those who meditate long upon them are changed forever as a result of the reflection. Relating these great truths to your life and ministry can transform them; the price is concentrated application of the Word of God to your own life. As you meditate on the teaching in this lesson, ask the Lord how he might want you to enrich, change, or alter your ministry approach because of the truths the Holy Spirit has pointed out to you here. As you meditate on these truths, and think about your own life and ministry connected to them, seek to discern what the Spirit might be calling you to do right now, if anything, about these truths. Spend time before the Lord meditating on the truth of God's nature and greatness, and ask him how and in what way you might creatively apply the teaching here. Also, as you consider writing your ministry project for this module, you might want to connect your assignment to some theme here. Seek the Lord regarding his direction, and come back next week ready to share your insights with the other learners in your class.

Counseling and Prayer

In pondering these truths on the nature of God as triune Lord and on the greatness of God the Father Almighty, one begins to see the sufficiency of our God to meet every need, not only in one's personal life but in the lives of those whom we love and serve. Maybe in the course of this lesson, while meditating on the greatness of the Father, some pressing need has been made known to you. The Holy Spirit has caused you, perhaps, to focus on a particular issue, need, or concern, and you need to seek the Lord for his strength and aid in it. Now is the time to share your need and pray for one another. If time does not permit for you to intercede together now, enlist a prayer partner with whom you can share your burden and who will lift up your requests to the Lord. Of course, know that your instructor will be willing and open to pray with you, as well as your church leaders, especially your pastor. Listen to the Lord, and allow the Holy Spirit to lead you into sharing your needs with the Father Almighty, our great and sovereign Lord of all.

Scripture Memory

Matthew 3.16-17

Reading Assignment

To prepare for class, please visit *www.tumi.org/books* to find next week's reading assignment, or ask your mentor.

Other Assignments

page 287 7

Please turn in to your instructor your reading assignment sheet containing your summary of the reading material for the week. Make certain that you have selected your Bible passage for your exegetical project, and make sure that you understand the standards and due dates for your ministry project. *Word to the wise:* it is better to be organized and ahead of schedule than be forced into last minute cramming. Talk with your Mentor, and make sure that you have all the necessary information, and have turned in your selections in plenty of time so you can begin to complete these assignments on time.

Looking Forward to the Next Lesson

Our final lesson will concentrate on the attributes of God's *goodness*. God's marvelous goodness is expressed in his moral attributes of his perfect moral purity, absolute integrity, and unbounded love. In regards to his perfect moral purity, we'll examine his holiness, righteousness, and justice. In connection to his integrity, we'll explore his genuineness, veracity, and faithfulness. Finally, in regards to his love, we will highlight his benevolence, grace, mercy, and persistence. We will also explore together the relationship between God's goodness and his severity, examining the wrath of God and its relationship to his wonderful love.

Capstone Curriculum

Module 6: God the Father
Reading Completion Sheet

Name _____

Date _____

For each assigned reading, write a brief summary (one or two paragraphs) of the author's main point. (For additional readings, use the back of this sheet.)

Reading 1

Title and Author: _____   Pages _____

Reading 2

Title and Author: _____   Pages _____

LESSON 4

God as Father
The Goodness of God

page 289

Lesson Objectives

Welcome in the strong name of Jesus Christ! After your reading, study, discussion, and application of the materials in this lesson, you will be able to:

- Provide an outline of God's marvelous goodness expressed in his moral attributes of his perfect moral purity, absolute integrity, and unbounded love.

- Show how God's perfect moral purity is demonstrated through his holiness, righteousness, and justice.

- Clarify those qualities associated with God's integrity, i.e., his genuineness, veracity, and faithfulness.

- Recite an overview of the attributes associated with the love of God, his benevolence, grace, mercy, and persistence.

- Detail the biblical basis for the wrath of God as a moral quality usually associated with God's severity.

- Explain the relationship between God's goodness and severity, his love and justice.

- Express the need for an understanding of God's attributes and nature that prevents any confusion or conflict about the Lord and his actions.

Devotion

Please Don't Fool Yourself

page 290

Rom. 2.3-11 - Do you suppose, O man—you who judge those who do such things and yet do them yourself—that you will escape the judgment of God? [4] Or do you presume on the riches of his kindness and forbearance and patience, not knowing that God's kindness is meant to lead you to repentance? [5] But because of your hard and impenitent heart you are storing up wrath for yourself on the day of wrath when God's righteous judgment will be revealed. [6] He will render to each one according to his works: [7] to those who by patience in well-doing seek for glory and honor and immortality, he will give eternal life; [8] but for those who are self-seeking and do not obey the truth, but obey unrighteousness, there will be wrath and fury. [9] There will be tribulation and distress for every human being who does evil, the Jew first and also the Greek, [10] but glory and honor and peace for everyone who does good, the Jew first and also the Greek. [11] For God shows no partiality.

If there is anything that hampers people from becoming all that God wants them to become it is the tendency for people to make God into their own image, to take liberties with his goodness, to view his graciousness as weakness, and his love as license to do wrong. Truly, "The fear of the Lord is the beginning of wisdom, and the knowledge of the Holy One is insight," (Prov. 9.10). Many interpreters of God's fear lessen the importance of this kind of angst and dread of our living God, making fear here and other places in Scripture only refer to the noble concept of awe and reverence for God.

This text, however, can legitimately be interpreted as genuine fear, real dread, deep hearted angst of a mighty God who displays his kindness to us. This great overflowing kindness, God's goodness and grace, according to Paul in his letter to the Romans, "is meant to lead you to repentance," not to make us the judges of others or lackadaisical in our response to God's standards of holiness. The riches of God's kindness and forbearance and patience should prod and move us to do good, to seek immortality, to live for the Kingdom of God, to exalt Messiah in all we do, to care for our brothers and sisters in Christ, and to make disciples of all nations. In other words, the goodness of God should move you to action, change your identity, transform your life. We ought not fool ourselves or others; any understanding of God's kindness and goodness that does not give the sense of gratitude, fear, and willingness to obey God is a poor or flawed one. God's goodness enables us to escape his judgment, quite literally, by the skin of our teeth.

Let us, then, embrace the goodness of God not as if we deserve it or could ever earn it. Let us not judge anyone else, knowing full well that we are saved purely because of the mercy and kindness of the Lord. Please, don't fool yourself. The goodness of God should lead you to repentance and transformation, not judgment and self-satisfaction.

Let the goodness of God have its way in your life so you may remain humble, focused, and grateful as you seek immortality through faith in Messiah.

Nicene Creed and Prayer

After reciting and/or singing the Nicene Creed (located in the Appendix), pray the following prayer:

You are holy, Lord, the only God, and your deeds are wonderful. You are strong. You are great. You are the Most High, you are almighty. You, holy Father, are King of heaven and earth. You are Three and One, Lord God, all good. You are Good, all Good, supreme Good, Lord God, living and true. You are love, you are Wisdom. You are humility, you are endurance. You are rest, you are peace. You are joy and gladness. You are justice and moderation. You are all our riches, and you suffice for us. You are beauty. You are gentleness. You are protector, you are our guardian and defender. You are courage. You are our haven and our hope. You are our faith, our great consolation. You are our eternal life. Great and wonderful Lord, God almighty, merciful Savior.

~ St. Francis of Assisi, 1181-1226.
Appleton, George, ed. **The Oxford Book of Prayer**.
Oxford; New York: Oxford University Press, 1988. pp. 62-63

Quiz

Put away your notes, gather up your thoughts and reflections, and take the quiz for Lesson 3, *The Triune God: The Greatness of God*.

Scripture Memorization Review

Review with a partner, write out and/or recite the text for last class session's assigned memory verse: Matthew 3.16-17.

Assignments Due

Turn in your summary of the reading assignment for last week, that is, your brief response and explanation of the main points that the authors were seeking to make in the assigned reading (Reading Completion Sheet).

Freedom or License?

The entire church has been stirred after a series on the nature of God's grace in Christ by the youth pastor. His clear biblical teaching of the grace of God was well received, and he excellently outlined for the youth our freedom in Christ from the law, the power of the old sin nature, and all fleshly attempts to please God without the blood of Christ. A few of the kids, after hearing that they did not have to do anything to win the favor of God, have begun to "express their freedom" in ways that appear to some in the church to look more like license than freedom in Christ. They have begun to dress "worldly," bring secular music into the fellowship hall, and want to throw "dances" at the church. Some think it is wonderful, while others blame the youth pastor for placing these worldly ideas about freedom into the minds of the kids. How do you so address this issue as to help the students understand what the freedom of Christ really means as a response to the goodness of God?

"Making People Afraid Just Doesn't Work."

An older parishioner who for years has been a part of the fellowship commented one day to the pastor, "I have now been listening to you for four years, and I do not think I have ever heard you teach on the wrath of God. I mean never–you've never taught it in a Bible study, a sermon, a workshop, seminar–nowhere. I know that there is probably a good reason for this, but why don't you ever mention it? The Bible sure does!" The pastor nodded at the church member, and replied, "You're right, I haven't preached on this since I have been here. I just don't believe that teaching the wrath of God helps people really understand what God's intention is for today. Christ came to save, not to condemn, and people need to know that God cares for them, not be frightened into coming to Jesus out of dread and fear. Honestly, through my ministry over the years, if there is one thing I've learned is that making people afraid doesn't work. People don't need to be frightened into faith; rather, they need to be loved into it." Do you agree with this pastor's assessment of our task in communicating to people about God's love and wrath? Where is he right and where is he wrong?

"Just Too Mean."

In commenting on the reason why he just couldn't become a Christian, a coworker says to you during lunch break, "I like Jesus and all the talk about love and everything, but the thing I notice is that most Christians are really nasty people. They oppose too many things, they hate all kinds of groups, and just seem to be disagreeable about a lot of stuff. And, seeing the way they treated some of those fallen televangelists, they shoot their wounded, too. For all the talk about God's grace and goodness, they don't seem to be gracious to anybody, and they don't tend to find much good in anything. I just couldn't become a Christian. They are just too mean!" How would you respond to a person who had this perception of the Christian experience of grace?

CONTENT **God as Father: The Goodness of God**

Segment 1: Moral Qualities of Goodness

Rev. Dr. Don L. Davis

Summary of Segment 1

page 291

God expresses his goodness through his moral attributes of perfect moral purity, absolute integrity, and unbounded love. He demonstrates his perfect moral purity through his holiness, righteousness, and justice. He expresses his absolute integrity through his attributes of genuineness, veracity, and faithfulness. Finally, God expresses his unbounded love through his attributes of his benevolence, grace, mercy, and persistence.

Our objective for this segment, *Moral Qualities of Goodness,* is to enable you to see that:

- God's marvelous goodness is expressed through the moral attributes of his perfect moral purity, absolute integrity, and unbounded love.

- God's perfect moral purity is manifested through his holiness, righteousness, and justice.

- God the Father Almighty also expresses his goodness by those qualities associated with God's integrity, i.e., his genuineness, veracity, and faithfulness.

- The love of God, as an expression of his divine goodness, is associated with his attributes of benevolence, grace, mercy, and persistence.

- Understanding the goodness of God boosts our confidence and conviction to trust and serve our infinitely lovely God.

Video Segment 1 Outline

I. God the Father Almighty Possesses Perfect Moral Purity.

Theologians refer to the moral purity of God as his absolute holiness, perfect beauty demonstrated in his complete separation and freedom from anything malicious, sinful, chaotic, or evil. This perfect moral perfection is revealed in his holiness, righteousness, and justice.

A. God is holy (God is morally perfect and completely separate and free from all forms of evil and wickedness).

  1. He is absolutely unique.

     a. Exod. 15.11

     b. 1 Sam. 2.2

     c. Isa. 6.1-4

  2. He is absolutely pure in all respects.

     a. Hab. 1.13

     b. James 1.13

  3. He is beautiful and full of splendor.

     a. Ps. 104.1-4

     b. Ps. 22.3

     c. Rev. 4.8

4. Implications of God's holiness

   a. God's holiness is the standard of our lives–we are to reflect his moral character in our pursuits and relationships.

      (1) Lev. 11.44-45

      (2) 1 Pet. 1.15-16

   b. God deserves our praise, reverence, and delight.

      (1) 1 Chron. 16.10

      (2) Rev. 15.4

   c. God demands our personal sanctified service, Ps. 93.5.

B. God is righteous (the righteousness of God refers to his holiness applied to his relationship to other beings), Ps. 48.10; 71.15; 97.2; 111.3.

   1. The law of God is righteous, Ps. 19.7-9.

   2. God's actions correspond to his character.

      a. Judg. 5.11

      b. 1 Sam. 12.7

      c. Ps. 145.17

3. God is his own standard for right relationships and his own person is the standard for his will.

   a. Jer. 9.23-24

   b. John 17.25

4. Implications of God's righteousness

   a. God has done and can do no wrong to anyone or anything.

   b. God's ways are always beneficial, correct, and helpful.

   c. God's righteousness should engender confidence and hope.

C. God is just (God administers all his affairs with his universe according to his good will and just law).

1. God is impartial in his dealings, and does not give any respect to external categories or persons.

   a. 2 Chron. 19.7

   b. Jer. 32.19

   c. Col. 3.25

d. 1 Pet. 1.17

2. His government, judgments, and decrees are just.

    a. Gen. 18.25

    b. Ps. 9.4

    c. Rev. 19.2

3. God demonstrates justice in all of his actions and dealings, i.e., all his "ways."

    a. Deut. 32.4

    b. Isa. 45.21

4. Implications of God's justice

    a. As children of God, we are to show no partiality in our dealings with others.

        (1) Amos 5.15

        (2) Amos 5.24

        (3) James 2.9

b. God's justice should produce our worship and praise, Ps. 99.3-4.

c. Don't mess with the Lord, Jer. 50.7.

II. God the Father Almighty Possesses Absolute Integrity.

God is a God of truth: he is genuine, veracious, and faithful.

A. God is genuine (God is true in all he is, says, and does).

1. God is the only true God.

   a. 1 Thess. 1.9

   b. 1 Tim. 1.17

   c. 1 John 5.20

   d. Rev. 6.10

2. God is real and dwells in the realm which is the "really real," Ps. 100.3.

3. God delights in truth for this is his very nature.

   a. Ps. 31.5

b. Ps. 51.6

c. Jer. 10.17

d. John 17.3

4. Implications of God's genuineness

 a. All other gods are untrue: Yahweh is the only true God.

 b. Who God is, is the ground of all that God says and does.

 c. Doubting God is never permissible or sensible; he simply is truthful in his very being.

B. God is veracious (God represents things as they really are).

 1. God cannot lie.

 a. Num. 23.19

 b. 1 Sam. 15.29

 c. Titus 1.2

2. He fulfills to the final particulars all of his covenant promises.

    a. Mic. 7.20

    b. 2 Cor. 1.20

3. God's Word is absolutely trustworthy; it cannot be broken or changed.

    a. Ps. 119.160

    b. Isa. 55.8-11

    c. John 17.17

4. Implications of God's veracity

    a. God's veracity invites us to know, believe, and act on God's sure and certain promises.

    b. As God's children we must, like him, be truthful in all our ways.

    c. God's veracity asks us to wait upon the fulfillment of God's promises in his own time and his own way, Isa. 40.28-31.

C. God is faithful (God proves to be true in all things he does).

1. God proves true in all he does and carries through on.

    a. Num. 23.19

    b. 1 Kings 8.20

    c. 1 Thess. 5.24

    d. Heb. 10.23

2. God remains faithful, even when everyone and everything else fails, 2 Tim. 2.13.

3. God's faithfulness makes his actions and promises solidly predictable.

    a. Ps. 89.2

    b. Ps. 89.33

    c. Lam. 3.23

    d. 1 Cor. 1.9

    e. 1 Pet. 4.19

4. Implications of God's faithfulness

   a. We are to plead God's faithfulness in prevailing prayer, Ps. 143.1

   b. We are to proclaim God's faithfulness abroad

      (1) Ps. 40.10
      (2) Ps. 89.1

   c. God's faithfulness should spawn new forms of heartfelt worship and praise, Ps. 89.5

III. God the Father Almighty Possesses and Demonstrates Unbounded Love.

A. God is benevolent (God is concerned for the well-being and welfare of those whom he loves).

   1. He seeks and purposes our personal welfare.

      a. Jer. 29.11-13

      b. Matt. 6.25-33

   2. He fulfills his good will on our behalf, Deut. 7.7-8.

   3. God monitors our need in order to provide precisely the things which we require.

a. Ps. 103.9-18

b. Rom. 5.6-10

c. 1 John 4.10

4. Implications of God's benevolence

a. God will supply our need, Phil. 4.19.

b. We need never fret over our needs, lacks, or concerns, Matt. 6.25-33.

c. God is neither stingy nor cruel; he gives to all who ask him liberally, James 1.5.

B. God is gracious (God does not deal with us on the basis of our merit, but on the basis of his own goodness and kindness).

1. God provides his bounty to people without regard to their merit, Eph. 2.7-10.

2. He offers his mercy to the undeserving, Titus 2.11-15.

3. No one can earn their favors with him.

a. 2 Thess. 2.16

b. Heb. 4.16

4. Implications of God's gracious acts

   a. Do not take his grace for granted, Rom. 3.8; 6.1, 15.

   b. We are never to receive the grace of God in vain, 2 Cor. 6.1.

   c. We are to offer grace as we have received it from the Lord, Matt. 18.

C. God is merciful (God is filled with tender-hearted, loving compassion for those who are needy and broken).

   1. God is tender toward the hurting, oppressed, and the needy.

      a. Deut. 5.10

      b. Ps. 57.10

      c. Ps. 103.13

      d. Isa. 54.7

      e. Hos. 14.3

2. His mercies are tender and freshly available each day.

   a. Ps. 25.6

   b. Lam. 3.32-33

3. The mercies of God touch all his creatures and works.

   a. 1 Chron. 16.34

   b. Ps. 89.28

   c. Ps. 103.8-11

   d. Ps. 119.64

4. Implications of the mercies of God

   a. We should seek his mercy for ourselves and others.
      (1) Ps. 6.2
      (2) Gal. 6.16

   b. We should celebrate his mercies with song and worship.
      (1) Ps. 115.1
      (2) Ps. 118.1-4

c. We should unashamedly preach it to those who do not know him, Matt. 9.35-38.

D. God is persistent (God is patient and longsuffering in withholding judgment from us).

1. God is willing to withhold judgment of the guilty for the sake of their salvation.

    a. Ps. 86.15

    b. Rom. 2.4

    c. Rom. 9.22

    d. 1 Pet. 3.20

2. God's persistence is revealed clearly in his forgiveness of sins, Rom. 3.25.

3. God is patient in all his dealings toward his very own children.

    a. Isa. 30.18

    b. Ezek. 20.17

4. Implications of the persistence of God

   a. God's patience can encourage others to repent.

      (1) Joel 2.13

      (2) Rom. 2.4

      (3) 2 Pet. 3.9

   b. God's kind persistence in relationship with us should never be abused or despised

      (1) Eccles. 8.11

      (2) Matt. 24.46-49

      (3) Rom. 2.4-5

   c. We ought to remember that limits do exist in regards to God's loving persistence and patience in our lives

      (1) Gen. 6.3

      (2) Jer. 44.22

Conclusion

» The *goodness* of God is demonstrated in his moral attributes of perfect moral purity, absolute integrity, and unbounded love.

» His perfect moral purity is shown in his holiness, righteousness, and justice.

» God's integrity is revealed through his genuineness, veracity, and faithfulness.

» The Father's eternal love is displayed through his benevolence, grace, mercy, and persistence.

Now, take some time to discuss with your colleagues some clarifying questions regarding the ideas and concepts that the video brought out. In some sense, a full and rich understanding of what the Scriptures teach about the goodness of God the Father Almighty is absolutely necessary for the person who would give a clear and persuasive account of the Lord to others. The goodness of the Lord serves as the basis of our salvation, our repentance, even our very relationship with God through Jesus Christ, whose grace led us to God. Make sure, therefore, that you understand the goodness of God and those attributes which surround it. Be clear and concise in your answers, and where possible, support with Scripture!

Segue 1

Student Questions and Response

page 292 4

1. What is the relationship between God's marvelous goodness and his moral nature? What does it mean that "God expresses his moral perfection through *the moral attributes* of his perfect moral purity, absolute integrity, and unbounded love?"

2. What is the definition of God's holiness? What is the relationship of God's righteousness to his holiness? In what ways does God demonstrate his perfect *moral purity* through his justice in the universe?

3. As an expression of his integrity, what does it mean to say that God the Father Almighty is genuine? What meanings are attached to the idea that God is veracious? What elements are included in the assertion that the Father is faithful?

4. God's love includes his benevolence; what exactly is it? Explain the meaning of God's graciousness. How does God's grace relate to his mercy? In what sense does God's longsuffering persistence display his goodness to us and to his creation?

5. In seeking to understand the attributes of God's *goodness*, is there a way to see them together, as a whole, to "put them all together" as we ponder them? Explain your answer.

6. How might a full biblical understanding of God's goodness greatly impact our personal lives and ministries? In your opinion, what would you consider to be the best way to communicate the goodness of God to others? Explain your answer.

God as Father: The Goodness of God

Segment 2: Moral Qualities of Severity

Rev. Dr. Don L. Davis

Summary of Segment 2

An understanding of the *wrath of God*, a moral attribute usually associated with God's severity and not his goodness, is absolutely essential for anyone claiming to communicate a fully biblical picture of God the Father Almighty. As a central doctrine of Scripture, we must strive to understand God's wrath in connection to his goodness, which can only be accomplished by a close examination of the relationship between God's goodness and his severity. While we may struggle with understanding their relationship, there has never been or never will be any confusion or conflict within God. He is and will forever be the one true God, always acting everywhere with love and justice, in grace and truth.

Our objective for this segment, *Moral Qualities of Severity*, is to enable you to see that:

- The wrath of God the Father Almighty is a central doctrine of the Holy Scriptures, and a key dimension of God's revelation to us concerning his person.

- The wrath of God, as a moral quality usually associated with God's severity and not his goodness, must be examined in conjunction to God's goodness. Love and justice must be comprehended together.

- Any apparent tensions we might perceive between God's holiness and his love are not real conflicts but merely difficulties in our understanding of God's perfect attributes and his single nature as God.

- In God's own mind and character, there has not been nor will there ever be any confusion or conflict between himself or his attributes.

- Everywhere God acts and works, he is and will forever be the one true God, always acting everywhere in perfect harmony with his love and his justice, his grace and his truth.

I. The Wrath of God the Father Almighty

A. Definition (J. I. Packer, wrath of God refers to "the outgoing of God in retributive action, by whatever means, against those who have defied him," *Knowing God*, p. 149).

1. The "outgoing of God . . .": the wrath of God is an expression of God's very nature and being (i.e., the Bible contains an equal amount of references on the subject of his anger, fury, and wrath as his love).

2. ". . . in retributive action . . .": the wrath of God is displayed in acts of retribution, as a response to those who have rejected his pleas for repentance and/or change.

3. ". . . by whatever means . . .": the wrath of God can be demonstrated by flood or fire; only his *sovereignty* determines his methods.

4. ". . . against those who have defied him": the wrath of God (like the love of God) is directed toward the objects of his wrath in actions he selects.

B. Aspects of God's wrath

1. Negative elements: what the wrath of God is not

    a. It is not done in a *capricious way* (impulsive, spontaneous, unthinking response).

    b. It is never applied *without cause* (applied foolishly or unjustly).

Video Segment 2 Outline

If we would know God, it is vital that we face the truth concerning his wrath, however unfashionable it may be, and however strong our initial prejudices against it. Otherwise, we shall not understand the Gospel of salvation from wrath, nor the propitiatory achievement of the cross, nor the wonder of the redeeming love of God.
~ J. I. Packer. *Knowing God*. Downers Grove: InterVarsity Press, 1993. p. 156.

c. It is always *rightly given* (in every case it is merited, deserved, and proportionate to the offenses).

2. God's wrath pursues those things out of sync with his own good, acceptable, and perfect will.

    a. Rom. 1.18

    b. Rom. 3.25

    c. 1 Thess. 1.9-10

    d. Rev. 6.16-17

    e. Rev. 16.19

3. It is judicial in nature (i.e., God's administrating the justice of his kingdom reign, cf. Matt. 25).

    a. Ps. 58.10-11

    b. Lam. 1.18

    c. John 5.22-23

    d. Rom. 2.6

e. Rom. 9.18-22

f. Rev. 16.6-7

4. It is in response to the choice of human and angelic rebellion.

a. Satan and his minions are condemned because they deliberately chose to defy God's sovereign choice, Isa. 14.12-15.

b. Human beings are condemned both due to their own individual rebellion as well as their relationship to the first human pair.

   (1) Isa. 55.7

   (2) 1 Pet. 3.18

   (3) Isa. 53.6

C. God's anger: how do we understand it best?

1. God directs his anger against all apostasy and idolatry.

    a. Deut. 29.27-28

    b. Ps. 78.58-59

    c. Heb. 10.26-27

2. It is directed against those who *defy him*.

a. Those who are not sorry for the harm and wrong they have done, Isa. 9.13-14

b. Those who forsake his offers of grace and mercy, Ezra 8.22

c. Those who reject and oppose the Gospel of his Son

   (1) Ps. 2.2-3

   (2) 1 Thess. 2.16

d. Those who resist his rule in their lives (i.e., the wicked)

   (1) Rom. 1.18

   (2) Rom. 2.8

   (3) Eph. 5.6

   (4) Col. 3.6

3. The wrath of God is not necessary to receive; it can be averted.

   a. The blood of Jesus as the propitiation (i.e., the appeasement of God's wrath against sin), 1 Pet. 1.18-21

   b. By faith in Jesus Christ

      (1) Rom. 5.9

      (2) 2 Cor. 5.18-19

      (3) Col. 1.20

      (4) 1 Thess. 1.10

c. Upon repentance and confession of sin, Jer. 3.12-13

4. It cannot be resisted or overcome once unleashed.

   a. Job 9.13

   b. Job 14.13

   c. Rev. 6.16-17

II. Does a Tension Exist between God's Goodness and His Wrath?

A. The nature of the debate

1. Side one: God's justice and wrath demands the judgment and punishment of every single person who has defied his holiness and offer of salvation in Jesus Christ.

2. Side two: God's mercy and grace move him to be both forgiving and longsuffering with every single person who has defied his holiness and offer of salvation in Jesus Christ.

3. Questions which arise from the debate

   a. Are there conflicts between God's love and justice, and if so, what is the nature of these conflicts?

b. Does God's nature suggest tension within his person, and therefore in the way he relates with his creation?

B. God's nature is one and in perfect harmony within himself.

1. God is one; his nature is integrated and whole.

    a. Our God is one (as the only God and within himself), Deut. 6.4.

    b. All his attributes are perfectly integrated in his person and actions, Deut. 4.35.

2. God's attributes can be analyzed separately, but God acts in perfect union within himself and his will.

    a. When God acts lovingly, it is always just love; when God demonstrates his justice, it is always loving justice.

    b. Love without justice = sentimentality; justice without love = harshness.

3. Tensions arise from *logical* analysis of God's attributes.

    a. Tendency of analysis toward *isolation* and *reductionism*

    b. Inability to see attributes as *dynamically integrated* within God's person and character

C. Calvary as the perfect, simultaneous display of God's love and wrath

1. Calvary is the display of the love of God for a fallen world.

    a. John 3.16

    b. Rom. 5.8

    c. 2 Cor. 5.19-21

    d. 1 John 4.9-10

    e. 1 John 4.19

2. Calvary is the display of God's wrath against human sin.

    a. Isa. 53.4-6

    b. Rom. 3.24-26

    c. 1 Cor. 6.20

    d. 1 Cor. 7.23

    e. Eph. 1.7

f. Titus 2.14

g. 1 Pet. 1.18-19

h. 1 John 2.2

III. The Heart of the Matter: Fear God and Keep His Commandments.

A. Fear God, Eccles. 12.13.

B. Hate sin, Prov. 8.13.

C. Cling to Christ, Phil. 3.8.

D. Share the Good News, Rom. 1.16-17.

Conclusion

» The wrath of God the Father Almighty is a moral attribute usually associated with God's severity, not his goodness.

» The so-called tensions between God's goodness and severity deal more with *our analysis of God's nature* than any conflict within the Godhead himself.

» Within our infinitely beautiful God, all of his marvelous qualities reveal his goodness and greatness, his love and his justice, his grace and his truth.

The questions below will facilitate your review of the material you just covered in the second video segment. The wrath of God, although a critically important doctrine of Scripture, is prone to be misunderstood and misapplied, or even worse, completely ignored. Reflect carefully as you provide your answers to the following questions, and support your argument with the Word of God.

1. Explain Packer's definition of the wrath of God the Father Almighty: "the outgoing of God in retributive action, by whatever means, against those who have defied him." How important is the wrath of God to a full and biblical understanding of the Father's person?

2. Why is it important to view God's wrath as his reaction to those things out of sync with his *good, acceptable, and perfect will*? Is God's wrath ever done in an arbitrary or unjust manner? Explain.

3. What are some of the ways that the Scriptures define the essence and expression of God's anger? Is it possible to avoid the punishment and experience of God's wrath and anger? Provide a detailed answer.

4. How are we to understand the relationship between God's mercy and his justice, his wrath and his love? What precisely is the conflict between these attributes which appear to be out of sync with one another?

5. How does the fact that God is one help us to solve these kinds of questions regarding apparent conflicts within the nature of God?

6. In what way is Calvary (Jesus' death on the cross) a perfect image of the display of God's wrath and his love, simultaneously?

7. What is the final heart of the matter in reflecting upon the wrath of God? What should a biblical understanding of the wrath of God produce in our lives?

God expresses his goodness through his moral attributes of perfect moral purity, absolute integrity, and unbounded love. An understanding of the wrath of God is critical to fully appreciate the glory of God the Father Almighty. We can only understand God's wrath in connection to his goodness, and while we may logically find it difficult to resolve the tension in our minds between the two, no tension exists in the infinitely lovely nature of the one true God.

Segue 2

Student Questions and Response

page 292 📖 5

Summary of Key Concepts

- The goodness of God the Father Almighty is expressed in *his moral attributes* of his perfect moral purity, absolute integrity, and unbounded love.

- The moral purity of the Father is demonstrated through his holiness, righteousness, and justice.

- God's absolute moral integrity is associated with the attributes of his genuineness, truth, and faithfulness.

- The love of God the Father is displayed through the attributes of his benevolence, grace, mercy, and persistence (longsuffering and patience).

- The wrath of God is a central and defining doctrine in the Word of God, and cannot be ignored without doing damage to one's overall picture of the glory of God.

- God expresses his wrath in outgoing action as retribution against those who defy him and his good will.

- The wrath of God is never directed in an impulsive, unjust, or unthinking manner. It is always rightly given and associated with his just anger against all those things that oppose his rule and will.

- God's wrath, as a moral quality usually associated with God's severity and not his goodness, must be examined in conjunction to God's goodness to be properly appreciated. Love and justice must be comprehended together.

- Any apparent tensions we may perceive between God's holiness and his love are not real conflicts in God but merely reflections of our limited understanding of God's perfect attributes and nature.

- No confusion or conflicts exists between God's attributes in his nature or being.

- Everywhere God acts and works, he is and will forever be the one true God, always acting everywhere in perfect harmony with his love *and* his justice, his grace *and* his truth.

Student Application and Implications

Ask and answer your own critical questions about the nature of God's goodness and his wrath. Ponder your own issues and concerns, and identify any specific questions you may have on the issues raised by the truths of God's goodness and his anger against evil. The questions below might spark some thoughts of your own!

* If God is absolutely holy, how can he have any kind of relationship with us or with creation, since we are all now living under the curse?

* If our God is a God of perfect and unbounded love, how can he truly send even a single soul to perish in hell?

* Since the blood of Jesus has appeased God's wrath (i.e., propitiated us before the Father), why aren't all people automatically saved, even without having to ask for forgiveness?

* In light of the fact that God is gracious and does not deal with us on the basis of our merits but on his sovereign grace and love, why hasn't God chosen to save everybody everywhere? If God does not desire a single soul to perish, why do they perish anyway?

* How do you resolve and connect the idea that God makes it rain on the just and the unjust, while at the same time, God's anger is against those who defy his will and his salvation through Jesus Christ? How can this be?

* What does it mean to receive the grace of God in vain? Is it possible for someone who was once the object of his love and grace, to become an object of his wrath and anger? Explain your answer.

CASE STUDIES

The People of Israel

Discuss and outline the way in which God's relationship with his people Israel may give us insight into the nature of God's love and justice in connection to his people. For instance, the same people that God rescued from the bondage and cruelty of Egyptian oppression, were judged by God to wander for forty years in the wilderness because of disobedience and unbelief. The same people who were rescued by God under the kings of Israel and Judah were sent into exile into the two respective kingdoms, Assyria in the northern kingdom, and Babylon in the southern kingdom. What clues or hints do we get from the case study of the Israelites that God's love and his justice are simultaneously in play when he relates to his own people?

page 293 6

There Is No Hell?

A number of key evangelicals are reviewing the historical doctrine of eternal punishment and redefining it in terms of "annihilation" rather than "unending, conscious torment outside of the presence of God forever." Deeply moved and affected by the Bible's teaching on the love and goodness of God the Father Almighty, they are looking closely again at the texts which have been made to argue for a place where those who defy God are consciously in agony forever. They are asserting, in place of this view, the idea that God will destroy or obliterate his enemies, but will not keep them conscious and alive forever for the purpose of tormenting them. Discuss the case study of the doctrine of hell as an example of the need for the Church to rediscover and re-articulate the biblical teaching on the wrath of God the Father Almighty. What do you make of these attempts to rethink the classic doctrine of hell? Do you agree, disagree?

Universal Salvation for All

A noted Catholic theologian (Karl Rahner) is today making the case for understanding the death of Christ as a *universal salvation*. In this view, the death of Christ is applied generically to all nations and peoples, and therefore all families and individuals, whether they are aware of Jesus' work on the cross or not. As a matter of fact, these who are covered by the grace of God on the cross are referred to as "anonymous Christians," those who are included in the saving work of Messiah Jesus on the cross, whether they are aware of it or not. Surely, there are texts in the Bible which seem to suggest that God's salvation is for all people everywhere (cf. 1 John 2.1-2; 4.14; 5.19; John 1.29; 4.42; 11.51-52; 2 Cor. 5.18-21; Rev. 12.9, etc.). Can one make a legitimate case from Scripture that the entire world is included in God's display of his goodness in Jesus Christ–will all be saved as a result of Jesus' death, or only a select number? What is the problem (if any exists) with the idea of universal salvation?

Restatement of the Lesson's Thesis

God expresses his goodness through his moral attributes of perfect moral purity, absolute integrity, and unbounded love. He demonstrates his *perfect moral purity* through his holiness, righteousness, and justice. He expresses his absolute integrity through his attributes of genuineness, truth, and faithfulness. Finally, God expresses his unbounded love through his attributes of his benevolence, grace, mercy, and persistence. An understanding of the *wrath of God*, is critical for a biblically accurate picture of God the Father Almighty. We understand this key doctrine of Scripture only when we examine the relationship between God's goodness and his severity. No tension exists between God's love and his wrath, for he is the one true God, always acting everywhere and in all things in perfect harmony with his love and justice, his grace and truth.

If you are interested in pursuing some of the ideas of the goodness and wrath of God the Father, you might want to give these books a try:

> Muncy, John. *Whatever Happened to the Wrath of God?* Library, PA: Ethnos Press, 1996.
>
> Yancey, Philip. *What's so Amazing about Grace?* Grand Rapids: Zondervan, 2002.

Resources and Bibliographies

Now it is time to relate the insights of your module to your ministry project, the letter that you will be writing either to an actual or an imaginary friend. To apply Scripture we must have a knowledge of the specific context and need we are seeking to address. This particular ministry project has been designed for you to think carefully and critically on just how you might apply the truths of this module to someone who needs to hear in a persuasive and clear manner the good news of God's offer in Jesus Christ. Your mentor by now has covered the details of the project with you, and now it is time for you to apply your insights in this creative work.

Remember, the goal of all learning is to grow in such a way that God, the Holy Spirit, may first of all *apply* those truths to your own life, and then use that learning *through you* as you equip, counsel, train, and encourage others. The ministry projects are designed to help you creatively apply the fruit of the Scriptures to your own life and ministry. As you work on your project, pray and ask the Lord to give you insight as you complete your work and share your insights with others.

Ministry Connections

In this final session, ask the Holy Spirit to search your heart and help you identify if there are any persons, situations, or opportunities that need to be prayed for as a result of your studies in this lesson, or beyond that, even in this module. Listen carefully to the Lord here; the Word of the Lord is always accompanied by the Spirit's leadings and promptings. What particular issues or people arise from this

Counseling and Prayer

lesson that require your focused supplication and prayer? Be obedient to the Lord; take some time to ponder this, and receive the necessary support in counsel and prayer for what the Spirit has shown you.

ASSIGNMENTS

Scripture Memory

No assignment due.

Reading Assignment

No assignment due.

Other Assignments

page 293  *7*

Your ministry project and your exegetical project should now be outlined, determined, and accepted by your instructor. There are no further sessions for the module, so you must make certain that you have communicated with your instructor, received all the standards and outlines for your assignments, and agreed upon a date for you to turn in your assignments.

Final Exam Notice

The final will be a take home exam, and will include questions taken from the first three quizzes, new questions on material drawn from this lesson, and essay questions which will ask for your short answer responses to key integrating questions. Also, you should plan on reciting or writing out the verses memorized for the course on the exam. When you have completed your exam, please notify your mentor and make certain that they get your copy.

Please note: Your module grade cannot be determined if you do not take the final exam and turn in all outstanding assignments to your mentor (reading completion sheets, ministry project, exegetical project, and final exam).

The Last Word about this Module

There is truly no way to describe the infinite beauty, power, and glory of our God, Father, Son and Holy Spirit, or the magnificence of the first person of the Trinity, God the Father Almighty. Jesus' words regarding the nature of eternal life cut to the very center of the importance of knowing and walking with God by faith in Jesus, "And this is eternal life, that they know you the only true God, and Jesus Christ whom you have sent" John 17.3. Our very salvation is linked to an accurate knowledge of God the Father Almighty, and his dear Son our Lord, Messiah Jesus.

Our sincere hope is that this module will simply be one of the first steps of a lifelong pursuit of our God. As a living God and the Maker of all things, he longs to be longed for, and can only be found when we give all ourselves to the quest. May the prayers of the sons of Korah become your personal heartfelt vision and life purpose:

> *Ps. 42.1-2 - "As a deer pants for flowing streams, so pants my soul for you, O God. [2] My soul thirsts for God, for the living God. When shall I come and appear before God?"*

May the greatness and goodness of God the Father Almighty fill your life with vision and power, so that you may represent the Lord honorably as his disciple for such a time as this!

Appendices

147	Appendix 1: **The Nicene Creed** *(with Scripture memory passages)*
148	Appendix 2: **We Believe: Confession of the Nicene Creed (Common Meter)**
149	Appendix 3: **The Story of God: Our Sacred Roots**
150	Appendix 4: **The Theology of Christus Victor**
151	Appendix 5: **Christus Victor: An Integrated Vision for the Christian Life**
152	Appendix 6: **Old Testament Witness to Christ and His Kingdom**
153	Appendix 7: **Summary Outline of the Scriptures**
155	Appendix 8: **From Before to Beyond Time**
157	Appendix 9: **There Is a River**
158	Appendix 10: **A Schematic for a Theology of the Kingdom and the Church**
159	Appendix 11: **Living in the Already and the Not Yet Kingdom**
160	Appendix 12: **Jesus of Nazareth: The Presence of the Future**
161	Appendix 13: **Traditions**
169	Appendix 14: **The Names of Almighty God**
173	Appendix 15: **Theological Visions and Approaches**
178	Appendix 16: **A Theology of the Church in Kingdom Perspective**
179	Appendix 17: **Apostolicity**
180	Appendix 18: **From Deep Ignorance to Credible Witness**
181	Appendix 19: **Picking Up on Different Wavelengths: Integrated vs. Fragmented Mindsets**
185	Appendix 20: **The Father, Son, and Holy Ghost Share the Same Divine Attributes and Works**
187	Appendix 21: **The Picture and the Drama**
188	Appendix 22: **The Self-Consciousness of Jesus Christ**

189	Appendix 23: **The Shadow and the Substance**
190	Appendix 24: **Theories of Inspiration**
191	Appendix 25: **Toward a Hermeneutic of Critical Engagement**
192	Appendix 26: **Ralph D. Winter Editorial**
196	Appendix 27: **When "Christian" Does Not Translate**
198	Appendix 28: **Pursuing Faith, Not Religion: The Liberating Quest for Contextualization**
202	Appendix 29: **Contextualization Among Hindus, Muslims, and Buddhists**
208	Appendix 30: **A People Reborn: Foundational Insights on People Movements**
212	Appendix 31: **Missions in the 21st Century: Working with Social Entrepreneurs?**
214	Appendix 32: **Giving Glory to God**
223	Appendix 33: **Your Kingdom Come: "The Story of God's Glory"**
237	Appendix 34: **God's Three-In-Oneness: The Trinity**
245	Appendix 35: **God's Sovereignty and Universal Revelation**
251	Appendix 36: **Substitution**
252	Appendix 37: **Suffering: The Cost of Discipleship and Servant-Leadership**
253	Appendix 38: **Documenting Your Work**

APPENDIX 1
The Nicene Creed

Memory Verses ⇩

Rev. 4.11 (ESV) *Worthy are you, our Lord and God, to receive glory and honor and power, for you created all things, and by your will they existed and were created.*

John 1.1 (ESV) *In the beginning was the Word, and the Word was with God, and the Word was God.*

1 Cor.15.3-5 (ESV) *For what I received I passed on to you as of first importance: that Christ died for our sins according to the Scriptures, that he was buried, that he was raised on the third day according to the Scriptures, and that he appeared to Peter, and then to the Twelve.*

Rom. 8.11 (ESV) *If the Spirit of him who raised Jesus from the dead dwells in you, he who raised Christ Jesus from the dead will also give life to your mortal bodies through his Spirit who dwells in you.*

1 Pet. 2.9 (ESV) *But you are a chosen race, a royal priesthood, a holy nation, a people for his own possession, that you may proclaim the excellencies of him who called you out of darkness into his marvelous light.*

1 Thess. 4.16-17 (ESV) *For the Lord himself will descend from heaven with a cry of command, with the voice of an archangel, and with the sound of the trumpet of God. And the dead in Christ will rise first. Then we who are alive, who are left, will be caught up together with them in the clouds to meet the Lord in the air, and so we will always be with the Lord.*

We believe in one God, *(Deut. 6.4-5; Mark 12.29; 1 Cor. 8.6)*
  the Father Almighty, *(Gen. 17.1; Dan. 4.35; Matt. 6.9; Eph. 4.6; Rev. 1.8)*
  Maker of heaven and earth *(Gen 1.1; Isa. 40.28; Rev. 10.6)*
  and of all things visible and invisible. *(Ps. 148; Rom. 11.36; Rev. 4.11)*

We believe in one Lord Jesus Christ, the only Begotten Son of God,
  begotten of the Father before all ages,
  God from God, Light from Light, True God from True God,
  begotten not created,
  of the same essence as the Father, *(John 1.1-2; 3.18; 8.58; 14.9-10; 20.28; Col. 1.15, 17; Heb. 1.3-6)*
  through whom all things were made. *(John 1.3; Col. 1.16)*

Who for us men and for our salvation came down from heaven
  and was incarnate by the Holy Spirit and the virgin Mary
  and became human. *(Matt. 1.20-23; John 1.14; 6.38; Luke 19.10)*
  Who for us too, was crucified under Pontius Pilate,
  suffered, and was buried. *(Matt. 27.1-2; Mark 15.24-39, 43-47; Acts 13.29; Rom. 5.8; Heb. 2.10; 13.12)*
  The third day he rose again
  according to the Scriptures, *(Mark 16.5-7; Luke 24.6-8; Acts 1.3; Rom. 6.9; 10.9; 2 Tim. 2.8)*
  ascended into heaven,
  and is seated at the right hand of the Father. *(Mark 16.19; Eph. 1.19-20)*
  He will come again in glory
  to judge the living and the dead,
  and his Kingdom will have no end.
    (Isa. 9.7; Matt. 24.30; John 5.22; Acts 1.11; 17.31; Rom. 14.9; 2 Cor. 5.10; 2 Tim. 4.1)

We believe in the Holy Spirit, the Lord and life-giver,
    (Gen. 1.1-2; Job 33.4; Ps. 104.30; 139.7-8; Luke 4.18-19; John 3.5-6; Acts 1.1-2; 1 Cor. 2.11; Rev. 3.22)
  who proceeds from the Father and the Son, *(John 14.16-18, 26; 15.26; 20.22)*
  who together with the Father and Son
  is worshiped and glorified, *(Isa. 6.3; Matt. 28.19; 2 Cor. 13.14; Rev. 4.8)*
  who spoke by the prophets. *(Num. 11.29; Mic. 3.8; Acts 2.17-18; 2 Pet. 1.21)*

We believe in one holy, catholic, and apostolic Church.
    (Matt. 16.18; Eph. 5.25-28; 1 Cor. 1.2; 10.17; 1 Tim. 3.15; Rev. 7.9)

We acknowledge one baptism for the forgiveness of sin, *(Acts 22.16: 1 Pet. 3.21; Eph. 4.4-5)*
  And we look for the resurrection of the dead
  And the life of the age to come. *(Isa. 11.6-10; Mic. 4.1-7; Luke 18.29-30; Rev. 21.1-5; 21.22-22.5)*

Amen.

APPENDIX 2
We Believe: Confession of the Nicene Creed (Common Meter*)

Rev. Dr. Don L. Davis, 2007. All Rights Reserved.

* This song is adapted from the Nicene Creed, and set to Common Meter (8.6.8.6.), meaning it can be sung to tunes of the same meter, such as: *O, for a Thousand Tongues to Sing; Alas, and Did My Savior Bleed?; Amazing Grace; All Hail the Power of Jesus' Name; There Is a Fountain; Joy to the World*

The Father God Almighty rules, Maker of earth and heav'n.
Yes, all things seen and those unseen, by him were made, and given!

We hold to one Lord Jesus Christ, God's one and only Son,
Begotten, not created, too, he and our Lord are one!

Begotten from the Father, same, in essence, God and Light;
Through him all things were made by God, in him were given life.

Who for us all, for salvation, came down from heav'n to earth,
Was incarnate by the Spirit's pow'r, and the Virgin Mary's birth.

Who for us too, was crucified, by Pontius Pilate's hand,
Suffered, was buried in the tomb, on third day rose again.

According to the Sacred text all this was meant to be.
Ascended to heav'n, to God's right hand, now seated high in glory.

He'll come again in glory to judge all those alive and dead.
His Kingdom rule shall never end, for he will reign as Head.

We worship God, the Holy Spirit, our Lord, Life-giver known,
With Fath'r and Son is glorified, Who by the prophets spoke.

And we believe in one true Church, God's people for all time,
Cath'lic in scope, and built upon the apostolic line.

Acknowledging one baptism, for forgiv'ness of our sin,
We look for Resurrection day–the dead shall live again.

We look for those unending days, life of the Age to come,
When Christ's great Reign shall come to earth, and God's will shall be done!

APPENDIX 3

The Story of God: Our Sacred Roots

Rev. Dr. Don L. Davis

The Alpha and the Omega	Christus Victor	Come, Holy Spirit	Your Word Is Truth	The Great Confession	His Life in Us	Living in the Way	Reborn to Serve
The LORD God is the source, sustainer, and end of all things in the heavens and earth. All things were formed and exist by his will and for his eternal glory, the triune God, Father, Son, and Holy Spirit, Rom. 11.36.							
The Triune God's Unfolding Drama *God's Self-Revelation in Creation, Israel, and Christ*				**The Church's Participation in God's Unfolding Drama** *Fidelity to the Apostolic Witness to Christ and His Kingdom*			
The Objective Foundation: The Sovereign Love of God *God's Narration of His Saving Work in Christ*				**The Subjective Practice: Salvation by Grace through Faith** *The Redeemed's Joyous Response to God's Saving Work in Christ*			
The Author of the Story	*The Champion of the Story*	*The Interpreter of the Story*	*The Testimony of the Story*	*The People of the Story*	*Re-enactment of the Story*	*Embodiment of the Story*	*Continuation of the Story*
The Father as Director	Jesus as Lead Actor	The Spirit as Narrator	Scripture as Script	As Saints, Confessors	As Worshipers, Ministers	As Followers, Sojourners	As Servants, Ambassadors
Christian Worldview	Communal Identity	Spiritual Experience	Biblical Authority	Orthodox Theology	Priestly Worship	Congregational Discipleship	Kingdom Witness
Theistic and Trinitarian Vision	Christ-centered Foundation	Spirit-Indwelt and -Filled Community	Canonical and Apostolic Witness	Ancient Creedal Affirmation of Faith	Weekly Gathering in Christian Assembly	Corporate, Ongoing Spiritual Formation	Active Agents of the Reign of God
Sovereign Willing	Messianic Representing	Divine Comforting	Inspired Testifying	Truthful Retelling	Joyful Excelling	Faithful Indwelling	Hopeful Compelling
Creator True Maker of the Cosmos	Recapitulation Typos and Fulfillment of the Covenant	Life-Giver Regeneration and Adoption	Divine Inspiration God-breathed Word	The Confession of Faith Union with Christ	Song and Celebration Historical Recitation	Pastoral Oversight Shepherding the Flock	Explicit Unity Love for the Saints
Owner Sovereign Disposer of Creation	Revealer Incarnation of the Word	Teacher Illuminator of the Truth	Sacred History Historical Record	Baptism into Christ Communion of Saints	Homilies and Teachings Prophetic Proclamation	Shared Spirituality Common Journey through the Spiritual Disciplines	Radical Hospitality Evidence of God's Kingdom Reign
Ruler Blessed Controller of All Things	Redeemer Reconciler of All Things	Helper Endowment and the Power	Biblical Theology Divine Commentary	The Rule of Faith Apostles' Creed and Nicene Creed	The Lord's Supper Dramatic Re-enactment	Embodiment Anamnesis and Prolepsis through the Church Year	Extravagant Generosity Good Works
Covenant Keeper Faithful Promisor	Restorer Christ, the Victor over the powers of evil	Guide Divine Presence and Shekinah	Spiritual Food Sustenance for the Journey	The Vincentian Canon Ubiquity, antiquity, universality	Eschatological Foreshadowing The Already/Not Yet	Effective Discipling Spiritual Formation in the Believing Assembly	Evangelical Witness Making Disciples of All People Groups

APPENDIX 4

The Theology of Christus Victor
A Christ-Centered Biblical Motif for Integrating and Renewing the Urban Church

Rev. Dr. Don L. Davis

	The Promised Messiah	The Word Made Flesh	The Son of Man	The Suffering Servant	The Lamb of God	The Victorious Conqueror	The Reigning Lord in Heaven	The Bridegroom and Coming King
Biblical Framework	Israel's hope of Yahweh's anointed who would redeem his people	In the person of Jesus of Nazareth, the Lord has come to the world	As the promised king and divine Son of Man, Jesus reveals the Father's glory and salvation to the world	As Inaugurator of the Kingdom of God, Jesus demonstrates God's reign present through his words, wonders, and works	As both High Priest and Paschal Lamb, Jesus offers himself to God on our behalf as a sacrifice for sin	In his resurrection from the dead and ascension to God's right hand, Jesus is proclaimed as Victor over the power of sin and death	Now reigning at God's right hand till his enemies are made his footstool, Jesus pours out his benefits on his body	Soon the risen and ascended Lord will return to gather his Bride, the Church, and consummate his work
Scripture References	Isa. 9.6-7 Jer. 23.5-6 Isa. 11.1-10	John 1.14-18 Matt. 1.20-23 Phil. 2.6-8	Matt. 2.1-11 Num. 24.17 Luke 1.78-79	Mark 1.14-15 Matt. 12.25-30 Luke 17.20-21	2 Cor. 5.18-21 Isa. 52-53 John 1.29	Eph. 1.16-23 Phil. 2.5-11 Col. 1.15-20	1 Cor. 15.25 Eph. 4.15-16 Acts. 2.32-36	Rom. 14.7-9 Rev. 5.9-13 1 Thess. 4.13-18
Jesus' History	The pre-incarnate, only begotten Son of God in glory	His conception by the Spirit, and birth to Mary	His manifestation to the Magi and to the world	His teaching, exorcisms, miracles, and mighty works among the people	His suffering, crucifixion, death, and burial	His resurrection, with appearances to his witnesses, and his ascension to the Father	The sending of the Holy Spirit and his gifts, and Christ's session in heaven at the Father's right hand	His soon return from heaven to earth as Lord and Christ: the Second Coming
Description	The biblical promise for the seed of Abraham, the prophet like Moses, the son of David	In the Incarnation, God has come to us; Jesus reveals to humankind the Father's glory in fullness	In Jesus, God has shown his salvation to the entire world, including the Gentiles	In Jesus, the promised Kingdom of God has come visibly to earth, demonstrating his binding of Satan and rescinding the Curse	As God's perfect Lamb, Jesus offers himself up to God as a sin offering on behalf of the entire world	In his resurrection and ascension, Jesus destroyed death, disarmed Satan, and rescinded the Curse	Jesus is installed at the Father's right hand as Head of the Church, Firstborn from the dead, and supreme Lord in heaven	As we labor in his harvest field in the world, so we await Christ's return, the fulfillment of his promise
Church Year	Advent	Christmas	Season after Epiphany Baptism and Transfiguration	Lent	Holy Week Passion	Eastertide Easter, Ascension Day, Pentecost	Season after Pentecost Trinity Sunday	Season after Pentecost All Saints Day, Reign of Christ the King
	The Coming of Christ	*The Birth of Christ*	*The Manifestation of Christ*	*The Ministry of Christ*	*The Suffering and Death of Christ*	*The Resurrection and Ascension of Christ*	*The Heavenly Session of Christ*	*The Reign of Christ*
Spiritual Formation	As we await his Coming, let us proclaim and affirm the hope of Christ	O Word made flesh, let us every heart prepare him room to dwell	Divine Son of Man, show the nations your salvation and glory	In the person of Christ, the power of the reign of God has come to earth and to the Church	May those who share the Lord's death be resurrected with him	Let us participate by faith in the victory of Christ over the power of sin, Satan, and death	Come, indwell us, Holy Spirit, and empower us to advance Christ's Kingdom in the world	We live and work in expectation of his soon return, seeking to please him in all things

APPENDIX 5
Christus Victor
An Integrated Vision for the Christian Life
Rev. Dr. Don L. Davis

For the Church
- The Church is the primary extension of Jesus in the world
- Ransomed treasure of the victorious, risen Christ
- *Laos:* The people of God
- God's new creation: presence of the future
- Locus and agent of the Already/Not Yet Kingdom

For Theology and Doctrine
- The authoritative Word of Christ's victory: the Apostolic Tradition: the Holy Scriptures
- Theology as commentary on the grand narrative of God
- *Christus Victor* as core theological framework for meaning in the world
- The Nicene Creed: the Story of God's triumphant grace

For Spirituality
- The Holy Spirit's presence and power in the midst of God's people
- Sharing in the disciplines of the Spirit
- Gatherings, lectionary, liturgy, and our observances in the Church Year
- Living the life of the risen Christ in the rhythm of our ordinary lives

For Gifts
- God's gracious endowments and benefits from *Christus Victor*
- Pastoral offices to the Church
- The Holy Spirit's sovereign dispensing of the gifts
- Stewardship: divine, diverse gifts for the common good

Christus Victor
Destroyer of Evil and Death
Restorer of Creation
Victor o'er Hades and Sin
Crusher of Satan

For Worship
- People of the Resurrection: unending celebration of the people of God
- Remembering, participating in the Christ event in our worship
- Listen and respond to the Word
- Transformed at the Table, the Lord's Supper
- The presence of the Father through the Son in the Spirit

For Evangelism and Mission
- Evangelism as unashamed declaration and demonstration of *Christus Victor* to the world
- The Gospel as Good News of kingdom pledge
- We proclaim God's Kingdom come in the person of Jesus of Nazareth
- The Great Commission: go to all people groups making disciples of Christ and his Kingdom
- Proclaiming Christ as Lord and Messiah

For Justice and Compassion
- The gracious and generous expressions of Jesus through the Church
- The Church displays the very life of the Kingdom
- The Church demonstrates the very life of the Kingdom of heaven right here and now
- Having freely received, we freely give (no sense of merit or pride)
- Justice as tangible evidence of the Kingdom come

Appendix 6

Old Testament Witness to Christ and His Kingdom

Rev. Dr. Don L. Davis

Christ Is Seen in the OT's:	Covenant Promise and Fulfillment	Moral Law	Christophanies	Typology	Tabernacle, Festival, and Levitical Priesthood	Messianic Prophecy	Salvation Promises
Passage	Gen. 12.1-3	Matt. 5.17-18	John 1.18	1 Cor. 15.45	Heb. 8.1-6	Mic. 5.2	Isa. 9.6-7
Example	The Promised Seed of the Abrahamic covenant	The Law given on Mount Sinai	Commander of the Lord's army	Jonah and the great fish	Melchizedek, as both High Priest and King	The Lord's Suffering Servant	Righteous Branch of David
Christ As	Seed of the woman	The Prophet of God	God's present Revelation	Antitype of God's drama	Our eternal High Priest	The coming Son of Man	Israel's Redeemer and King
Where Illustrated	Galatians	Matthew	John	Matthew	Hebrews	Luke and Acts	John and Revelation
Exegetical Goal	To see Christ as heart of God's sacred drama	To see Christ as fulfillment of the Law	To see Christ as God's revealer	To see Christ as antitype of divine typos	To see Christ in the Temple *cultus*	To see Christ as true Messiah	To see Christ as coming King
How Seen in the NT	As fulfillment of God's sacred oath	As *telos* of the Law	As full, final, and superior revelation	As substance behind the historical shadows	As reality behind the rules and roles	As the Kingdom made present	As the One who will rule on David's throne
Our Response in Worship	God's veracity and faithfulness	God's perfect righteousness	God's presence among us	God's inspired Scripture	God's ontology: his realm as primary and determinative	God's anointed servant and mediator	God's resolve to restore his kingdom authority
How God Is Vindicated	God does not lie: he's true to his word	Jesus fulfills all righteousness	God's fulness is revealed to us in Jesus of Nazareth	The Spirit spoke by the prophets	The Lord has provided a mediator for humankind	Every jot and tittle written of him will occur	Evil will be put down, creation restored, under his reign

APPENDIX 7
Summary Outline of the Scriptures
Rev. Dr. Don L. Davis

1. GENESIS - Beginnings
   a. Adam
   b. Noah
   c. Abraham
   d. Isaac
   e. Jacob
   f. Joseph

2. EXODUS - Redemption, (out of)
   a. Slavery
   b. Deliverance
   c. Law
   d. Tabernacle

3. LEVITICUS - Worship and Fellowship
   a. Offerings, sacrifices
   b. Priests
   c. Feasts, festivals

4. NUMBERS - Service and Walk
   a. Organized
   b. Wanderings

5. DEUTERONOMY - Obedience
   a. Moses reviews history and law
   b. Civil and social laws
   c. Palestinian Covenant
   d. Moses' blessing and death

6. JOSHUA - Redemption (into)
   a. Conquer the land
   b. Divide up the land
   c. Joshua's farewell

7. JUDGES - God's Deliverance
   a. Disobedience and judgment
   b. Israel's twelve judges
   c. Lawless conditions

8. RUTH - Love
   a. Ruth chooses
   b. Ruth works
   c. Ruth waits
   d. Ruth rewarded

9. 1 SAMUEL - Kings, Priestly Perspective
   a. Eli
   b. Samuel
   c. Saul
   d. David

10. 2 SAMUEL - David
    a. King of Judah
       (9 years - Hebron)
    b. King of all Israel
       (33 years - Jerusalem)

11. 1 KINGS - Solomon's Glory, Kingdom's Decline
    a. Solomon's glory
    b. Kingdom's decline
    c. Elijah the prophet

12. 2 KINGS - Divided Kingdom
    a. Elisha
    b. Israel (N. Kingdom falls)
    c. Judah (S. Kingdom falls)

13. 1 CHRONICLES - David's Temple Arrangements
    a. Genealogies
    b. End of Saul's reign
    c. Reign of David
    d. Temple preparations

14. 2 CHRONICLES - Temple and Worship Abandoned
    a. Solomon
    b. Kings of Judah

15. EZRA - The Minority (Remnant)
    a. First return from exile - Zerubbabel
    b. Second return from exile - Ezra (priest)

16. NEHEMIAH - Rebuilding by Faith
    a. Rebuild walls
    b. Revival
    c. Religious reform

17. ESTHER - Female Savior
    a. Esther
    b. Haman
    c. Mordecai
    d. Deliverance: Feast of Purim

18. JOB - Why the Righteous Suffer
    a. Godly Job
    b. Satan's attack
    c. Four philosophical friends
    d. God lives

19. PSALMS - Prayer and Praise
    a. Prayers of David
    b. Godly suffer; deliverance
    c. God deals with Israel
    d. Suffering of God's people - end with the Lord's reign
    e. The Word of God (Messiah's suffering and glorious return)

20. PROVERBS - Wisdom
    a. Wisdom versus folly
    b. Solomon
    c. Solomon - Hezekiah
    d. Agur
    e. Lemuel

21. ECCLESIASTES - Vanity
    a. Experimentation
    b. Observation
    c. Consideration

22. SONG OF SOLOMON - Love Story

23. ISAIAH - The Justice (Judgment) and Grace (Comfort) of God
    a. Prophecies of punishment
    b. History
    c. Prophecies of blessing

24. JEREMIAH - Judah's Sin Leads to Babylonian Captivity
    a. Jeremiah's call; empowered
    b. Judah condemned; predicted Babylonian captivity
    c. Restoration promised
    d. Prophesied judgment inflicted
    e. Prophesies against Gentiles
    f. Summary of Judah's captivity

25. LAMENTATIONS - Lament over Jerusalem
    a. Affliction of Jerusalem
    b. Destroyed because of sin
    c. The prophet's suffering
    d. Present desolation versus past splendor
    e. Appeal to God for mercy

26. EZEKIEL - Israel's Captivity and Restoration
    a. Judgment on Judah and Jerusalem
    b. Judgment on Gentile nations
    c. Israel restored; Jerusalem's future glory

27. DANIEL - The Time of the Gentiles
    a. History; Nebuchadnezzar, Belshazzar, Daniel
    b. Prophecy

28. HOSEA - Unfaithfulness
    a. Unfaithfulness
    b. Punishment
    c. Restoration

29. JOEL - The Day of the Lord
    a. Locust plague
    b. Events of the future day of the Lord
    c. Order of the future day of the Lord

30. AMOS - God Judges Sin
    a. Neighbors judged
    b. Israel judged
    c. Visions of future judgment
    d. Israel's past judgment blessings

31. OBADIAH - Edom's Destruction
    a. Destruction prophesied
    b. Reasons for destruction
    c. Israel's future blessing

32. JONAH - Gentile Salvation
    a. Jonah disobeys
    b. Other suffer
    c. Jonah punished
    d. Jonah obeys; thousands saved
    e. Jonah displeased, no love for souls

33. MICAH - Israel's Sins, Judgment, and Restoration
    a. Sin and judgment
    b. Grace and future restoration
    c. Appeal and petition

34. NAHUM - Nineveh Condemned
    a. God hates sin
    b. Nineveh's doom prophesied
    c. Reasons for doom

35. HABAKKUK - The Just Shall Live by Faith
    a. Complaint of Judah's unjudged sin
    b. Chaldeans will punish
    c. Complaint of Chaldeans' wickedness
    d. Punishment promised
    e. Prayer for revival; faith in God

36. ZEPHANIAH - Babylonian Invasion Prefigures the Day of the Lord
    a. Judgment on Judah foreshadows the Great Day of the Lord
    b. Judgment on Jerusalem and neighbors foreshadows final judgment of all nations
    c. Israel restored after judgments

37. HAGGAI - Rebuild the Temple
    a. Negligence
    b. Courage
    c. Separation
    d. Judgment

38. ZECHARIAH - Two Comings of Christ
    a. Zechariah's vision
    b. Bethel's question; Jehovah's answer
    c. Nation's downfall and salvation

39. MALACHI - Neglect
    a. The priest's sins
    b. The people's sins
    c. The faithful few

Summary Outline of the Scriptures (continued)

1. MATTHEW - Jesus the King
   a. The Person of the King
   b. The Preparation of the King
   c. The Propaganda of the King
   d. The Program of the King
   e. The Passion of the King
   f. The Power of the King

2. MARK - Jesus the Servant
   a. John introduces the Servant
   b. God the Father identifies the Servant
   c. The temptation initiates the Servant
   d. Work and word of the Servant
   e. Death, burial, resurrection

3. LUKE - Jesus Christ the Perfect Man
   a. Birth and family of the Perfect Man
   b. Testing of the Perfect Man; hometown
   c. Ministry of the Perfect Man
   d. Betrayal, trial, and death of the Perfect Man
   e. Resurrection of the Perfect Man

4. JOHN - Jesus Christ is God
   a. Prologue - the Incarnation
   b. Introduction
   c. Witness of Jesus to his Apostles
   d. Passion - witness to the world
   e. Epilogue

5. ACTS - The Holy Spirit Working in the Church
   a. The Lord Jesus at work by the Holy Spirit through the Apostles at Jerusalem
   b. In Judea and Samaria
   c. To the uttermost parts of the Earth

6. ROMANS - The Righteousness of God
   a. Salutation
   b. Sin and salvation
   c. Sanctification
   d. Struggle
   e. Spirit-filled living
   f. Security of salvation
   g. Segregation
   h. Sacrifice and service
   i. Separation and salutation

7. 1 CORINTHIANS - The Lordship of Christ
   a. Salutation and thanksgiving
   b. Conditions in the Corinthian body
   c. Concerning the Gospel
   d. Concerning collections

8. 2 CORINTHIANS - The Ministry in the Church
   a. The comfort of God
   b. Collection for the poor
   c. Calling of the Apostle Paul

9. GALATIANS - Justification by Faith
   a. Introduction
   b. Personal - Authority of the Apostle and glory of the Gospel
   c. Doctrinal - Justification by faith
   d. Practical - Sanctification by the Holy Spirit
   e. Autographed conclusion and exhortation

10. EPHESIANS - The Church of Jesus Christ
    a. Doctrinal - the heavenly calling of the Church
        A Body
        A Temple
        A Mystery
    b. Practical - The earthly conduct of the Church
        A New Man
        A Bride
        An Army

11. PHILIPPIANS - Joy in the Christian Life
    a. Philosophy for Christian living
    b. Pattern for Christian living
    c. Prize for Christian living
    d. Power for Christian living

12. COLOSSIANS - Christ the Fullness of God
    a. Doctrinal - In Christ believers are made full
    b. Practical - Christ's life poured out in believers, and through them

13. 1 THESSALONIANS - The Second Coming of Christ:
    a. Is an inspiring hope
    b. Is a working hope
    c. Is a purifying hope
    d. Is a comforting hope
    e. Is a rousing, stimulating hope

14. 2 THESSALONIANS - The Second Coming of Christ
    a. Persecution of believers now; judgment of unbelievers hereafter (at coming of Christ)
    b. Program of the world in connection with the coming of Christ
    c. Practical issues associated with the coming of Christ

15. 1 TIMOTHY - Government and Order in the Local Church
    a. The faith of the Church
    b. Public prayer and women's place in the Church
    c. Officers in the Church
    d. Apostasy in the Church
    e. Duties of the officer of the Church

16. 2 TIMOTHY - Loyalty in the Days of Apostasy
    a. Afflictions of the Gospel
    b. Active in service
    c. Apostasy coming; authority of the Scriptures
    d. Allegiance to the Lord

17. TITUS - The Ideal New Testament Church
    a. The Church is an organization
    b. The Church is to teach and preach the Word of God
    c. The Church is to perform good works

18. PHILEMON - Reveal Christ's Love and Teach Brotherly Love
    a. Genial greeting to Philemon and family
    b. Good reputation of Philemon
    c. Gracious plea for Onesimus
    d. Guiltless illustration of Imputation
    e. General and personal requests

19. HEBREWS - The Superiority of Christ
    a. Doctrinal - Christ is better than the Old Testament economy
    b. Practical - Christ brings better benefits and duties

20. JAMES - Ethics of Christianity
    a. Faith tested
    b. Difficulty of controlling the tongue
    c. Warning against worldliness
    d. Admonitions in view of the Lord's coming

21. 1 PETER - Christian Hope in the Time of Persecution and Trial
    a. Suffering and security of believers
    b. Suffering and the Scriptures
    c. Suffering and the sufferings of Christ
    d. Suffering and the Second Coming of Christ

22. 2 PETER - Warning Against False Teachers
    a. Addition of Christian graces gives assurance
    b. Authority of the Scriptures
    c. Apostasy brought in by false testimony
    d. Attitude toward Return of Christ: test for apostasy
    e. Agenda of God in the world
    f. Admonition to believers

23. 1 JOHN - The Family of God
    a. God is Light
    b. God is Love
    c. God is Life

24. 2 JOHN - Warning against Receiving Deceivers
    a. Walk in truth
    b. Love one another
    c. Receive not deceivers
    d. Find joy in fellowship

25. 3 JOHN - Admonition to Receive True Believers
    a. Gaius, brother in the Church
    b. Diotrephes
    c. Demetrius

26. JUDE - Contending for the Faith
    a. Occasion of the epistle
    b. Occurrences of apostasy
    c. Occupation of believers in the days of apostasy

27. REVELATION - The Unveiling of Christ Glorified
    a. The person of Christ in glory
    b. The possession of Jesus Christ - the Church in the World
    c. The program of Jesus Christ - the scene in Heaven
    d. The seven seals
    e. The seven trumpets
    f. Important persons in the last days
    g. The seven vials
    h. The fall of Babylon
    i. The eternal state

APPENDIX 8
From Before to Beyond Time:
The Plan of God and Human History
Adapted from: Suzanne de Dietrich. **God's Unfolding Purpose.** *Philadelphia: Westminster Press, 1976.*

I. **Before Time (Eternity Past) 1 Cor. 2.7**
   A. The Eternal Triune God
   B. God's Eternal Purpose
   C. The Mystery of Iniquity
   D. The Principalities and Powers

II. **Beginning of Time (Creation and Fall) Gen. 1.1**
   A. Creative Word
   B. Humanity
   C. Fall
   D. Reign of Death and First Signs of Grace

III. **Unfolding of Time (God's Plan Revealed Through Israel) Gal. 3.8**
   A. Promise (Patriarchs)
   B. Exodus and Covenant at Sinai
   C. Promised Land
   D. The City, the Temple, and the Throne (Prophet, Priest, and King)
   E. Exile
   F. Remnant

IV. **Fullness of Time (Incarnation of the Messiah) Gal. 4.4-5**
   A. The King Comes to His Kingdom
   B. The Present Reality of His Reign
   C. The Secret of the Kingdom: the Already and the Not Yet
   D. The Crucified King
   E. The Risen Lord

V. **The Last Times (The Descent of the Holy Spirit) Acts 2.16-18**
   A. Between the Times: the Church as Foretaste of the Kingdom
   B. The Church as Agent of the Kingdom
   C. The Conflict Between the Kingdoms of Darkness and Light

VI. **The Fulfillment of Time (The Second Coming) Matt. 13.40-43**
   A. The Return of Christ
   B. Judgment
   C. The Consummation of His Kingdom

VII. **Beyond Time (Eternity Future) 1 Cor. 15.24-28**
   A. Kingdom Handed Over to God the Father
   B. God as All in All

From Before to Beyond Time
Scriptures for Major Outline Points

I. Before Time (Eternity Past)

1 Cor. 2.7 (ESV) - But we impart a secret and hidden wisdom of God, *which God decreed before the ages* for our glory (cf. Titus 1.2).

II. Beginning of Time (Creation and Fall)

Gen. 1.1 (ESV) - *In the beginning*, God created the heavens and the earth.

III. Unfolding of Time (God's Plan Revealed Through Israel)

Gal. 3.8 (ESV) - And the Scripture, foreseeing that God would justify the Gentiles by faith, *preached the Gospel beforehand to Abraham*, saying, "In you shall all the nations be blessed" (cf. Rom. 9.4-5).

IV. Fullness of Time (The Incarnation of the Messiah)

Gal. 4.4-5 (ESV) - *But when the fullness of time had come*, God sent forth his Son, born of woman, born under the law, to redeem those who were under the law, so that we might receive adoption as sons.

V. The Last Times (The Descent of the Holy Spirit)

Acts 2.16-18 (ESV) - But this is what was uttered through the prophet Joel: "'*And in the last days it shall be*,' God declares, 'that I will pour out my Spirit on all flesh, and your sons and your daughters shall prophesy, and your young men shall see visions, and your old men shall dream dreams; even on my male servants and female servants in those days I will pour out my Spirit, and they shall prophesy.'"

VI. The Fulfillment of Time (The Second Coming)

Matt. 13.40-43 (ESV) - Just as the weeds are gathered and burned with fire, *so will it be at the close of the age*. The Son of Man will send his angels, and they will gather out of his kingdom all causes of sin and all lawbreakers, and throw them into the fiery furnace. In that place there will be weeping and gnashing of teeth. Then the righteous will shine like the sun in the Kingdom of their Father. He who has ears, let him hear.

VII. Beyond Time (Eternity Future)

1 Cor. 15.24-28 (ESV) - Then comes the end, when he delivers the Kingdom to God the Father after destroying every rule and every authority and power. For he must reign until he has put all his enemies under his feet. The last enemy to be destroyed is death. For "God has put all things in subjection under his feet." But when it says, "all things are put in subjection," it is plain that he is excepted who put all things in subjection under him. When all things are subjected to him, then the Son himself will also be subjected to him who put all things in subjection under him, that God may be all in all.

APPENDIX 9
"There Is a River"
Identifying the Streams of a Revitalized Authentic Christian Community in the City[1]

Rev. Dr. Don L. Davis • Psalm 46.4 (ESV) - There is a river whose streams make glad the city of God, the holy habitation of the Most High.

Tributaries of Authentic Historic Biblical Faith			
Recognized Biblical Identity	*Revived Urban Spirituality*	*Reaffirmed Historical Connectivity*	*Refocused Kingdom Authority*
The Church Is **One**	The Church Is **Holy**	The Church Is **Catholic**	The Church Is **Apostolic**
A Call to Biblical Fidelity — Recognizing the Scriptures as the anchor and foundation of the Christian faith and practice	A Call to the Freedom, Power, and Fullness of the Holy Spirit — Walking in the holiness, power, gifting, and liberty of the Holy Spirit in the body of Christ	A Call to Historic Roots and Continuity — Confessing the common historical identity and continuity of authentic Christian faith	A Call to the Apostolic Faith — Affirming the apostolic tradition as the authoritative ground of the Christian hope
A Call to Messianic Kingdom Identity — Rediscovering the story of the promised Messiah and his Kingdom in Jesus of Nazareth	A Call to Live as Sojourners and Aliens as the People of God — Defining authentic Christian discipleship as faithful membership among God's people	A Call to Affirm and Express the Global Communion of Saints — Expressing cooperation and collaboration with all other believers, both local and global	A Call to Representative Authority — Submitting joyfully to God's gifted servants in the Church as undershepherds of true faith
A Call to Creedal Affinity — Embracing the Nicene Creed as the shared rule of faith of historic orthodoxy	A Call to Liturgical, Sacramental, and Catechetical Vitality — Experiencing God's presence in the context of the Word, sacrament, and instruction	A Call to Radical Hospitality and Good Works — Expressing kingdom love to all, and especially to those of the household of faith	A Call to Prophetic and Holistic Witness — Proclaiming Christ and his Kingdom in word and deed to our neighbors and all peoples

[1] This schema is an adaptation and is based on the insights of the **Chicago Call** statement of May 1977, where various leading evangelical scholars and practitioners met to discuss the relationship of modern evangelicalism to the historic Christian faith.

APPENDIX 10
A Schematic for a Theology of the Kingdom and the Church
The Urban Ministry Institute

The Reign of the One, True, Sovereign, and Triune God, the LORD God, Yahweh, God the Father, Son, and Holy Spirit			
The Father Love - 1 John 4.8 Maker of heaven and earth and of all things visible and invisible	**The Son** Faith - Heb. 12.2 Prophet, Priest, and King	**The Spirit** Hope - Rom. 15.13 Lord of the Church	
Creation All that exists through the creative action of God.	**Kingdom** The Reign of God expressed in the rule of his Son Jesus the Messiah.	**Church** The one, holy, apostolic community which functions as a witness to (Acts 28.31) and a foretaste of (Col. 1.12; James 1.18; 1 Pet. 2.9; Rev. 1.6) the Kingdom of God.	
The eternal God, sovereign in power, infinite in wisdom, perfect in holiness, and steadfast in love, is the source and goal of all things.	**Freedom** (Slavery) Jesus answered them, "Truly, truly, I say to you, everyone who commits sin is a slave to sin. The slave does not remain in the house forever; the son remains forever. So if the Son sets you free, you will be free indeed." - John 8.34-36 (ESV)		*The Church is an Apostolic Community Where the Word is Rightly Preached, Therefore it is a Community of:* **Calling** - For freedom Christ has set us free; stand firm therefore, and do not submit again to a yoke of slavery. - Gal. 5.1 (ESV) (cf. Rom. 8.28-30; 1 Cor. 1.26-31; Eph. 1.18; 2 Thess. 2.13-14; Jude 1.1) **Faith** - "... for unless you believe that I am he you will die in your sins"... So Jesus said to the Jews who had believed in him, "If you abide in my word, you are truly my disciples, and you will know the truth, and the truth will set you free." - John 8.24b, 31-32 (ESV) (cf. Ps. 119.45; Rom. 1.17; 5.1-2; Eph. 2.8-9; 2 Tim. 1.13-14; Heb. 2.14-15; James 1.25) **Witness** - The Spirit of the Lord is upon me, because he has anointed me to proclaim good news to the poor. He has sent me to proclaim liberty to the captives and recovering of sight to the blind, to set at liberty those who are oppressed, to proclaim the year of the Lord's favor. - Luke 4.18-19 (ESV) (cf. Lev. 25.10; Prov. 31.8; Matt. 4.17; 28.18-20; Mark 13.10; Acts 1.8; 8.4, 12; 13.1-3; 25.20; 28.30-31)
Rom. 8.18-21 → O, the depth of the riches and wisdom and knowledge of God! How unsearchable are his judgments, and how inscrutable his ways! For who has known the mind of the Lord, or who has been his counselor? Or who has ever given a gift to him, that he might be repaid?" For from him and through him and to him are all things. To him be glory forever! Amen! - Rom. 11.33-36 (ESV) (cf. 1 Cor. 15.23-28; Rev.)	**Wholeness** (Sickness) But he was wounded for our transgressions; he was crushed for our iniquities; upon him was the chastisement that brought us peace, and with his stripes we are healed. - Isa. 53.5 (ESV)		*The Church is One Community Where the Sacraments are Rightly Administered, Therefore it is a Community of:* **Worship** - You shall serve the Lord your God, and he will bless your bread and your water, and I will take sickness away from among you. - Exod. 23.25 (ESV) (cf. Ps. 147.1-3; Heb. 12.28; Col. 3.16; Rev. 15.3-4; 19.5) **Covenant** - And the Holy Spirit also bears witness to us; for after the saying, "This is the covenant that I will make with them after those days, declares the Lord: I will put my laws on their hearts, and write them on their minds," then he adds, "I will remember their sins and their lawless deeds no more." - Heb. 10.15-17 (ESV) (cf. Isa. 54.10-17; Ezek. 34.25-31; 37.26-27; Mal. 2.4-5; Luke 22.20; 2 Cor. 3.6; Col. 3.15; Heb. 8.7-13; 12.22-24; 13.20-21) **Presence** - In him you also are being built together into a dwelling place for God by his Spirit. - Eph. 2.22 (ESV) (cf. Exod. 40.34-38, Ezek. 48.35; Matt. 18.18-20)
Rev. 21.1-5 →			
	Justice (Selfishness) Behold, my servant whom I have chosen, my beloved with whom my soul is well pleased. I will put my Spirit upon him, and he will proclaim justice to the Gentiles. He will not quarrel or cry aloud, nor will anyone hear his voice in the streets; a bruised reed he will not break, and a smoldering wick he will not quench, until he brings justice to victory. - Matt. 12.18-20 (ESV)		*The Church is a Holy Community Where Discipline is Rightly Ordered, Therefore it is a Community of:* **Reconciliation** - For he himself is our peace, who has made us both one and has broken down in his flesh the dividing wall of hostility by abolishing the law of commandments and ordinances, that he might create in himself one new man in place of the two, so making peace, and might reconcile us both to God in one body through the cross, thereby killing the hostility. And he came and preached peace to you who were far off and peace to those who were near. For through him we both have access in one Spirit to the Father. - Eph. 2.14-18 (ESV) (cf. Exod. 23.4-9; Lev. 19.34; Deut. 10.18-19; Ezek. 22.29; Mic. 6.8; 2 Cor. 5.16-21) **Suffering** - Since therefore Christ suffered in the flesh, arm yourselves with the same way of thinking, for whoever has suffered in the flesh has ceased from sin, so as to live for the rest of the time in the flesh no longer for human passions but for the will of God. - 1 Pet. 4.1-2 (ESV) (cf. Luke 6.22; 10.3; Rom. 8.17; 2 Tim. 2.3; 3.12; 1 Pet. 2.20-24; Heb. 5.8; 13.11-14) **Service** - But Jesus called them to him and said, "You know that the rulers of the Gentiles lord it over them, and their great ones exercise authority over them. It shall not be so among you. But whoever would be great among you must be your servant, and whoever would be first among you must be your slave even as the Son of Man came not to be served but to serve, and to give his life as a ransom for many." - Matt. 20.25-28 (ESV) (cf. 1 John 4.16-18, Gal. 2.10)
Isa. 11.6-9 →			

APPENDIX 11
Living in the Already and the Not Yet Kingdom
Rev. Dr. Don L. Davis

The Spirit: The pledge of the inheritance (***arrabon***)
The Church: The foretaste (***aparche***) of the Kingdom
"In Christ": The rich life (***en Christos***) we share as citizens of the Kingdom

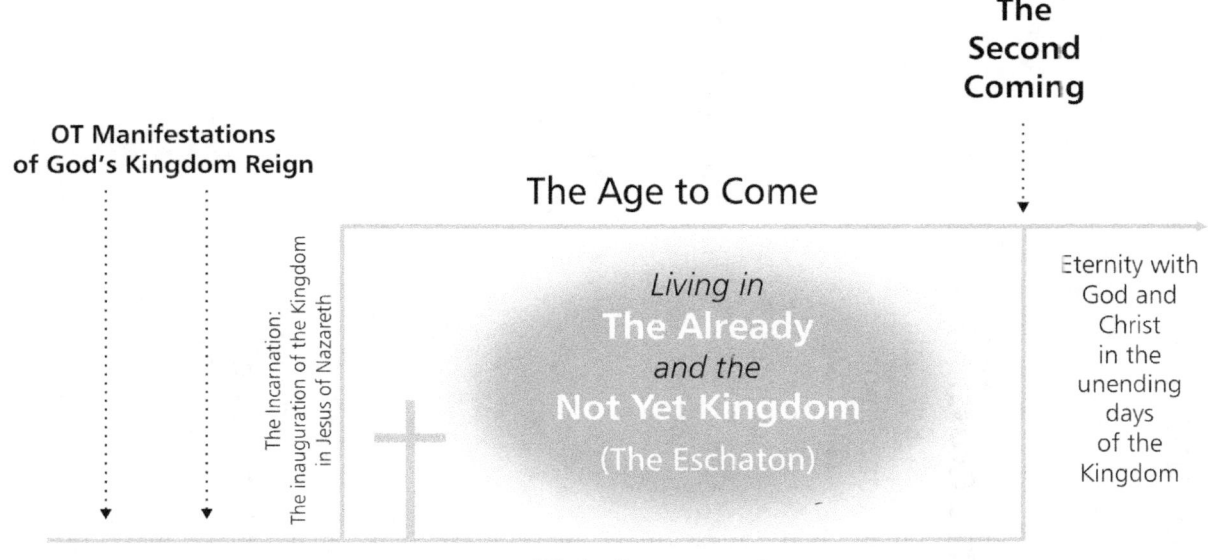

Internal enemy: The flesh (*sarx*) and the sin nature
External enemy: The world (*kosmos*) the systems of greed, lust, and pride
Infernal enemy: The devil (*kakos*) the animating spirit of falsehood and fear

Jewish View of Time

This Present Age — The Age to Come

The Coming of Messiah
The restoration of Israel
The end of Gentile oppression
The return of the earth to Edenic glory
Universal knowledge of the Lord

APPENDIX 12

Jesus of Nazareth: The Presence of the Future

Rev. Dr. Don L. Davis

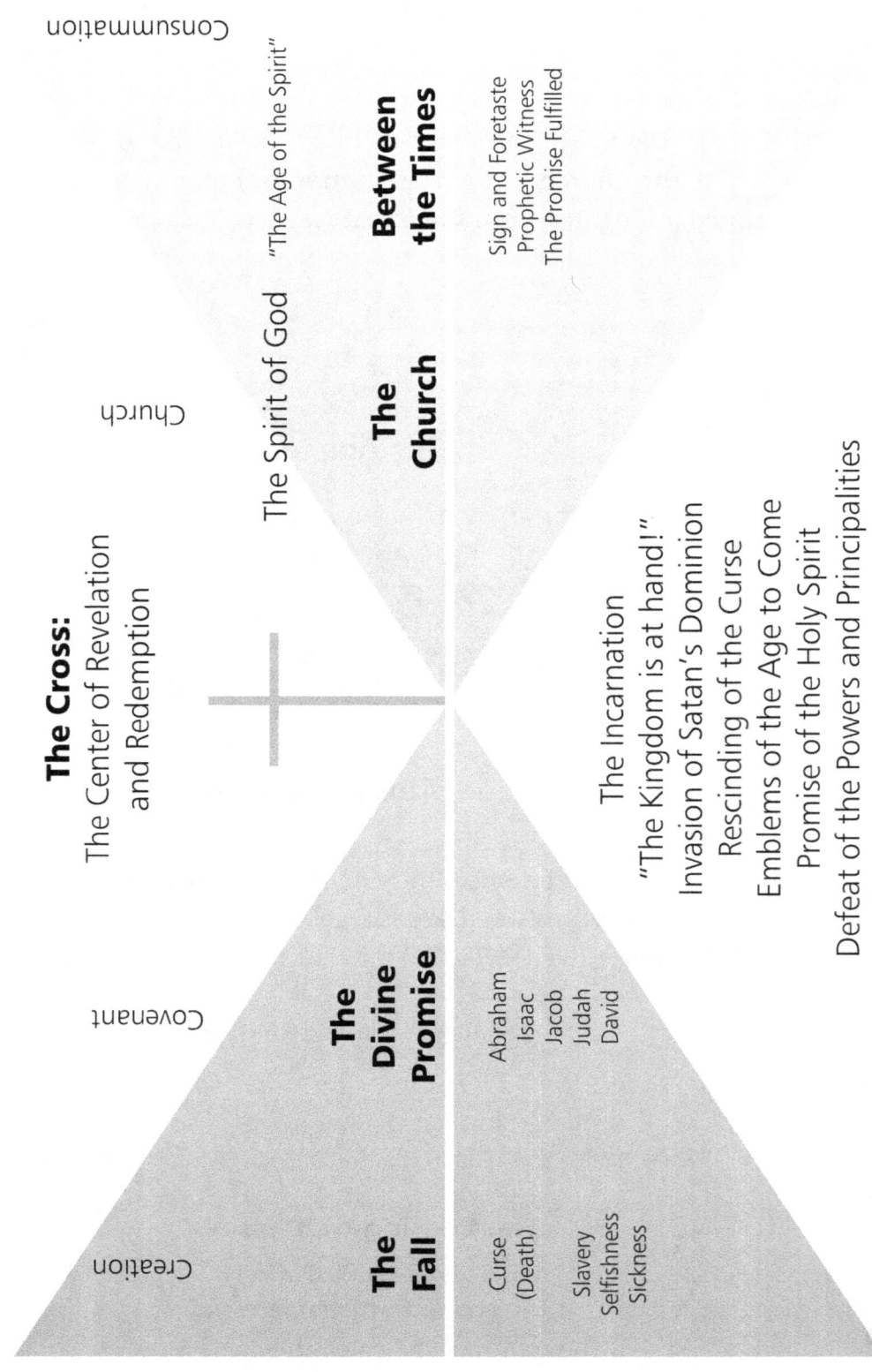

APPENDIX 13
Traditions
(Paradosis)

Dr. Don L. Davis and Rev. Terry G. Cornett

Strong's Definition

Paradosis. Transmission, i.e. (concretely) a precept; specifically, the Jewish traditionary law

Vine's Explanation

denotes "a tradition," and hence, by metonymy, (a) "the teachings of the rabbis," . . . (b) "apostolic teaching," . . . of instructions concerning the gatherings of believers, of Christian doctrine in general . . . of instructions concerning everyday conduct.

1. **The concept of tradition in Scripture is essentially positive.**

   Jer. 6.16 (ESV) - Thus says the Lord: "Stand by the roads, and look, and ask for the ancient paths, where the good way is; and walk in it, and find rest for your souls. But they said, 'We will not walk in it'" (cf. Exod. 3.15; Judg. 2.17; 1 Kings 8.57-58; Ps. 78.1-6).

   2 Chron. 35.25 (ESV) - Jeremiah also uttered a lament for Josiah; and all the singing men and singing women have spoken of Josiah in their laments to this day. They made these a rule in Israel; behold, they are written in the Laments (cf. Gen. 32.32; Judg. 11.38-40).

   Jer. 35.14-19 (ESV) - The command that Jonadab the son of Rechab gave to his sons, to drink no wine, has been kept, and they drink none to this day, for they have obeyed their father's command. I have spoken to you persistently, but you have not listened to me. I have sent to you all my servants the prophets, sending them persistently, saying, 'Turn now every one of you from his evil way, and amend your deeds, and do not go after other gods to serve them, and then you shall dwell in the land that I gave to you and your fathers.' But you did not incline your ear or listen to me. The sons of Jonadab the son of Rechab have kept the command that their father gave them, but this people has not obeyed me. Therefore, thus says the

Traditions (continued)

Lord, the God of hosts, the God of Israel: Behold, I am bringing upon Judah and all the inhabitants of Jerusalem all the disaster that I have pronounced against them, because I have spoken to them and they have not listened, I have called to them and they have not answered." But to the house of the Rechabites Jeremiah said, "Thus says the Lord of hosts, the God of Israel: Because you have obeyed the command of Jonadab your father and kept all his precepts and done all that he commanded you, therefore thus says the Lord of hosts, the God of Israel: Jonadab the son of Rechab shall never lack a man to stand before me."

2. Godly tradition is a wonderful thing, but not all tradition is godly.

Any individual tradition must be judged by its faithfulness to the Word of God and its usefulness in helping people maintain obedience to Christ's example and teaching.[1] In the Gospels, Jesus frequently rebukes the Pharisees for establishing traditions that nullify rather than uphold God's commands.

Mark 7.8 (ESV) - You leave the commandment of God and hold to the tradition of men" (cf. Matt. 15.2-6; Mark 7.13).

Col. 2.8 (ESV) - See to it that no one takes you captive by philosophy and empty deceit, according to human tradition, according to the elemental spirits of the world, and not according to Christ.

3. Without the fullness of the Holy Spirit, and the constant edification provided to us by the Word of God, tradition will inevitably lead to dead formalism.

Those who are spiritual are filled with the Holy Spirit, whose power and leading alone provides individuals and congregations a sense of freedom and vitality in all they practice and believe. However, when the practices and teachings of any given tradition are no longer infused by the power of the Holy Spirit and the Word of God, tradition loses its effectiveness, and may actually become counterproductive to our discipleship in Jesus Christ.

Eph. 5.18 (ESV) - And do not get drunk with wine, for that is debauchery, but be filled with the Spirit.

---

[1] *"All Protestants insist that these traditions must ever be tested against Scripture and can never possess an independent apostolic authority over or alongside of Scripture." (J. Van Engen, "Tradition,"* **Evangelical Dictionary of Theology**, *Walter Elwell, Gen. ed.) We would add that Scripture is itself the "authoritative tradition" by which all other traditions are judged. See "Appendix A, The Founders of Tradition: Three Levels of Christian Authority," p. 4.*

Traditions (continued)

Gal. 5.22-25 (ESV) - But the fruit of the Spirit is love, joy, peace, patience, kindness, goodness, faithfulness, gentleness, self-control; against such things there is no law. And those who belong to Christ Jesus have crucified the flesh with its passions and desires. If we live by the Spirit, let us also walk by the Spirit.

2 Cor. 3.5-6 (ESV) - Not that we are sufficient in ourselves to claim anything as coming from us, but our sufficiency is from God, who has made us competent to be ministers of a new covenant, not of the letter but of the Spirit. For the letter kills, but the Spirit gives life.

4. **Fidelity to the Apostolic Tradition (teaching and modeling) is the essence of Christian maturity.**

    2 Tim. 2.2 (ESV) - and what you have heard from me in the presence of many witnesses entrust to faithful men who will be able to teach others also.

    1 Cor. 11.1-2 (ESV) - Be imitators of me, as I am of Christ. Now I commend you because you remember me in everything and maintain the traditions even as I delivered them to you (cf.1 Cor. 4.16-17, 2 Tim. 1.13-14, 2 Thess. 3.7-9, Phil. 4.9).

    1 Cor. 15.3-8 (ESV) - For I delivered to you as of first importance what I also received: that Christ died for our sins in accordance with the Scriptures, that he was buried, that he was raised on the third day in accordance with the Scriptures, and that he appeared to Cephas, then to the twelve. Then he appeared to more than five hundred brothers at one time, most of whom are still alive, though some have fallen asleep. Then he appeared to James, then to all the apostles. Last of all, as to one untimely born, he appeared also to me.

5. **The Apostle Paul often includes an appeal to the tradition for support in doctrinal practices.**

    1 Cor. 11.16 (ESV) - If anyone is inclined to be contentious, we have no such practice, nor do the churches of God (cf. 1 Cor. 1.2, 7.17, 15.3).

Traditions (continued)

> 1 Cor. 14.33-34 (ESV) - For God is not a God of confusion but of peace. As in all the churches of the saints, the women should keep silent in the churches. For they are not permitted to speak, but should be in submission, as the Law also says.

6. When a congregation uses received tradition to remain faithful to the "Word of God," they are commended by the apostles.

> 1 Cor. 11.2 (ESV) - Now I commend you because you remember me in everything and maintain the traditions even as I delivered them to you.

> 2 Thess. 2.15 (ESV) - So then, brothers, stand firm and hold to the traditions that you were taught by us, either by our spoken word or by our letter.

> 2 Thess. 3.6 (ESV) - Now we command you, brothers, in the name of our Lord Jesus Christ, that you keep away from any brother who is walking in idleness and not in accord with the tradition that you received from us.

Appendix A

The Founders of Tradition: Three Levels of Christian Authority

Exod. 3.15 (ESV) - God also said to Moses, "Say this to the people of Israel, 'The Lord, the God of your fathers, the God of Abraham, the God of Isaac, and the God of Jacob, has sent me to you.' This is my name forever, and thus I am to be remembered throughout all generations."

1. The Authoritative Tradition: the Apostles and the Prophets (The Holy Scriptures)

Eph. 2.19-21 (ESV) - So then you are no longer strangers and aliens, but you are fellow citizens with the saints and members of the household of God, built on the foundation of the apostles and prophets, Christ Jesus himself being the cornerstone, in whom the whole structure, being joined together, grows into a holy temple in the Lord.

~ The Apostle Paul

Traditions (continued)

Those who gave eyewitness testimony to the revelation and saving acts of Yahweh, first in Israel, and ultimately in Jesus Christ the Messiah. This testimony is binding for all people, at all times, and in all places. It is the authoritative tradition by which all subsequent tradition is judged.

2. The Great Tradition: the Ecumenical Councils and their Creeds[2]

[2] See Appendix B, "Defining the Great Tradition."

What has been believed everywhere, always, and by all.

~ Vincent of Lerins

The Great Tradition is the core dogma (doctrine) of the Church. It represents the teaching of the Church as it has understood the Authoritative Tradition (the Holy Scriptures), and summarizes those essential truths that Christians of all ages have confessed and believed. To these doctrinal statements the whole Church, (Catholic, Orthodox, and Protestant)[3] gives its assent. The worship and theology of the Church reflects this core dogma, which finds its summation and fulfillment in the person and work of Jesus Christ. From earliest times, Christians have expressed their devotion to God in its Church calendar, a yearly pattern of worship which summarizes and reenacts the events of Christ's life.

[3] Even the more radical wing of the Protestant reformation (Anabaptists) who were the most reluctant to embrace the creeds as dogmatic instruments of faith, did not disagree with the essential content found in them. "They assumed the Apostolic Creed–they called it 'The Faith,' **Der Glaube**, as did most people." See John Howard Yoder, **Preface to Theology: Christology and Theological Method**. Grand Rapids: Brazos Press, 2002. pp. 222-223.

3. Specific Church Traditions: the Founders of Denominations and Orders

The Presbyterian Church (U.S.A.) has approximately 2.5 million members, 11,200 congregations and 21,000 ordained ministers. Presbyterians trace their history to the 16th century and the Protestant Reformation. Our heritage, and much of what we believe, began with the French lawyer John Calvin (1509-1564), whose writings crystallized much of the Reformed thinking that came before him.

~ The Presbyterian Church, U.S.A.

Christians have expressed their faith in Jesus Christ in various ways through specific movements and traditions which embrace and express the Authoritative Tradition and the Great Tradition in unique ways. For instance,

Traditions (continued)

Catholic movements have arisen around people like Benedict, Francis, or Dominic, and among Protestants people like Martin Luther, John Calvin, Ulrich Zwingli, and John Wesley. Women have founded vital movements of Christian faith (e.g., Aimee Semple McPherson of the Foursquare Church), as well as minorities (e.g., Richard Allen of the African Methodist Episcopal Church or Charles H. Mason of the Church of God in Christ, who also helped to spawn the Assemblies of God), all which attempted to express the Authoritative Tradition and the Great Tradition in a specific way consistent with their time and expression.

The emergence of vital, dynamic movements of the faith at different times and among different peoples reveal the fresh working of the Holy Spirit throughout history. Thus, inside Catholicism, new communities have arisen such as the Benedictines, Franciscans, and Dominicans; and outside Catholicism, new denominations have emerged (Lutherans, Presbyterians, Methodists, Church of God in Christ, etc.). Each of these specific traditions have "founders," key leaders whose energy and vision helped to establish a unique expression of Christian faith and practice. Of course, to be legitimate, these movements must adhere to and faithfully express both the Authoritative Tradition and the Great Tradition. Members of these specific traditions embrace their own unique practices and patterns of spirituality, but these unique features are not necessarily binding on the Church at large. They represent the unique expressions of that community's understanding of and faithfulness to the Authoritative and Great Traditions.

Specific traditions seek to express and live out this faithfulness to the Authoritative and Great Traditions through their worship, teaching, and service. They seek to make the Gospel clear within new cultures or sub-cultures, speaking and modeling the hope of Christ into new situations shaped by their own set of questions posed in light of their own unique circumstances. These movements, therefore, seek to contextualize the Authoritative tradition in a way that faithfully and effectively leads new groups of people to faith in Jesus Christ, and incorporates those who believe into the community of faith that obeys his teachings and gives witness of him to others.

Traditions (continued)

Appendix B

Defining the "Great Tradition"

The Great Tradition (sometimes called the "classical Christian tradition") is defined by Robert E. Webber as follows:

[It is] the broad outline of Christian belief and practice developed from the Scriptures between the time of Christ and the middle of the fifth century

~ Webber. **The Majestic Tapestry**.
Nashville: Thomas Nelson Publishers, 1986. p. 10.

This tradition is widely affirmed by Protestant theologians both ancient and modern.

Thus those ancient Councils of Nicea, Constantinople, the first of Ephesus, Chalcedon, and the like, which were held for refuting errors, we willingly embrace, and reverence as sacred, in so far as relates to doctrines of faith, for they contain nothing but the pure and genuine interpretation of Scripture, which the holy Fathers with spiritual prudence adopted to crush the enemies of religion who had then arisen.

~ John Calvin. **Institutes**. IV, ix. 8.

. . . most of what is enduringly valuable in contemporary biblical exegesis was discovered by the fifth century.

~ Thomas C. Oden. **The Word of Life**.
San Francisco: HarperSanFrancisco, 1989. p. xi

The first four Councils are by far the most important, as they settled the orthodox faith on the Trinity and the Incarnation.

~ Philip Schaff. **The Creeds of Christendom**. Vol. 1.
Grand Rapids: Baker Book House, 1996. p. 44.

Our reference to the Ecumenical Councils and Creeds is, therefore, focused on those Councils which retain a widespread agreement in the Church among Catholics, Orthodox, and Protestants. While Catholic and Orthodox share common agreement on the first seven councils, Protestants tend to affirm and use primarily the first four. Therefore, those councils which continue to be shared by the whole Church are completed with the Council of Chalcedon in 451.

Traditions (continued)

It is worth noting that each of these four Ecumenical Councils took place in a pre-European cultural context and that none of them were held in Europe. They were councils of the whole Church and they reflected a time in which Christianity was primarily an eastern religion in it's geographic core. By modern reckoning, their participants were African, Asian, and European. The councils reflected a church that ". . . has roots in cultures far distant from Europe and preceded the development of modern European identity, and [of which] some of its greatest minds have been African" (Oden, *The Living God*, San Francisco: HarperSanFrancisco, 1987, p. 9).

Perhaps the most important achievement of the Councils was the creation of what is now commonly called the Nicene Creed. It serves as a summary statement of the Christian faith that can be agreed on by Catholic, Orthodox, and Protestant Christians.

The first four Ecumenical Councils are summarized in the following chart:

Name/Date/Location	Purpose
First Ecumenical Council 325 A.D. Nicea, Asia Minor	Defending against: *Arianism* Question answered: *Was Jesus God?* Action: *Developed the initial form of the Nicene Creed to serve as a summary of the Christian faith*
Second Ecumenical Council 381 A.D. Constantinople, Asia Minor	Defending against: *Macedonianism* Question answered: *Is the Holy Spirit a personal and equal part of the Godhead?* Action: *Completed the Nicene Creed by expanding the article dealing with the Holy Spirit*
Third Ecumenical Council 431 A.D. Ephesus, Asia Minor	Defending against: *Nestorianism* Question answered: *Is Jesus Christ both God and man in one person?* Action: *Defined Christ as the Incarnate Word of God and affirmed his mother Mary as* **theotokos** *(God-bearer)*
Fourth Ecumenical Council 451 A.D. Chalcedon, Asia Minor	Defending against: *Monophysitism* Question answered: *How can Jesus be both God and man?* Action: *Explained the relationship between Jesus' two natures (human and Divine)*

APPENDIX 14
The Names of Almighty God
Rev. Dr. Don L. Davis

I. The Names of God

A. *Elohim*

1. *Elohim* is a Hebrew plural form used more than 2000 times in the Old Testament, usually termed a "plural of majesty" of the general name for God.

2. Derived from *El*, whose root meaning is "to be strong" (cf. Gen. 17.1; 28.3; 35.11; Josh. 3.10) or "to be preeminent." (cf. Frank M. Cross, "El," in *Theological Dictionary of the Old Testament*, 6 vols., revised, edited by G. Johannes Botterweck and Helmer Ringgren (Grand Rapids: Eerdmans, 1977, 1:244.)

3. *Elohim* is usually translated "God" in English translations.

4. This name *emphasizes God's transcendence* (cf. that God is above all others who are called God). *Elohim* is the plural form of *El*; the terms seem to be interchangeable (cf. Exod. 34.14; Ps. 18.31; Deut. 32.17, 21).

5. *El* may signify in some texts (such as Isa. 31.3) the "power and strength of God and the defenselessness of human enemies" (cf. Hos. 11.9). (Cf. 34. Helmer Ringgren, "*Elohim*," in *Theological Dictionary of the Old Testament*, 1:273-74.)

B. *Adonai*

1. The term *Adonai* (Heb. *Adhon* or *Adhonay*) in its root means "lord" or "master" and is usually translated "Lord" in English Bibles.

2. It occurs 449 times in the Old Testament and 315 times with Yahweh. *Adhon* emphasizes the servant-master relationship (cf. Gen. 24.9) and suggests God's authority as Master, i.e., the One rules with absolute authority (cf. Ps. 8.1; Hos. 12.14).

The Names of Almighty God (continued)

3. *Adonai* can be understood to mean "*Lord of all*" or "*Lord par excellence*" (cf. Deut. 10.17; Josh. 3.11). (Cf. Merrill F. Unger and William White, Jr., eds., *Nelson's Expository Dictionary of the Old Testament* [Nashville: Nelson, 1980], pp. 228-29; and Otto Eissfeldt, "*Adhon*," in *Theological Dictionary of the Old Testament*, 1:59-72.)

C. *Yahweh* (Jehovah)

1. The name *Yahweh* translates the Hebrew *tetragrammaton* (four lettered expression) YHWH. Since the original name contained no vowels, it is uncertain how it should be pronounced. (For instance, the ASV translates it "Jehovah," whereas most modern translations simply render it "LORD" [to distinguish it from *Adonai*, "Lord"]).

2. Jewish scholars generally pronounce it as "*Adonai*" rather than voicing YHWH, out of respect for its sacredness.

3. It is used as a common designation (used 6,828 times in the Old Testament), and some suggest it may be related to the verb "to be." (Cf. Exod. 3.14-15 the Lord declares, "I AM WHO I AM...The Lord . . . has sent me to you. This is my name forever.)

4. *Yahweh* as the I AM connects to the "I AM" claims of Messiah Jesus (cf. John 6.35; 8.12; 10.9, 11; 11.25; 14.6; 15.1), who claimed equality with Yahweh.

5. *Yahweh*, the name of covenant relationship

   a. The name of the Abrahamic Covenant (Gen. 12.8)

   b. The name of the Exodus (Exod. 6.6; 20.2)

   c. *A unique relationship*: although the terms *Elohim* and *Adonai* were terms known to other peoples, Yahweh was unique to Israel.

The Names of Almighty God (continued)

II. Compound Names: the Name of God Involving the Names *El* (or *Elohim*) and *Yahweh*

A. *El Shaddai*

1. Translated "God Almighty"

2. Probably relates to the word *mountain*, suggesting the power or strength of God

3. The name of God as a covenant-keeping God (Gen. 17.1; cf. vv. 1–8)

B. *El Elyon*

1. Translated "God Most High"

2. This terms refers to *the supremacy of God*

3. *Yahweh* God is a god above all so-called gods (cf. Gen. 14.18–22). Melchizedek recognized him as "God Most High" inasmuch as he is possessor of heaven and earth (v. 19).

C. *El Olam*

1. Translated the "Everlasting God"

2. Emphasizes *the unchanging character of God* (Gen. 21.33; Isa. 40.28)

D. *Yahweh* compound names

1. Adonai-Yahweh, "*The Lord our Sovereign,*" Gen. 15.2, 8

2. Yahweh-Jireh, "*The Lord will provide,*" Gen. 22.14

3. Yahweh Elohim, "*The Lord God,*" Gen. 2.4-25

4. Yahweh-Nissi , "*The Lord our banner,*" Exod. 17.15

5. Yahweh-Rapha, "*The Lord our healer,*" Exod. 15.26

6. Yahweh-Rohi, "*The Lord our shepherd,*" Ps. 23.1

The Names of Almighty God (continued)

7. Yahweh-Shammah, "*The Lord is there,*" Ezek. 48.35

8. Yahweh-Hoseenu, "*The Lord our Maker,*" Ps. 95.6

9. Yahweh-Shalom, "*The Lord our peace,*" Judg. 6.24

10. Yahweh-Sabbaoth, "*The Lord of armies,*" 1 Sam. 1.3

11. Yahweh-Mekaddishkem, "*The Lord your sanctifier,*" Exod. 31.13

12. Yahweh-Tsidkenu, "*The Lord our righteousness,*" Jer. 23.6

APPENDIX 15
Theological Visions and Approaches
The Urban Ministry Institute

The following outline provides a bare bones overview of some of the philosophical approaches and understandings related to God and his relationship to the universe. Individuals pose different arguments for the existence of God and the relationship between God and his universe based on their 1) understanding of Scripture, 2) underlying assumptions about the existence of God, 3) view of the material universe and world, and 4) the human capacity to know God (if he exists), and what that knowledge involves. Many modern approaches think of God's existence and all speech about God as the possibility of religion *within the bounds of knowledge*.

I. Principles of Natural Theology

    A. *Ontological argument* - Anselm *Proslogion*

        1. Logical necessity of God's existence by reason alone

        2. God = that than which no greater can be thought

        3. To exist in reality is greater than to exist merely in thought.

        4. "That than which no greater can be thought" must exist both in reality and in thought.

        5. Tautology – (argument in a circle) merely to define an entity as existing does not provide grounds for inferring its existence.

        6. Kant – a merchant cannot increase his wealth by adding zeroes to the figures in his accounts.

    B. *Cosmological argument* – existence of a first cause of the cosmos

        1. The things we observe in the world all have antecedent causes. Nothing is totally self-caused, and there must be a first cause.

        2. God is the Prime Mover and the First Cause.

Theological Visions and Approaches (continued)

    C. *Teleological argument* – (physico-teleological)

        1. Telos = end

        2. Things in our experience appear to serve ends beyond their devising or control. Purpose observed in nature, implying a cosmic mind.

        3. Key warrant: purpose does not occur without a Purposer.

    D. *Moral argument* – People of different cultures and beliefs recognize certain basic moral values and obligations.

        1. These universal values cannot be reduced to mere conventions.

        2. These do not emerge from the material universe.

        3. We can, therefore, posit a personal, moral being as the source of all moral values and as the One to whom all moral beings are ultimately responsible.

II. Facts about Natural Theology

    A. Most prevalent in *Catholic theology*

    B. *Calvinistic theology*: believes in a general revelation of God in nature and providence

        1. Spoke of 'divinity' or 'sense of God' which was 'the seed of religion'

        2. For sure and certain knowledge of God we must turn to the Word of God in Scripture

    C. *Karl Barth*: rejected all natural theology on the grounds that God reveals himself in his Word, and is pointless to look elsewhere

Theological Visions and Approaches (continued)

D. *Emil Brunner*: argued for a natural theology based on such ideas as the image of God, general revelation, preserving grace, divine ordinances, point of contact, and the contention that race does not abolish nature but perfects it.

III. Dualism

A. A *dualism* exists when there are two substances, or powers, or modes, neither of which is reducible to the other.

1. Monism – there is only one substance, power, or mode.

2. Twins of all things

B. Four different contexts (God and creation)

1. Identifying God with his creation

    a. Metaphysical pantheism

    b. Mystical connection

2. God is distinct from his creation in the sense of its GROUND.

3. Unlike deism, God is its SUSTAINING CAUSE (both transcendently and imminently).

4. Difficulties: what is precisely the relationship between the divine and human action in creation

IV. Materialism

"The doctrine that whatever exists is either physical matter, or depends upon physical matter."

A. A philosophical position with definite ontological explanations (the denial of the existence of minds or spirits)

B. Research program and methodology with no such implications

Theological Visions and Approaches (continued)

    C. Opposed by mind-body dualism

    D. What of humanity as part of the creation, and life after death?

V. Deism

"Belief in a remote creator, uninvolved in the world whose mechanism he devised"

    A. Stands for the abolition of dogma founded on alleged revelation

    B. Promotes a natural religion with blessings bestowed on all by a beneficent God

    C. Religion of moral law: "rationalists with a heart hunger for religion"

    D. Non-christocentric worship of God

    E. Ecclesiastical power as a hindrance of free thinking people

    F. Fall and redemption is dismissed, its literary form regarded as crude, corrupt, and flawed

VI. Determinism

    A. *Scientific determinism* – the form of every physical event is determined uniquely by the conjunction of events preceding it; discovering the interdependence and expressing it in laws.

Theological Visions and Approaches (continued)

B. *Theological determinism* – the form of all events is determined according to the "determinate counsel and foreknowledge of God" (Acts 2.23).

C. What of the *theodicy* questions? (Theodicy as the problem of evil happening to good or innocent persons)

D. Limited freedom or no freedom at all: what of the relationship between the material world, causative events, and the sovereignty of God?

APPENDIX 16

A Theology of the Church in Kingdom Perspective

Terry Cornett and Don Davis

APPENDIX 17
Apostolicity
The Unique Place of the Apostles in Christian Faith and Practice
Rev. Dr. Don L. Davis

Gal. 1.8-9 (ESV) - But even if we or an angel from heaven should preach to you a gospel contrary to the one we preached to you, let him be accursed. **[9]** As we have said before, so now I say again: If anyone is preaching to you a gospel contrary to the one you received, let him be accursed.

2 Thess. 3.6 (ESV) - Now we command you, brothers, in the name of our Lord Jesus Christ, that you keep away from any brother who is walking in idleness and not in accord with the tradition that you received from us.

Luke 1.1-4 (ESV) - Inasmuch as many have undertaken to compile a narrative of the things that have been accomplished among us, **[2]** just as those who from the beginning were eyewitnesses and ministers of the word have delivered them to us, **[3]** it seemed good to me also, having followed all things closely for some time past, to write an orderly account for you, most excellent Theophilus, **[4]** that you may have certainty concerning the things you have been taught.

John 15.27 (ESV) - And you also will bear witness, because you have been with me from the beginning.

Acts 1.3 (ESV) - To them he presented himself alive after his suffering by many proofs, appearing to them during forty days and speaking about the kingdom of God.

Acts 1.21-22 (ESV) - So one of the men who have accompanied us during all the time that the Lord Jesus went in and out among us, **[22]** beginning from the baptism of John until the day when he was taken up from us—one of these men must become with us a witness to his resurrection.

1 John 1.1-3 (ESV) - That which was from the beginning, which we have heard, which we have seen with our eyes, which we looked upon and have touched with our hands, concerning the word of life— **[2]** the life was made manifest, and we have seen it, and testify to it and proclaim to you the eternal life, which was with the Father and was made manifest to us— **[3]** that which we have seen and heard we proclaim also to you, so that you too may have fellowship with us; and indeed our fellowship is with the Father and with his Son Jesus Christ.

"Apostolicity"

- **Focused on Messiah Jesus**
- **Infallible (Authoritative)**
- **Universally acknowledged among the churches**
- **Clear standard for credentialing ordained leaders**
- **Standard for NT canon**

APPENDIX 18
From Deep Ignorance to Credible Witness
Rev. Dr. Don L. Davis

Level	Stage	Description / Scripture References	Key Quote
8	**Witness**	Ability to give witness and teach 2 Tim. 2.2 Matt. 28.18-20 1 John 1.1-4 Prov. 20.6 2 Cor. 5.18-21	*And the things you have heard me say in the presence of many witnesses entrust to reliable men who will also be qualified to teach others.* - 2 Tim. 2.2
7	**Lifestyle**	Consistent appropriation and habitual practice based on beliefs Heb. 5.11-6.2 Eph. 4.11-16 2 Pet. 3.18 1 Tim. 4.7-10	*And Jesus increased in wisdom and in stature, and in favor with God and man.* - Luke 2.52
6	**Demonstration**	Expressing conviction in corresponding conduct, speech, and behavior James 2.14-26 2 Cor. 4.13 2 Pet. 1.5-9 1 Thess. 1.3-10	*Nevertheless, at your word I will let down the net.* - Luke 5.5
5	**Conviction**	Committing oneself to think, speak, and act in light of information Heb. 2.3-4 Heb. 11.1, 6 Heb. 3.15-19 Heb. 4.2-6	*Do you believe this?* - John 11.26
4	**Discernment**	Understanding the meaning and implications of information John 16.13 Eph. 1.15-18 Col. 1.9-10 Isa. 6.10; 29.10	*Do you understand what you are reading?* - Acts 8.30
3	**Knowledge**	Ability to recall and recite information 2 Tim. 3.16-17 1 Cor. 2.9-16 1 John 2.20-27 John 14.26	*For what does the Scripture say?* - Rom. 4.3
2	**Interest**	Responding to ideas or information with both curiosity and openness Ps. 42.1-2 Acts 9.4-5 John 12.21 1 Sam. 3.4-10	*We will hear you again on this matter.* - Acts 17.32
1	**Awareness**	General exposure to ideas and information Mark 7.6-8 Acts 19.1-7 John 5.39-40 Matt. 7.21-23	*At that time, Herod the tetrarch heard about the fame of Jesus.* - Matt. 14.1
0	**Ignorance**	Unfamiliarity with information due to naivete, indifference, or hardness Eph. 4.17-19 Ps. 2.1-3 Rom. 1.21; 2.19 1 John 2.11	*Who is the Lord that I should heed his voice?* - Exod. 5.2

APPENDIX 19
Picking Up on Different Wavelengths
Integrated vs. Fragmented Mindsets and Lifestyles
Dr. Don L. Davis

A Fragmented Mindset and Lifestyle	An Integrated Lifestyle and Mindset
Sees things primarily in relation to one's own needs	Sees all things as one and whole
Sees something other than God as a substitute point of reference and coordination for meaning and truth	Sees God in Christ as the ultimate point of reference and coordination for all meaning and truth
Seeks God's blessing upon one's own personal enhancement	Aligns personal goals with God's ultimate plan and purposes
Understands the purpose of life to experience the greatest level of personal fulfillment and enhancement possible	Understands the purpose of life to make the maximum contribution possible to God's purpose in the world
Only relates to others in connection to their effect upon and place within one's individual personal space	Deeply identifies with all people and things as an integral part of God's great plan for his own glory
Defines theology as seeking to express someone's perspective on some religious idea or concept	Defines theology as seeking to comprehend God's ultimate designs and plans for himself in Jesus Christ
Applications are rooted in seeking right responses to particular issues and situations	Applications are byproducts of understanding what God is doing for himself in the world
Focuses on the style of analysis (to discern the processes and make-up of things)	Focuses on the style of synthesis (to discern the connection and unity of all things)
Seeks to understand biblical revelation primarily from the standpoint of one's private life ("God's plan for my life")	Seeks to understand biblical revelation primarily from the standpoint of God's plan for whole ("God's plan for the ages")
Governed by pressing concerns to ensure one's own security and significance in one's chosen endeavors ("My personal life plan")	Decision making is governed by commitment to participate as co-workers with God in the overall vision ("God's working in the world")
Coordinates itself around personal need as a working paradigm and project	Connects and correlates itself around God's vision and plan as a working paradigm
Sees mission and ministry as the expression of one's personal giftedness and burden, bringing personal satisfaction and security	Sees mission and ministry as the present, practical expression of one's identity vis-a-vis the panoramic vision of God
Relates knowledge, opportunity, and activity to the goals of personal enhancement and fulfillment	Relates knowledge, opportunity, and activity to a single, integrated vision and purpose
All of life is perceived to revolve around the personal identity and needs of the individual	All of life is perceived to revolve around a single theme: the revelation of God in Jesus of Nazareth

Picking Up on Different Wavelengths (continued)

Scriptures on the Validity of Seeing All Things as Unified and Whole

Ps. 27.4 (ESV) - One thing have I asked of the Lord, that will I seek after: that I may dwell in the house of the Lord all the days of my life, to gaze upon the beauty of the Lord and to inquire in his temple.

Luke 10.39-42 (ESV) - And she had a sister called Mary, who sat at the Lord's feet and listened to his teaching. [40] But Martha was distracted with much serving. And she went up to him and said, "Lord, do you not care that my sister has left me to serve alone? Tell her then to help me." [41] But the Lord answered her, "Martha, Martha, you are anxious and troubled about many things, [42] but one thing is necessary. Mary has chosen the good portion, which will not be taken away from her."

Phil. 3.13-14 (ESV) - Brothers, I do not consider that I have made it my own. But one thing I do: forgetting what lies behind and straining forward to what lies ahead [14] I press on toward the goal for the prize of the upward call of God in Christ Jesus.

Ps. 73.25 (ESV) - Whom have I in heaven but you? And there is nothing on earth that I desire besides you.

Mark 8.36 (ESV) - For what does it profit a man to gain the whole world and forfeit his life?

Luke 18.22 (ESV) - When Jesus heard this, he said to him, "One thing you still lack. Sell all that you have and distribute to the poor, and you will have treasure in heaven; and come, follow me."

John 17.3 (ESV) - And this is eternal life, that they know you the only true God, and Jesus Christ whom you have sent.

1 Cor. 13.3 (ESV) - If I give away all I have, and if I deliver up my body to be burned, but have not love, I gain nothing.

Gal. 5.6 (ESV) - For in Christ Jesus neither circumcision nor uncircumcision counts for anything, but only faith working through love.

Picking Up on Different Wavelengths (continued)

Col. 2.8-10 (ESV) - See to it that no one takes you captive by philosophy and empty deceit, according to human tradition, according to the elemental spirits of the world, and not according to Christ. [9] For in him the whole fullness of deity dwells bodily, [10] and you have been filled in him, who is the head of all rule and authority.

1 John 5.11-12 (ESV) - And this is the testimony, that God gave us eternal life, and this life is in his Son. [12] Whoever has the Son has life; whoever does not have the Son of God does not have life.

Ps. 16.5 (ESV) - The Lord is my chosen portion and my cup; you hold my lot.

Ps. 16.11 (ESV) - You make known to me the path of life; in your presence there is fullness of joy; at your right hand are pleasures forevermore.

Ps. 17.15 (ESV) - As for me, I shall behold your face in righteousness; when I awake, I shall be satisfied with your likeness.

Eph. 1.9-10 (ESV) - making known to us the mystery of his will, according to his purpose, which he set forth in Christ [10] as a plan for the fullness of time, to unite all things in him, things in heaven and things on earth.

John 15.5 (ESV) - I am the vine; you are the branches. Whoever abides in me and I in him, he it is that bears much fruit, for apart from me you can do nothing.

Ps. 42.1 (ESV) - As a deer pants for flowing streams, so pants my soul for you, O God.

Hab. 3.17-18 (ESV) - Though the fig tree should not blossom, nor fruit be on the vines, the produce of the olive fail and the fields yield no food, the flock be cut off from the fold and there be no herd in the stalls, [18] yet I will rejoice in the Lord; I will take joy in the God of my salvation.

Matt. 10.37 (ESV) - Whoever loves father or mother more than me is not worthy of me, and whoever loves son or daughter more than me is not worthy of me.

Ps. 37.4 (ESV) - Delight yourself in the Lord, and he will give you the desires of your heart.

Ps. 63.3 (ESV) - Because your steadfast love is better than life, my lips will praise you.

Picking Up on Different Wavelengths (continued)

Ps. 89.6 (ESV) - For who in the skies can be compared to the Lord? Who among the heavenly beings is like the Lord

Phil. 3.8 (ESV) - Indeed, I count everything as loss because of the surpassing worth of knowing Christ Jesus my Lord. For his sake I have suffered the loss of all things and count them as rubbish, in order that I may gain Christ

1 John 3.2 (ESV) - Beloved, we are God's children now, and what we will be has not yet appeared; but we know that when he appears we shall be like him, because we shall see him as he is.

Rev. 21.3 (ESV) - And I heard a loud voice from the throne saying, "Behold, the dwelling place of God is with man. He will dwell with them, and they will be his people, and God himself will be with them as their God.

Rev. 21.22-23 (ESV) - And I saw no temple in the city, for its temple is the Lord God the Almighty and the Lamb. [23] And the city has no need of sun or moon to shine on it, for the glory of God gives it light, and its lamp is the Lamb.

Ps. 115.3 (ESV) - Our God is in the heavens; he does all that he pleases.

Jer. 32.17 (ESV) - Ah, Lord God! It is you who has made the heavens and the earth by your great power and by your outstretched arm! Nothing is too hard for you.

Dan. 4.35 (ESV) - all the inhabitants of the earth are accounted as nothing, and he does according to his will among the host of heaven and among the inhabitants of the earth; and none can stay his hand or say to him, "What have you done?"

Eph. 3.20-21 (ESV) - Now to him who is able to do far more abundantly than all that we ask or think, according to the power at work within us, [21] to him be glory in the Church and in Christ Jesus throughout all generations, forever and ever. Amen.

APPENDIX 20
The Father, Son, and Holy Ghost Share the Same Divine Attributes and Works
Supporting Scriptures

Adapted from Edward Henry Bickersteth, **The Trinity**. *Grand Rapids: Kregel Publications, 1957. Rpt. 1980.*

Attribute of God	God the Father	God the Son	God the Holy Spirit
God Is Eternal (Deut. 33.27)	Isa. 44.6; Rom. 16.26	John 8.58; Rev. 1.17-18	Heb. 9.14
God Created All Things (Rev. 4.11) and Is the Source of Life (Deut. 30.20)	Pss. 36.9; 100.3; 1 Cor. 8.6	John 1.3, 4; Col. 1.16	Gen. 1.2; Pss. 33.6; 104.30; Job 33.4; John 7.38-39; Rom. 8.11
God Is Incomprehensible (1 Tim. 6.16) and Omniscient (Jer. 16.17)	Isa. 46.9-10; Matt. 11.27; Heb. 4.13	Matt. 11.27; John 21.17	Isa. 40.13-14; 1 Cor. 2.10; John 16.15
God Is Omnipresent (Jer. 23.24)	Acts 17.27-28	Matt. 18.20; 28.20	Ps. 139.7-10
God Is Omnipotent (2 Chron. 20.6) and Sovereignly Acts as He Chooses (Job 42.2)	Luke 1.37; Eph. 1.11	John 14.14; Matt. 11.27	Zech. 4.6; Rom. 15.19; 1 Cor. 12.11
God Is True, Holy, Righteous, and Good (Ps. 119)	Ps. 34.8; John 7.28; 17.11, 25	John 14.6; 10.11; Acts 3.14	1 John 5.6; John 14.26; Ps. 143.10
God is the Source of Strength for His People (Exod. 15.2)	Ps. 18.32	Phil. 4.13	Eph. 3.16
God Alone Forgives and Cleanses from Sin (Pss. 51.7; 130.3-4)	Exod. 34.6-7	Mark 2.7-11	1 Cor. 6.11; Heb. 9.14

The Father, Son, and Holy Ghost Share the Same Divine Attributes and Works (continued)

Attribute of God	God the Father	God the Son	God the Holy Spirit
God Gave Humanity the Divine Law Which Revealed His Character and Will (2 Tim. 3.16)	Ezek. 2.4; Isa. 40.8; Deut. 9.10	Matt. 24.35; John 5.39; Heb. 1.1-2	2 Sam. 23.2; 2 Pet. 1.21; Rom. 8.2
God Dwells in and among the People Who Believe in Him (Isa. 57.15)	2 Cor. 6.16; 1 Cor. 14.25	Eph. 3.17; Matt. 18.20	John 14.17; 1 Cor. 6.19; Eph. 2.22
God Is the Supreme, Highest Being Who Has No Equal, Who Reigns as Lord and King over All Creation, and Who Alone Is to Be Worshiped and Glorified	Isa. 42.8; Ps. 47.2; 1 Tim. 6.15; Matt. 4.10; Rev. 22.8-9	John 20.28-29; Rev. 17.14; Heb. 1.3, 6-8	Matt. 12.31; Luke 1.35; 2 Cor. 3.18; 1 Pet. 4.14; John 4.24

APPENDIX 21

The Picture and the Drama

Image and Story in the Recovery of Biblical Myth

Don L. Davis

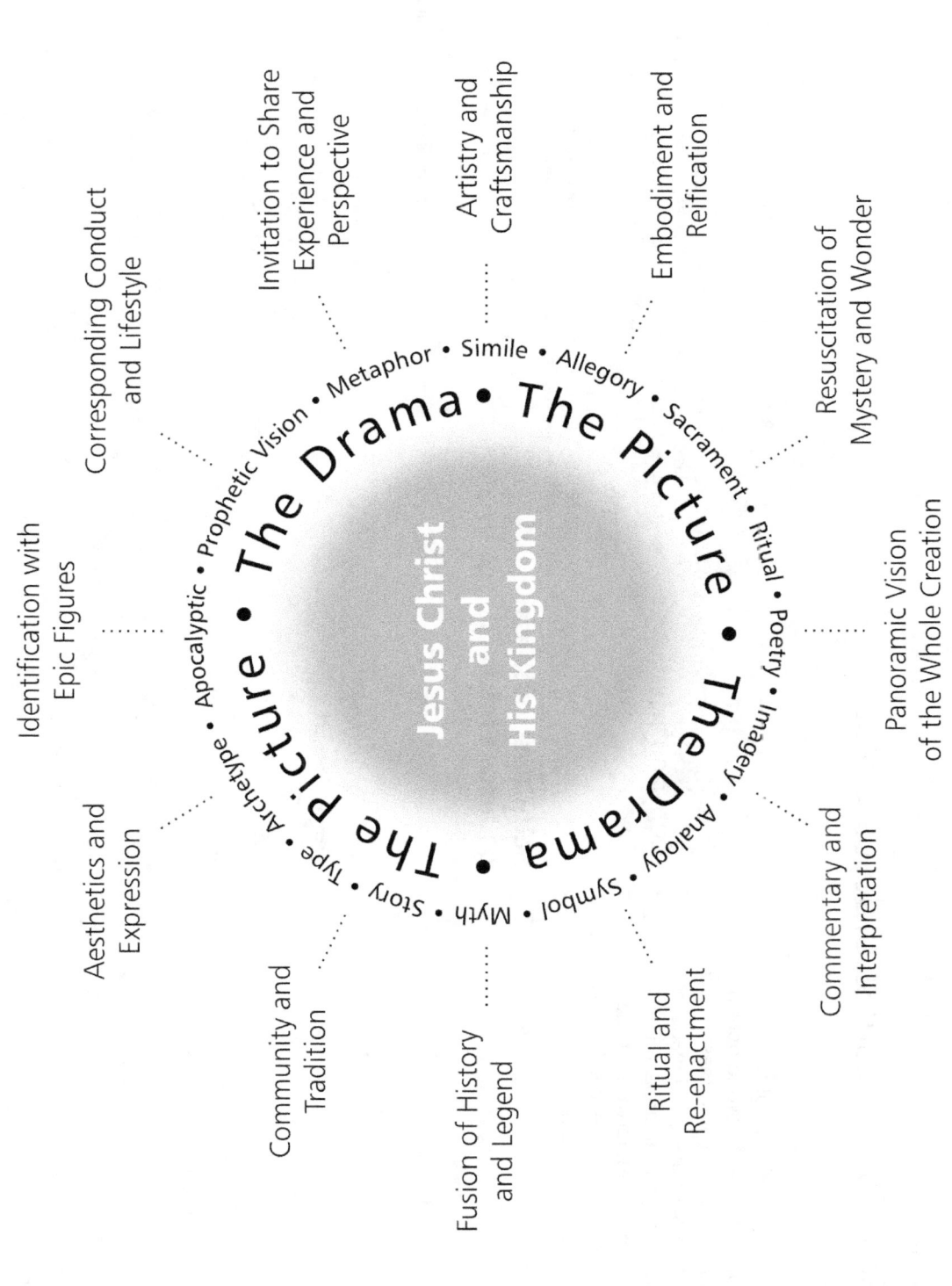

APPENDIX 22
The Self-Consciousness of Jesus Christ
Rev. Dr. Don L. Davis

John 17.25-26 (ESV) - O righteous Father, even though the world does not know you, I know you, and these know that you have sent me. [26] I made known to them your name, and I will continue to make it known, that the love with which you have loved me may be in them, and I in them.

Prophetic Orientation

John 5.34 (ESV) - Not that the testimony that I receive is from man, but I say these things so that you may be saved.

John 3.11 (ESV) - Truly, truly, I say to you, we speak of what we know, and bear witness to what we have seen, but you do not receive our testimony.

John 5.30 (ESV) - I can do nothing on my own. As I hear, I judge, and my judgment is just, because I seek not my own will but the will of him who sent me.

John 8.26 (ESV) - I have much to say about you and much to judge, but he who sent me is true, and I declare to the world what I have heard from him.

John 12.47-49 (ESV) - If anyone hears my words and does not keep them, I do not judge him; for I did not come to judge the world but to save the world. [48] The one who rejects me and does not receive my words has a judge; the word that I have spoken will judge him on the last day. [49] For I have not spoken on my own authority, but the Father who sent me has himself given me a commandment--what to say and what to speak.

The Self-Consciousness of Jesus Christ

God-Consciousness

John 5.17 (ESV) - But Jesus answered them, "My Father is working until now, and I am working."

John 5.19-20 (ESV) - So Jesus said to them, "Truly, truly, I say to you, the Son can do nothing of his own accord, but only what he sees the Father doing. For whatever the Father does, that the Son does likewise. [20] For the Father loves the Son and shows him all that he himself is doing. And greater works than these will he show him, so that you may marvel."

John 8.26 (ESV) - I have much to say about you and much to judge, but he who sent me is true, and I declare to the world what I have heard from him.

John 8.42 (ESV) - Jesus said to them, "If God were your Father, you would love me, for I came from God and I am here. I came not of my own accord, but he sent me."

John 14.10 (ESV) - Do you not believe that I am in the Father and the Father is in me? The words that I say to you I do not speak on my own authority, but the Father who dwells in me does his works.

Divine Representation

John 5.30 (ESV) - "I can do nothing on my own. As I hear, I judge, and my judgment is just, because I seek not my own will but the will of him who sent me.

John 6.38 (ESV) - For I have come down from heaven, not to do my own will but the will of him who sent me.

John 14.10 (ESV) - Do you not believe that I am in the Father and the Father is in me? The words that I say to you I do not speak on my own authority, but the Father who dwells in me does his works.

John 17.8 (ESV) - For I have given them the words that you gave me, and they have received them and have come to know in truth that I came from you; and they have believed that you sent me.

Apocalyptic Imagination

John 5.21-22 (ESV) - For as the Father raises the dead and gives them life, so also the Son gives life to whom he will. [22] The Father judges no one, but has given all judgment to the Son.

John 11.23-26 (ESV) - Jesus said to her, "Your brother will rise again." [24] Martha said to him, "I know that he will rise again in the resurrection on the last day." [25] Jesus said to her, "I am the resurrection and the life. Whoever believes in me, though he die, yet shall he live, [26] and everyone who lives and believes in me shall never die. Do you believe this?"

John 4.25-26 (ESV) - The woman said to him, "I know that Messiah is coming (he who is called Christ). When he comes, he will tell us all things." [26] Jesus said to her, "I who speak to you am he."

Mark 14.61-62 (ESV) - But he remained silent and made no answer. Again the high priest asked him, "Are you the Christ, the Son of the Blessed?" [62] And Jesus said, "I am, and you will see the Son of Man seated at the right hand of Power, and coming with the clouds of heaven."

APPENDIX 23

The Shadow and the Substance

Understanding the Old Testament as God's Witness to Jesus Christ

Rev. Dr. Don L. Davis

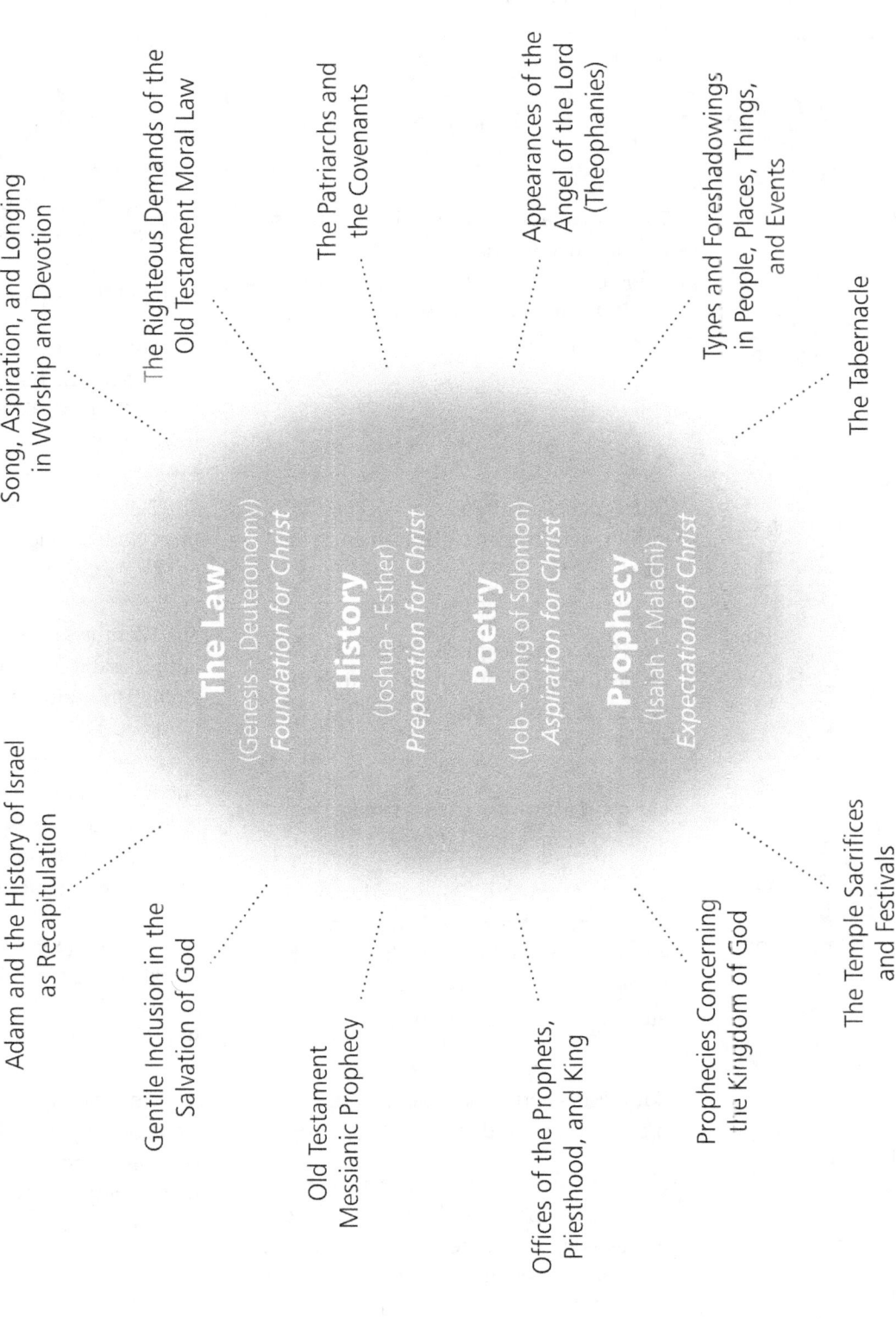

The Law (Genesis – Deuteronomy) *Foundation for Christ*

History (Joshua – Esther) *Preparation for Christ*

Poetry (Job – Song of Solomon) *Aspiration for Christ*

Prophecy (Isaiah – Malachi) *Expectation of Christ*

- Song, Aspiration, and Longing in Worship and Devotion
- The Righteous Demands of the Old Testament Moral Law
- The Patriarchs and the Covenants
- Appearances of the Angel of the Lord (Theophanies)
- Types and Foreshadowings in People, Places, Things, and Events
- The Tabernacle
- The Temple Sacrifices and Festivals
- Prophecies Concerning the Kingdom of God
- Offices of the Prophets, Priesthood, and King
- Old Testament Messianic Prophecy
- Gentile Inclusion in the Salvation of God
- Adam and the History of Israel as Recapitulation

APPENDIX 24
Theories of Inspiration
Rev. Terry G. Cornett

Theory of Inspiration	Explanation	Possible Objection(s)
Mechanical or Dictation	The human author is a passive instrument in God's hands. The author simply writes down each word as God speaks it. This direct dictation is what protects the text from human error.	The books of Scripture show diverse writing styles, vocabularies, and manners of expression which vary with each human author. This theory doesn't seem to explain why God would use human authors rather than giving us a direct written word from himself.
Intuition or Natural	Gifted people with exceptional spiritual insight were chosen by God to write the Bible	The Bible indicates that Scripture came from God, through human authors (2 Pet. 1.20-21).
Illumination	The Holy Spirit heightened the normal capacities of human authors so that they had special insight into spiritual truth.	The Scriptures indicate that the human authors expressed the very words of God ("Thus saith the Lord" passages; Rom. 3.2.)
Degrees of Inspiration	Certain parts of the Bible are more inspired than others. Sometimes this position is used to argue that portions dealing with key doctrines or ethical truths are inspired while portions dealing with history, economics, culture, etc. are less inspired or not inspired.	The biblical authors never indicate that some of Scripture is more inspired or treat only one kind of biblical material as inspired in their use of it. Jesus speaks about the entire scriptural revelation up to his day as an unchanging word from God (Matt. 5.17-18; John 3.34-35).
Verbal-Plenary	Both divine and human elements are present in the production of Scripture. The entire text of Scripture, including the words, are a product of the mind of God expressed in human terms and conditions, through human authors that he foreknew (Jer. 1.5) and chose for the task.	It seems unlikely that the human elements which are finite and culture-bound could be described as the unchanging words of God.

APPENDIX 25
Toward a Hermeneutic of Critical Engagement
Rev. Dr. Don L. Davis

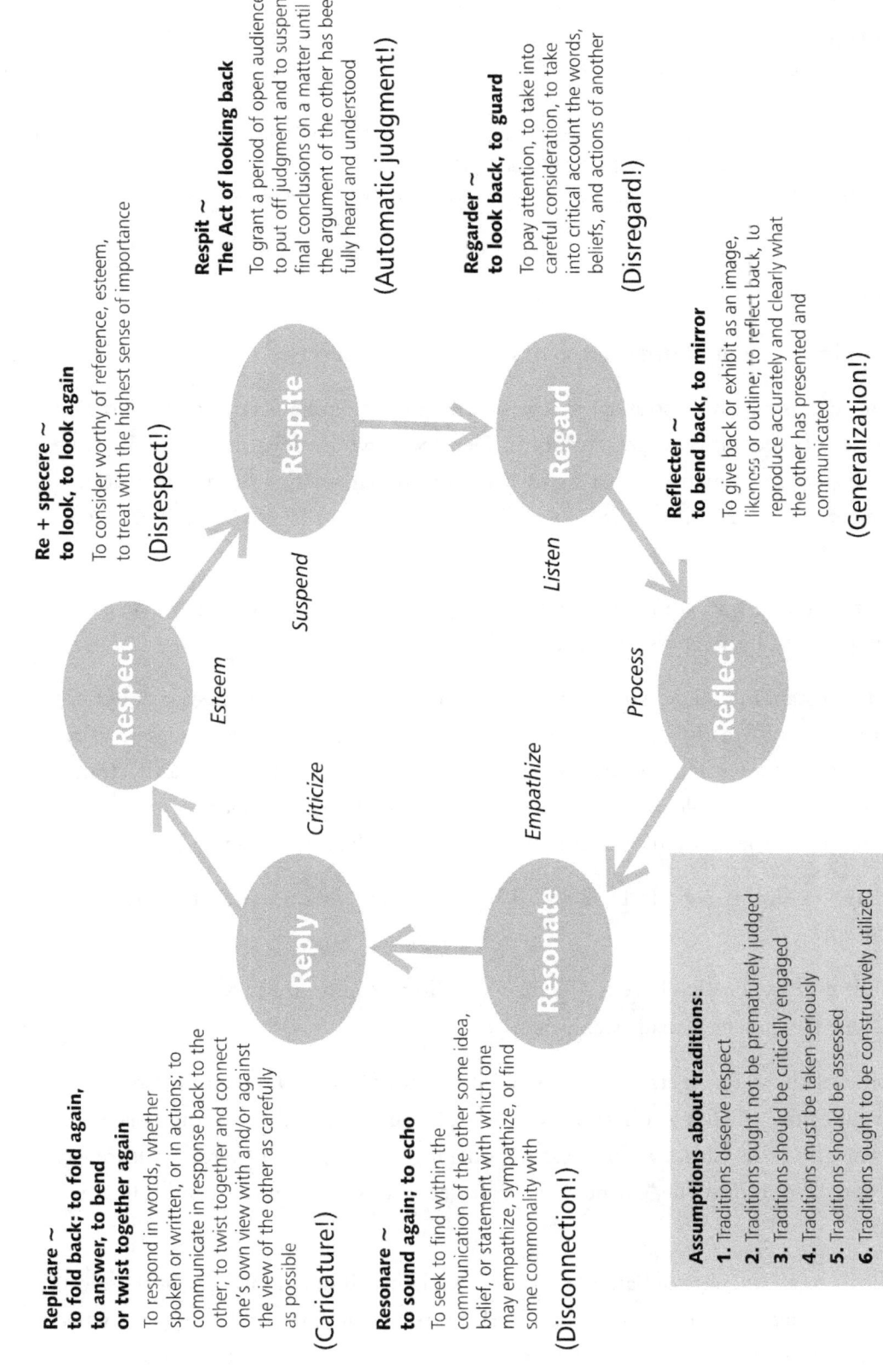

Replicare ~
to fold back; to fold again, to answer, to bend or twist together again

To respond in words, whether spoken or written, or in actions; to communicate in response back to the other; to twist together and connect one's own view with and/or against the view of the other as carefully as possible

(Caricature!)

Resonare ~
to sound again; to echo

To seek to find within the communication of the other some idea, belief, or statement with which one may empathize, sympathize, or find some commonality with

(Disconnection!)

Re + specere ~
to look, to look again

To consider worthy of reference, esteem, to treat with the highest sense of importance

(Disrespect!)

Respit ~
The Act of looking back

To grant a period of open audience, to put off judgment and to suspend final conclusions on a matter until the argument of the other has been fully heard and understood

(Automatic judgment!)

Regarder ~
to look back, to guard

To pay attention, to take into careful consideration, to take into critical account the words, beliefs, and actions of another

(Disregard!)

Reflecter ~
to bend back, to mirror

To give back or exhibit as an image, likeness or outline; to reflect back, to reproduce accurately and clearly what the other has presented and communicated

(Generalization!)

Assumptions about traditions:
1. Traditions deserve respect
2. Traditions ought not be prematurely judged
3. Traditions should be critically engaged
4. Traditions must be taken seriously
5. Traditions should be assessed
6. Traditions ought to be constructively utilized

APPENDIX 26
Editorial
Ralph D. Winter

This article was taken from Mission Frontiers: The Bulletin of the US Center for World Mission, Vol. 27, No. 5; September-October 2005; ISSN 0889-9436.
Copyright 2005 by the U.S. Center for World Mission. Used by permission. All Rights Reserved.

Ralph D. Winter is the Editor of Mission Frontiers and the General Director of the Frontier Mission Fellowship.

Dear Reader,

This time you must learn a new phrase: Insider Movements.

This idea as a mission strategy was so shockingly new in Paul's day that almost no one (either then or now) gets the point. That's why we are devoting this entire issue to "Insider Movements." That's why the 2005 annual meeting of the International Society for Frontier Missiology is devoted to the same subject. (See *www.ijfm.org/isfm*.)

First of all, be warned: many mission donors and prayer warriors, and even some missionaries, heartily disagree with the idea.

One outstanding missionary found that even his mission board director could not agree. He was finally asked to find another mission agency to work under. Why? His director was a fine former pastor who had never lived among a totally strange people. After a couple of years of increasingly serious correspondence between the director and the missionary family, the relationship had to come to an end.

Okay, so this is serious business. Why is *Insider Movements* such a troubling concept?

Well, everywhere Paul went "Judaizers" followed him and tried to destroy the Insider Movement he had established.

Some of those Judaizers were earnest followers of Christ who simply could not imagine how a Greek – still a Greek in dress, language and culture – could become a believer in Jesus Christ without casting off a huge amount of his Greek culture, get circumcised, follow the "kosher" dietary rules and the "new moons and Sabbaths", etc.

The flagrant language of Paul's letter to the Galatians is one result. The very serious text of his letter to the Romans is another. Years ago the scales fell off my eyes when I read that "Israel, who pursued a law of righteousness, has not attained it ... Why

Ralph D. Winter Editorial (continued)

not? Because they pursued it not by faith but as if it were by works" (Rom. 9:32 NIV).

Paul was not saying the Jewish religious culture was defective or that the Greek culture was superior. He was emphasizing that heart faith is the key element in any culture—that *forms* were not the key thing but the *faith*. Greeks who yielded in heart faith to the Gospel did not need to become Jews culturally and follow Jewish forms.

Paul said, in effect, "I am very, very proud of a Gospel that is the power of God to save people who obey God in faith, no matter whether they follow Jewish or Greek customs" (Rom. 1:16).

But the real trick is not simply for people of faith in every culture to stay and stagnate in their own cultural cul-de-sac, but both to retain their own culture and at the same time recognize the validity of versions of the faith within other cultures and the universality of the Body of Christ.

Different sources of European Christianity flowed over into the United States, producing some 200 different "flavors" of Christianity—some born here (Mormons, Jehovah's Witnesses), some quite biblical, some not so biblical, some very strange.

The same thing happens on the mission field: a lot of different movements emerge. The ideal is for the Gospel to become effectively expressed within the language and culture of a people and not just be a transplant from the missionary's culture.

H. Richard Niebhur's famous book, *Social Sources of Denominationalism*, is known for pointing out that different denominations did not just have doctrinal differences (often very minor) but usually reflected, at least for a time, social differences that were the real difference. Note, however, the Christian faith was in many cases an "Insider Movement" and was expressed within different social streams, taking on characteristics of those different streams.

But, back to missions. The Jewish/Greek thing is far more and far "worse" than the differences between Methodists who pray that their trespasses be forgiven and Presbyterians who pray that their debts be forgiven!

No, in Paul's day circumcision was undoubtedly a major barrier to adult Greek men becoming culturally Jewish followers of Christ. Another sensitive point was the question of eating meat that had been offered to idols, and so on.

Ralph D. Winter Editorial (continued)

Later in history, the Jewish/Greek tension was paralleled by a Latin/German tension. This time, we see a profound difference in attitudes toward clerical marriage vs. celibacy and the use of Latin in church services.

For centuries Latin was *the language* of Europe, enabling ministers, attorneys, medical doctors, and public officials to read the books of their trade in a single language. That lasted a long time! For centuries a unifying reading language did a lot of good. But the Bible did not come into its own until it was translated into the heart languages of Europe.

The deep rumbling that modernized Europe was the unleashed Bible.

It is an exciting and maybe disturbing thing—the idea that biblical faith can be clothed in any language and culture. Witness the awesome reality in the so-called mission lands today. Whether Africa, India or China, it may well be that the largest number of genuine believers in Jesus Christ do not show up in what we usually call Christian churches!

Can you believe it? They may still consider themselves Muslims or Hindus (in a cultural sense).

Alas, today Christianity itself is identified with the cultural vehicle of the civilization of the West. People in mission lands who do not wish to be "westernized" feel they need to stay clear of the Christian Church, which in their own country is often a church highly Western in its culture, theology, interpretation of the Bible, etc.

For example, in Japan there are "churches" that are so Western that in the last forty years they have not grown by a single member. Many astute observers have concluded that there is not yet "a Japanese form of Christianity." When one emerges, it may not want to associate with the Western Christian tradition except in a fraternal way.

In India we now know that there are actually millions of Hindus who have chosen to follow Christ, reading the Bible daily and worshipping at the household level, but not often frequenting the West-related Christian churches of that land.

In some places thousands of people who consider themselves Muslims are nevertheless heart-and-soul followers of Jesus Christ who carry the New Testament with them into the mosques.

Ralph D. Winter Editorial (continued)

In Africa there are more than 50 million believers (of a sort) within a vast sphere called "the African Initiated Churches." The people in the more formally "Christian church" may not regard these others as Christians at all. Indeed, some of them are a whole lot further from pure biblical faith than Mormons. But, if they revere and study the Bible, we need to let the Bible do its work. These groups range from the wildly heretical to the seriously biblical within over ten thousand "denominations" which are not related to any overt Christian body.

Thus, not all "insider" movements are ideal. Our own Christianity is not very successfully [*sic*] "inside" our culture, since many "Christians" are Christian in name only. Even mission "church planting" activities may or may not be "insider" at all, and even if they are they may not be ideal.

Around the world some of these movements do not baptize. In other cases they do. I have been asked, "Are you promoting the idea of non-baptized believers?" No, in reporting the existence of these millions of people, we are reporting on the incredible power of the Bible. We are not promoting all the ideas they reflect or the practices they follow. The Bible is like an underground fire burning out of control! In one sense we can be very happy.

APPENDIX 27
When "Christian" Does Not Translate
Frank Decker

This article was taken from Mission Frontiers: The Bulletin of the US Center for World Mission, Vol. 27, No. 5; September-October 2005; ISSN 0889-9436.
Copyright 2005 by the U.S. Center for World Mission. Used by permission. All Rights Reserved.

"I grew up as a Muslim, and when I gave my life to Jesus I became a Christian. Then I felt the Lord saying, 'Go back to your family and tell them what the Lord has done for you.'" Such was the beginning of the testimony of a sweet sister in Christ named Salima. As she stood before the microphone at a conference held recently in Asia, I thought about how her story would have been applauded by my Christian friends back home.

But then she said something that would have probably shocked most American Christians. She told us that in order to share Christ with her family, she now identifies herself as a Muslim rather than a Christian. "But," she added, "I could never go back to Islam without Jesus whom I love as my Lord."

Like this woman, countless people, primarily in Asia, who live in Muslim, Buddhist, and Hindu contexts are saying *yes* to Jesus, but *no* to Christianity. As Westerners, we assume that the word "Christian" *ipso facto* refers to someone who has given his or her life to Jesus, and a "non-Christian" is an unbeliever. However, in the words of one Asian attendee, "The word 'Christian' means something different here in the East."

Consider the story of Chai, a Buddhist from Thailand. "Thailand has not become a Christian country, because in the eyes of the Thai, to become a Christian means you can no longer be Thai. That's because in Thailand 'Christian' equals 'foreigner.'" So when Chai gave his life to Jesus, he began referring to himself as a "Child of God" and a "new Buddhist." He then related a subsequent incident in which he had a conversation with a Buddhist monk on a train. "After I listened to his story, I told him that he was missing one thing in life. He asked me what that was and I told him it was Jesus."

Chai continued to tell us the story in which the monk not only gave his life to Christ, but also invited Chai to come to his Buddhist temple to share about Jesus. Then Chai said, "At the beginning of our conversation the monk asked me, 'Are you a Christian?' and I said *no*. I explained that Christianity and Jesus are two

A former missionary in Ghana, Frank Decker currently serves as Vice President for Field Operations for the Mission Society for United Methodists.

When "Christian" Does Not Translate (continued)

different things. Salvation is in Jesus, not in Christianity. If I had said I was a 'Christian,' the conversation would have ended at that point." But it didn't end. And the monk now walks with Jesus.

Indeed, an American missionary that has been working in Asia for about two decades said, "For the first five or seven years of our ministry in [a Muslim country] we were frustrated because we were trying to get people to change their religion." He went on to say how in evangelical circles we talk a lot about how it is not our religion that saves us; it is *Jesus*. "If we really believe that, why do we insist that people change their religion?"

Asif is a brother in Christ with whom I have spent time in his village in a country that is 90 percent Muslim. Traditional Christian organizations in that country have only had a significant impact on the other ten percent that has never been Muslim. Make no mistake – Asif is sold out to Jesus, as are the other members of this Muslim Background Believers (MBB) movement. I will never forget seeing the tears stream down Asif's face as he told me how he and his brother, also a believer in Jesus, were beaten in an attack that his brother did not survive. These are Muslims who walk with Jesus and openly share with their Muslim friends about the Lord, who in Arabic is referred to as "Isa al-Masih" (Jesus the Messiah).

These "insider movements" are not intended to *hide* a believer's spiritual identity, but rather to enable those within the movement to *go deeper* into the cultural community – be it Islamic, Hindu, or Buddhist – and be witnesses for Jesus within the context of that culture. In some countries, such movements are just getting started. In other places, estimates of adherents are in the hundreds of thousands.

As the Body of Christ, we should be very careful that the things we uphold as sacred are not post-biblical accoutrements, but are indeed transcendent. If we are not open to "new wineskins," we may unwittingly find ourselves attached to traditions, as were the Pharisees in the day of Jesus.

The names in this story have been changed. This article is excerpted by permission from the May/June 2005 issue of Good News Magazine, a renewal ministry within the United Methodist Church (www.goodnewsmag.org).

APPENDIX 28
Pursuing Faith, Not Religion
The Liberating Quest for Contextualization
Charles Kraft

This article was taken from Mission Frontiers: The Bulletin of the US Center for World Mission, Vol. 27, No. 5; September-October 2005; ISSN 0889-9436.
Copyright 2005 by the U.S. Center for World Mission. Used by permission. All Rights Reserved.

The following is excerpted from chapters 5 and 6 of **Appropriate Christianity** *(William Carey Library Publishers, 2005).*

It is not widely understood either outside of or even inside of Christianity that our faith is intended to be different from the religions in its relationship to the culture of the people who practice it. Whereas religions such as Islam, Buddhism and Hinduism require a sizeable chunk of the culture in which they were developed, Christianity rightly understood does not. Jesus came to bring life (Jn. 10:10), not a religion. It is people who have reduced our faith to a religion and exported it as if it is simply a competitor with the religions. And so, those receiving our message tend to interpret Christianity as if it was simply another religion—a culturally-encapsulated religion—rather than a faith that can be expressed in terms of any culture.

But Christianity correctly understood is commitment- and meaning-based, not form-based. A commitment to Jesus Christ and the meanings associated with that commitment can, therefore, be practiced in a wide variety of cultural forms. This is what contextualization is all about. And this is an important feature of Christianity that is often misunderstood by advocates as well as potential receptors.

Still another part of the reputation of Christianity worldwide is that it is more a matter of thinking than of practicality. For many, our faith has little to do with the issues of real life such as how to gain protection from evil spirits, how to gain and keep physical health and how to maintain good family relationships. Instead, Christianity is often seen as a breaker-up of families. And when the issue is a need for spiritual power and protection, even Christians need to keep on good terms with a shaman, priest or medicine man/woman since, in spite of biblical promises, Christian pastors can only recommend secular approaches to healing and protection.

A Christianity that is appropriate both to the Bible and to the receiving culture will confront these misperceptions and, hopefully, get them changed.

Dr. Charles H. Kraft has served as a missionary in Nigeria, taught African languages and linguistics at Michigan State University and UCLA for ten years, and taught Anthropology and Intercultural Communication in the School of Intercultural Studies, Fuller Seminary for the past 35 years. He travels widely, has pioneered in the field of Contextualization, and is widely used in a ministry of inner healing. He is the author or editor of many books, including Appropriate Christianity (William Carey Library Publishers, 2005).

Pursuing Faith, Not Religion (continued)

Traditions Die Hard

Any discussion of this topic needs to take into account the fact that the situations most cross-cultural workers are working in nowadays are seldom pioneer situations. Thus, we who teach contextualization are dealing primarily with those whose major concern will have to be on how to bring about change in already existing situations rather than on how to plant culturally appropriate churches.

Typically, then, those who learn what contextualization is all about find themselves working with churches that are quite committed to their Western approach to Christianity. This has become their tradition and they are not open to changing it.

The leaders of many such churches may never have seen culturally appropriate Christianity and probably lack the ability to imagine it. And if they can imagine such an approach, they are unlikely to want to risk what they are familiar with in hopes of gaining greater cultural appropriateness. For many, the risk of losing their position may be very real since their colleagues, committed to preserving the "sacred" tradition, may turn against them and oust them from their parishes.

We need to learn, then, not only the principles of cultural appropriateness, but the principles of effective communication. And this needs to be coupled with patience and prayer plus a readiness to make the right kind of suggestions if asked to.

Fear of Syncretism

A major hindrance to many, especially those who have received theological instruction, is the fear that they might open the door to an aberrant form of Christianity. They see Latin American "christo-paganism" and shy away from what is called Christian but is not really. Fearing that if they deviate from the Western Christianity that they have received they are in danger of people carrying things too far, they fall back on the familiar and do nothing to change it, no matter how much misunderstanding there might be in the community of unbelievers concerning the real meanings of Christianity.

There are, however, at least two roads to syncretism: an approach that is too nativistic and an approach that is too dominated by foreignness. With respect to the latter, it is easy to miss the fact that Western Christianity is quite syncretistic when it is very intellectualized, organized according to foreign patterns, weak on the Holy Spirit and spiritual power, strong on Western forms of communication (e.g.,

Pursuing Faith, Not Religion (continued)

preaching) and Western worship patterns and imposed on non-Western peoples as if it were scriptural. It is often easier to conclude that a form of Christian expression is syncretistic when it looks too much like the receiving culture than when it looks "normal," that is, Western.

But Western patterns are often farther from the Bible than non-Western patterns. And the amount of miscommunication of what the gospel really is can be great when people get the impression that ours is a religion rather than a faith and that, therefore, foreign forms are a requirement. To give that impression is surely syncretistic and heretical. I call this "communicational heresy."

But, what about the concept of syncretism? Is this something that can be avoided or is it a factor of human limitations and sinfulness? I vote for the latter and suggest that there is no way to avoid it. Wherever there are imperfect understandings made by imperfect people, there will be syncretism. That syncretism exists in all churches is not the problem. Helping people to move from where they are to more ideal expressions of Christian faith is what we need to address.

As long as we fear something that is inevitable, however, we are in bondage. I remember the words of one field missionary who was studying with us, "Until I stopped worrying about syncretism, I could not properly think about contextualization." Our advice to national leaders (and to missionaries), then, is to stop fearing syncretism. Deal with it in its various forms as a starting point, whether it has come from the receiving society or from the source society and help people to move toward more ideal expressions of their faith ....

Domestication and "Cultural Christianity"

[Down] through the centuries, those who have come to Christ have tended to "domesticate" their Christianity. Just as the early Jewish Christians who disagreed with Paul required Gentiles to accept Christ in a Jewish cultural package, so Romans and Germans and Americans have pressured those who convert to Christ to also convert to the culture of those who bring the message.

Thus, our faith has come to be known as primarily a cultural thing, a religion wrapped in the cultural forms of the group in power. And from about the fourth century on it has been seen largely as a European cultural thing—captured by our European ancestors and domesticated in cultures very different from that in which

Pursuing Faith, Not Religion (continued)

the faith was originally planted. Converts to Christianity, then, are seen as those who have abandoned their own cultural religion and chosen to adopt the religion and, usually, many of the forms of European culture. Often such converts are regarded as traitors to their own people and their ways.

If ours is simply a "form religion," ... it can be *adapted but not contextualized*, it can be in *competition with other forms of religion* but not flow through those forms because by definition it seeks to replace those forms. But biblical Christianity is not simply a set of cultural forms. Cultural Christianity, however, is. And we get tangled up in our discussions because it is often not clear whether we are speaking of essential, biblical Christianity or of the traditional religion of Western societies that is also called Christianity. In one of my books (1979a) I have attempted to make this distinction by spelling biblical Christianity with a capital C and cultural christianity with a small c....

I would ... call religion a form thing, the expression through cultural forms of deep-level (worldview) assumptions and meanings. Religious forms are culture-specific and, if the religion has been borrowed from another cultural context, it requires certain of the forms of that other culture to be borrowed. Islam, for example, requires certain forms of prayer, a specific pilgrimage, an untranslatable Arabic book, even clothing styles. Likewise Judaism, Hinduism, Buddhism and cultural christianity. These are religions.

Essential biblical Christianity, however, requires none of the original cultural forms. That's how it can be "captured" by the West and be considered Western even though its origin is not Western. *Essential Christianity is an allegiance, a relationship, from which flow a series of meanings that are intended to be expressed through the cultural forms of any culture.* These forms are intended, then, to be chosen for their appropriateness to convey proper biblical meanings in the receptors' contexts.

I believe Christianity is intended to be "a faith," not a set of cultural forms and therefore different in essence from the religions. Religions, because they are cultural things, can be *adapted* to new cultures. Adaptation is an external thing resulting in smaller or larger changes in the forms of the religion. Christianity, however, can be *contextualized*, a process in which appropriate meanings may be carried by quite different forms in various cultures. Unfortunately, due to the interference of cultural christianity, we have not seen all the variety that is possible . . . .

APPENDIX 29

Contextualization Among Muslims, Hindus, and Buddhists: A Focus on "Insider Movements"

John and Anna Travis

This article was taken from Mission Frontiers: The Bulletin of the US Center for World Mission, Vol. 27, No. 5; September-October 2005; ISSN 0889-9436.
Copyright 2005 by the U.S. Center for World Mission. Used by permission. All Rights Reserved.

The following is excerpted by permission of the authors. A larger version of this article is found in chapter 23 of **Appropriate Christianity** *(William Carey Library Publishers, 2005).*

Much has been written over the past 25 years on the application of contextualization in ministry among Muslims. In 1998 I (John) wrote an article for the *Evangelical Missions Quarterly* in which I presented a model for comparing six different types of *ekklesia* or congregations (which I refer to as "Christ-centered communities") found in the Muslim world today (Travis 1998). These six types of Christ-centered communities are differentiated in terms of three factors: language, cultural forms, and religious identity. This model, referred to as the C1-C6 spectrum (or continuum), has generated much discussion, especially around the issue of fellowships of "Muslim followers of Jesus" (the C5 position on the scale).

Parshall (1998), an advocate of contextualization, feels that C5 crosses the line and falls into dangerous syncretism. In subsequent writings many of Parshall's concerns have been addressed (see Massey 2000, Gilliland 1998, Winter 1999, Travis 1998 and 2000). *Yet in spite of concerns that some may have on this issue, the fact remains that in a number of countries today, there are groups of Muslims who have genuinely come to faith in Jesus Christ, yet have remained legally and socio-religiously within the local Muslim community.* . . .

We will not be contending that C5 is the best or only thing God is doing in the Muslim world today; indeed God is bringing Muslims to Himself in a great diversity of ways, some of which we may only understand in eternity. What we will argue, however, is that one way God is moving at this point in salvation history, is by sovereignly drawing Muslims to Himself, revolutionizing them spiritually, yet calling them to remain as salt and light in the religious community of their birth. . . .

In recent years we have had the privilege of meeting a number of C5 Muslims, and although our religious backgrounds and forms of worship are quite different, we have experienced sweet fellowship in Isa the Messiah. There is no question in our

---

John and Anna Travis, along with their two children, have lived in a tight-knit Asian Muslim neighborhood for nearly 20 years. They are involved in contextualized sharing of the good news, Bible translation and the ministry of prayer for inner healing. They have also helped train field workers in a number of Asian, Middle Eastern and North African countries. Both are pursuing graduate degrees, with John a Ph.D. candidate.

Contextualization Among Muslims, Hindus, and Buddhists (continued)

minds that these C5 Muslims are born-again members of the Kingdom of God, called to live out the Gospel inside the religious borders of their birth. As we have continued to see the limits of C4 in our context, and as our burden for lost Muslims only grows heavier, we have become convinced that a C5 expression of faith could actually be viable for our precious Muslim neighbors and probably large blocs of the Muslim world. We ourselves, being "Christian-background-believers," maintain a C4 lifestyle, but we believe God has called us to help "birth a C5 movement" in our context . . . .

We have attended many Muslim funerals. We grieve every time we see another Muslim friend buried, having passed into eternity without salvation in Christ. As we have seen the resistance toward changing religions and the huge gap between the Muslim and Christian communities, we feel that fighting the religion-changing battle is the wrong battle. We have little hope in our lifetime to believe for a major enough cultural, political and religious change to occur in our context such that Muslims would become open to entering Christianity on a wide scale.

But we do have great hope, as great as the promises of God, to believe that an "insider movement" could get off the ground – that vast numbers could discover that salvation in Isa the Messiah is waiting for every Muslim who will believe. We sense the desire of Jesus Himself to take the "yeast" of His Gospel to the inner chambers of Muslim communities, calling men, women and children to walk with Him as Lord and Savior, remaining vital members of their families and Muslim communities.

Theoretical and Theological Issues Regarding C5 Movements

. . . Our intent is not to prove if C5 *can* happen, as case studies already indicate that it *is* happening. Rather, we hope to help build a framework from which to understand this phenomenon and to answer some of the questions which have arisen such as: From a biblical perspective, can a person be truly saved and continue to be a Muslim? Doesn't a follower of Christ need to identify himself as a Christian and officially join the Christian faith? Can a Muslim follower of Christ retain all Muslim practices, in particular praying in the mosque toward Mecca and continuing to repeat the Muslim creed? This section will be framed around ten premises [elaborated in the full version of this article].

Contextualization Among Muslims, Hindus, and Buddhists (continued)

- *Premise 1*: For Muslims, culture, politics and religion are nearly inseparable, making changing religions a total break with society.

- *Premise 2*: Salvation is by grace alone through relationship / allegiance to Jesus Christ. Changing religions is not a prerequisite for nor a guarantee of salvation.

- *Premise 3*: Jesus' primary concern was the establishment of the Kingdom of God, not the founding of a new religion.

- *Premise 4*: The very term "Christian" is often misleading – not all called Christian are in Christ and not all in Christ are called Christian.

- *Premise 5*: Often gaps exist between what people actually believe and what their religion or group officially teaches.

- *Premise 6*: Some Islamic beliefs and practices are in keeping with the Word of God; some are not.

- *Premise 7*: Salvation involves a process. Often the exact point of transfer from the kingdom of darkness to the Kingdom of light is not known.

- *Premise 8*: A follower of Christ needs to be set free by Jesus from spiritual bondages in order to thrive in his/her life with Him.

- *Premise 9*: Due to the lack of Church structure and organization, C5 movements must have an exceptionally high reliance on the Spirit and the Word as their primary source of instruction.

- *Premise 10*: A contextual theology can only properly be developed through a dynamic interaction of actual ministry experience, the specific leading of the Spirit and the study of the Word of God.

A Look Beyond the Islamic Milieu

. . . An amazing book has just been republished by William Carey Library – *Churchless Christianity* (Hoefer 2001). The author, while formerly teaching at a seminary in India, began hearing stories of Hindus who in fact were worshipping and following Jesus in the privacy of their own homes. Knowing that there are many Hindus who have high regard for Jesus as a teacher, he set out to determine if

---

"The Church Emerges from the Inside"
A missionary couple working in Asia report, "In 1990 we were sent out into the field as church planters. But over the last year we have observed that when the gospel is sown on fertile soil within already established social groupings – like a circle of close neighbor friends, or the multi-generations an extended household – the church emerges from the inside. It is not so much that we are planting a church but that we are planting the gospel, and as the gospel seed grows, the church or churches form to the shape of existing networks."

Contextualization Among Muslims, Hindus, and Buddhists (continued)

indeed they had accepted Him as Lord and Savior or only as an enlightened guru. His quest became the basis of a doctoral dissertation in which he interviewed 80 such Hindu and Muslim families in the area of Madras, India.

Hoefer found that that a large number of these families, which have never been baptized or joined churches, indeed have a true relationship with Christ and pray and study His Word fervently. Hoefer says that most want baptism, but have never seen a baptism which is not one in the same with becoming an official member of a particular church. His conclusion after a very extensive process of interviews and statistical analysis is that in Madras there are 200,000 Hindus and Muslims who worship Jesus – an amount equal to the total number of Christians in that city!

It is instructive to note that 200 years ago, William Carey referred to Hindu followers of Jesus as "Christian Hindoos." Apparently this was due to the strong linkage in the minds of the Indians (and presumably William Carey) between being Hindu and being Indian (etymologically the word India comes from Hindia, the land of the Hindus). Rather than Hinduism being close to monotheistic faiths, it is just the opposite: adherents can worship any number of gods and goddesses. It appears that this openness allows room to exclusively worship the God of the Bible as the one true God (note the words of Joshua in Joshua 24:14-15).

In the early 1900s, Indian evangelist Sadhu Sundar Singh ran into hidden groups of Jesus followers among Hindus. As he preached the Gospel in Benares, his listeners told him of a Hindu holy man who had been preaching the same message. Singh spent the night at the man's home and heard his claim that his Hindu order had been founded long ago by the apostle Thomas, and now had up to 40,000 members. Singh later observed their services (including worship, prayer, baptism and communion) which were held in places which looked exactly like Hindu shrines and temples, minus the idols. "When Sundar tried to persuade them that they should openly declare themselves as Christians, they assured him that they were doing a more effective work as secret disciples, accepted as ordinary sadhus, but drawing men's minds toward the true faith in readiness for the day when open discipleship became possible" (Davey 1950:80) [*sic*].

Recently, we met a man doing outreach among Buddhists, among whom there is an extremely high fusion of culture and religion. To my surprise he had taken the C1-C6 continuum and adapted it to a Buddhist context. Though it appears impossible for the Gospel to thrive inside Buddhism, might there not be millions of Buddhists who are nominal believers and who are only Buddhist due to birth and

Contextualization Among Muslims, Hindus, and Buddhists (continued)

nationality? As Kraft has stated (1996:212-213), once this principle of true spiritual allegiance versus formal religion is grasped, "we begin to discover exciting possibilities for working within, say, Jewish or Islamic or Hindu or Buddhist or animistic cultures to reach people who will be culturally Jewish or Muslim or Hindu or animist to the end of their days but Christian in their faith allegiance". (Note: in his book Kraft defines Christian with a capital "C" as follower of Christ verses *christian* with a small "c" referring to the religious institution).

What is all of this leading to? Is there not blatant idolatry in traditional Hinduism? Yes, but not among those Hindu followers of Christ described by Hoefer and Davey. Is there not a denial by most Muslims that Jesus died on the cross? Yes, but not by those Muslims we have known who have put their faith in Christ. Is it not true that Jews teach the Messiah is yet to come? Yes, but thousands of Jews go to Messianic synagogues and believe, as did thousands of Jews in the first century, that Yeshua is indeed the long awaited Son of David.

We are tentatively coming to the conviction that God is doing a new thing to reach these remaining nations (*ta ethne*) dominated by mega-faiths. If Bosch had it right that faith in Christ wasn't meant to be a religion, could it be that we are witnessing some of the first fruits of vast movements where Jesus is causing the Gospel to break out of "Christianity"? Where those who know Jesus remain as a sweet fragrance inside the religion of their birth, and eventually the number of born-again adherents grows so large that a reform movement from inside that religion is birthed?

The process may be theologically messy, but we see no alternative. If we view both culture and religion as a person's own skin, we can look beyond it to the millions of human hearts longing for God yet longing to remain in community with their own people. This is in no way universalism (the belief that in the end all will be saved). Rather, this is a call to take much more seriously Christ's final words to go into all the world – Hindu, Buddhist, Muslim, Christian – and make disciples of all nations.

References

Bosch, David J. 1991 *Transforming Mission*. Maryknoll, NY: Orbis Books.

Davey, Cyril J. 1980 *Sadhu Sundar Singh*. Kent, UK: STL Books.

Contextualization Among Muslims, Hindus, and Buddhists (continued)

Gilliland, Dean S. 1998 "Context is Critical in Islampur Case." *Evangelical Missions Quarterly* 34(4): 415-417.

Hoefer, Herbert E. 2001 *Churchless Christianity*. Pasadena, CA: William Carey Library.

Kraft, Charles H. 1996 *Anthropology for Christian Witness*. Maryknoll, NY: Orbis Books.

Massey, Joshua. 2000 "God's Amazing Diversity in Drawing Muslims to Christ." *International Journal of Frontier Missions* 17 (1): 5-14.

Parshall, Phil. 1998 "Danger! New Directions in Contextualization." *Evangelical Missions Quarterly*. 43(4): 404-406, 409-410.

Travis, John. 1998 "Must all Muslims Leave Islam to Follow Jesus?" *Evangelical Missions Quarterly* 34(4): 411-415.

------. 2000 "Messianic Muslim Followers of Isa: A Closer Look at C5 Believers and Congregations." *International Journal of Frontier Missions* 17 (1): 53-59.

Winter, Ralph. 1999 "Going Far Enough? Taking Some Tips from the Historical Record." In *Perspectives on the World Christian Movement*. Ralph Winter and Steven Hawthorne, eds. Pp. 666-617. Pasadena, CA: William Carey Library.

APPENDIX 30
A People Reborn
Foundational Insights on People Movements
Donald McGavran

This article was taken from Mission Frontiers: The Bulletin of the US Center for World Mission, Vol. 27, No. 5; September-October 2005; ISSN 0889-9436.
Copyright 2005 by the U.S. Center for World Mission. Used by permission. All Rights Reserved.

Editor's note: What follows are excerpts from the late Donald McGavran's foreword to the English edition of Christian Keysser's classic book, A People Reborn (William Carey Library, 1980). McGavran's pen portraits and autobiographical notes reveal the extent to which, consciously or not, today's proponents of either insider movements or church-planting movements are building on foundations laid by pioneers such as Keysser, McGavran, and others in the first half of the 20th century. Note, in the final paragraph, McGavran's prescient observations about mission in the 21st century.

[Christian Keysser] was born in Bavaria in 1877, went to Kaiser Wilhelm Land (East New Guinea) in 1899, and remained in or near Sattelberg as a missionary till 1921, when he returned to Germany.... A literal translation of [Keysser's book] is *A New Guinean Congregation*. A truer, better title is: *A People Reborn: Caring Communities, Their Birth and Development*....

People Movements to Christ

... Around 1900 Keysser found himself evangelizing the Kate (pronounced Kawtai or kotte) tribe in the mountains near the sea.... Keysser's genius recognized that Christianization ought to preserve this people consciousness, and transform it into Tribal Christianity or Folk Christianity....

In 1935, largely through [Waskom] Pickett's writings and lectures, I woke to a discipling of ethnic units. I accompanied him while he studied missions in Mid-India and contributed several chapters to his *Christian Missions in Mid-India*, 1938. I, too, saw that the goal was not one-by-one conversion out of the castes and tribes, but rather the conversion of social units which remained part of the caste or tribe, and continued living in their ancestral homes. For the next two decades I worked at encouraging a Satnami people movement to develop – and failed. In 1955, my *Bridges of God* called castewise or tribal movements to Christian Faith "people

A People Reborn (continued)

movements".... What Keysser, Pickett and [Bruno] Gutmann had described in New Guinea, India and Tanganyika – *Bridges of God* – indebted only to Pickett, described in universal terms.

The discovery of all of us was that group decisions, which preserved the corporate life of the society and enabled men and women to become Christians without social dislocation, was the route by which most humans have moved to Christian Faith from non-Christian Faith, and was a good route. For all four of us, the discovery was difficult because missionaries came out of the most dedicated parts of the Western Church. They had learned that real Christians are those who individually and at great cost believe in Jesus Christ, love Him, obey His word, and venture out alone across the seven seas to do His bidding. They believed that "one-by-one-against-the-tide" was the right, the best, and often the only way for men and women to become Christians. . . .

Keysser's discovery in 1903 should be seen against his common erroneous conviction. He broke through that mindset to see that for a people to come to Christ "with social structure intact" was the best possible way. He, of course, went on immediately to describe the way in which such a people movement should be nurtured, guarded against formalism, fed on the Word, and made strong through constant exercise of its Christian options. This is his great contribution. His book is essential reading for any who wish to understand a) that discipling ethnic units is a splendid way for multitudes to become Christian, and b) how discipling and perfecting can be done so they result in genuine Christians in a truly Christian Congregation – a true Homogeneous Unit Church.

The Objective Thinker

. . . The people movement really began to roll. The outlying clans and villages clamored to become Christian, precisely because they saw that the Christians had become *greatly changed for the better.* This is the fundamental reason why people movements occur. Human beings are highly intelligent. After all, man is homo sapiens. When he sees that the new order, the Church, is actually different from and *superior* to the old order, then homo sapiens in corporate decisions moves to Christian Faith. A chain reaction runs through the tribal fabric. Congregations multiply. In general, it may be said that the higher the standard of Christianity

A People Reborn (continued)

achieved by the first groups to become Christian, the more influential is their example. Keysser, the objective thinker, saw this. . . .

Forming a True Congregation

[Another reason] why missiologists will profit from this book is Keysser's determined emphasis on the privilege and duty of the missionary *to form a Christian congregation out of various villages and clans.* By this he does not mean taking individuals, as separate pebbles, and forming them into a new organization called the church. Rather, he means taking the social organism, which the clan or village had been from time immemorial, and by exposing it to God's will and God's Word, and by leading it to act in a Christian fashion *transforming it into a Christian tribe.* This is not done simply by baptizing it. Hearing the Gospel, seeing the Gospel, receiving ample instruction, some of it in dramatic form, being baptized with clanal approval, and then for years led by the missionary and the Word, thinking through what in specific circumstances Christ requires the village, clan or tribe (the Christian Congregation) to do – all these steps are required to transform non-Christian social units into a Christian congregation. . . .

Dr. Keysser's adverse judgments concerning the churches in Germany must be seen as part of his convictions concerning the True Church. Throughout this volume he criticizes congregations in Germany for not being true communities, i.e. true *congregations*. . . . When in 1922 Keysser went back to Germany, he experienced culture shock in reverse. He found "churches" which as churches exercised little if any pastoral care of their members. . . . The congregations were not real communities. . . .

Today, when the establishment of caring communities in western churches has become one of the main purposes of contemporary Christianity, Keysser's comments about the German Church are particularly pertinent. They can be affirmed about the Church in most developed nations. When society becomes fragmented, individualism rages out of control and loneliness afflicts millions. The Church must provide loving, caring, powerful *communities*. Life is richest when lived in such. In the ancient world New Testament churches were such communities. Churches can again become such in New Guinea and New York, in Tokyo and Berlin, and in short, in every land. *True Churches are functioning communities.*

A People Reborn (continued)

. . . Professor Keysser has given the world of mission many insights which will be of great use in the coming century. In his day, animistic tribes were turning to Christ by people movements and forming genuine communities (congregations) in the Christian fold. In the twenty-first century, we shall see great segments of developing *and developed* nations turn to Christian Faith without social dislocation. They will remain real communities in becoming real congregations. Modern missiology is indebted to Christian Keysser.

APPENDIX 31
Missions in the 21st Century
Working with Social Entrepreneurs?
Rebecca Lewis

This article was taken from Mission Frontiers: The Bulletin of the US Center for World Mission, Vol. 27, No. 5; September-October 2005; ISSN 0889-9436.
Copyright 2005 by the U.S. Center for World Mission. Used by permission. All Rights Reserved.

The challenge is this: how to catalyze an "insider movement" to Christ in a society closed to traditional mission work? For this to happen, the gospel needs to spread through pre-existing social networks, which become the "church." People should not be drawn out of their families or communities into new social structures in order to become believers. God seems to be opening a new avenue of opportunity into closed societies through working with community agents of change – entrepreneurs working for social reform.

Historically, the most successful model for achieving lasting social change has been neither government nor business but the voluntary society (also known as the "citizen sector" or "civil society"). The idea of citizens banding together to reform society took a great step forward during the Evangelical Awakening, initiated by John Wesley in the 18th century. Out of this revival, and the Second Great Awakening in the early 19th century, came hundreds of voluntary, cross-denominational associations or "societies." Founded by visionary social entrepreneurs, each society attacked a certain issue, everything from abolishing slavery to creating special "Sunday schools" to teach reading to children who worked all week. Why not harness this successful model as a vehicle for advancing God's purposes among today's least-reached people groups?

Today the door is wide open in most countries to people who would catalyze grass-roots initiatives to address social problems. During the 1990s the number of international non-profit organizations jumped from 6000 to 26,000, a growth rate of over 400%. Likewise, hundreds of thousands of national NGOs (non-government organizations) have been formed in non-Western countries. Why the sudden growth? First, since the fall of the Soviet Union, many governments have been releasing control of the economy and nurturing the private sector. Second, social entrepreneurs and the civil society sector are now widely recognized for their success in solving formerly intractable problems.

Rebecca Lewis spent eight years in Morocco on a church planting team and currently creates curricula to help young people see how they can live their lives for God's purposes.

Missions in the 21st Century: Working with Social Entrepreneurs? (continued)

Third, governments are increasingly embarrassed if they try to block non-profit initiatives, because a global value for "empathy" has been established by the rapidly-spreading evangelical movement and the incorporation of Christian values in secular education worldwide. Fourth, there is a new openness to change in general. As people in remote places have become exposed to the rest of the world through mass media, they are reconsidering their behavior patterns and traditional beliefs. People everywhere are putting their hope in education and valuing progress as never before. As a result, local communities, as well as national governments, are getting behind citizen organizations seeking to implement solutions to systemic problems.

If the goal is to produce insider movements to Christ, why work with social entrepreneurs? Christian workers can build extensive relationships with leaders and families within a community by assisting social entrepreneurs (whether they are believers or not) with their vision to attack a problem. These types of broad relational networks – proactively bringing change to the community – form an excellent basis for the spread of the gospel in a way that leads to insider movements. Through helping the civil sector, workers have a role that is understandable and beneficial both in the eyes of the local people and the government. Also, like Jesus, they can announce the Kingdom in the context of bringing healing to the community.

To those who would like to learn more about finding and assisting social entrepreneurs, I recommend David Bornstein's fascinating book, *How to Change the World: Social Entrepreneurs and the Power of New Ideas* (Oxford University Press, 2003).

APPENDIX 32
Giving Glory to God
Rev. Dr. Don L. Davis

John 17.3-4 (ESV) - And this is eternal life, that they know you the only true God, and Jesus Christ whom you have sent. [4] I glorified you on earth, having accomplished the work that you gave me to do.

It is amazing how we can misunderstand things. We think we know what something is all about, and we act on our wrong assumptions, and then we are amazed at how bad things are going, or are surprised when we learn that we were off in our thinking.

> *One evening, a little girl was saying bedtime prayers with her mother. "Dear Harold, please bless Mother and Daddy and all my friends," she prayed. "Wait a minute", interrupted her mother, "who's Harold?" "That's God's name," was the answer. "Who told you that was God's name?" asked the mother. "I learned it in Sunday school, Mommy. 'Our Father, Who art in heaven, Harold be Thy name.'"*
>
> ~ Bruce Larson

I believe that for many Christians today, the Christian life is primarily misconceived and misconstrued. While they believe they have a proper understanding of things, they are wrong, and like the little child, they continue to go on with their error, not knowing they have misconceived the purpose of the entire Christian vision.

This morning we are going to speak about the final purpose of all things, and the high aim of the Christian religion, all church life, and our *raison d'etre* (our reason for being). We exist for the glory of God!

I. What is the Definition of Glorifying God?

    A. *To glorify God* means that we give him what he is worthy of; worship is "worth-ship," giving to God what he is due by virtue of his person and work.

Giving Glory to God (continued)

B. *Glorifying God* means acknowledging him as our source, our significance, and our security in all that we are and do.

II. All Heaven and Earth Were Created in Order to Bring God Glory.

All things that have life and exist, whether they are aware of it or not, were created by the hand of God in order to give him glory. He will get it from us, whether by life, or death, whether through honor or through tragedy.

A. Scriptures

1. Ps. 103.22
2. Ps. 145.10
3. Ps. 148.7-13
4. Prov. 16.4
5. Rom. 11.36
6. Phil. 2.9-11
7. Rev. 4.11

B. Illustrations and Principles

1. The key to effective living is living for the purpose that the Lord made you, understanding who you are, and why God put you here.

2. The Psalmist declares that everything that has breath ought to praise the Lord, Ps. 150.6.

3. In the not-too-distant future, God declares that all human beings everywhere will in fact acknowledge God as source, and give him the glory that he deserves, Rev. 5.12-14.

Giving Glory to God (continued)

III. The Redeemed of the Lord Were Selected by God in Order to Bring Glory to Him, 1 Pet. 4.11, 14

While God intends for all things to praise him, he has especially brought his people to him in order that they might praise him in a higher mode. God saved you, cleansed you, brought you back from a life of sin and disgrace in order that you might now be a light, a trophy, a shining example of his grace and power. He saved you in order that you might glorify his name.

A. Scriptures

1. Isa. 43.7, 21

2. 1 Pet. 2.9-10

3. 1 Cor. 10.31

4. Eph. 1.5, 6, 12

5. Col. 3.16-17

6. John 15.8

7. Eph. 5.19-20

B. Illustrations

1. What is the glory of a thing? To do well what it was made for!

   a. A chain saw

   b. A surgeon's scalpel

   c. A guitar

   d. We are his people, and the sheep of his hand, Ps. 95.6-7.

2. In letting our light shine, God receives more glory, Matt. 5.14-16.

3. We glorify God in proportion to our recognition of the good things that he has done for us.

   a. Isa. 63.7

   b. Ps. 9.13-14

Giving Glory to God (continued)

    4. We are called to glorify God for his doings.

        a. We praise him for *what he has done*: Calvary.

        b. We praise him for *what he is doing*: Redemption.

        c. We praise him for *what he is going to do*: the Second Coming.

C. God's glory must be supreme in our minds.

    1. More than our *safety*, Acts 20.24

    2. More than our *convenience*, Heb. 12.2-3

    3. More than *our very lives*, Phil 1.20

God wants to be glorified in us no matter what, when we are poor or rich, when we are happy or miserable, whether we are healthy or sick. Yes, God can even be glorified in our illness! The following is a wonderful prayer by a beloved Christian from Norway, Ole Hallesby, which captures the Christian's attitude regarding illness: "Lord, if it will be to Your glory, heal suddenly. If it will glorify You more, heal gradually; if it will glorify You even more, may your servant remain sick awhile; and if it will glorify Your name still more, take him to Yourself in heaven."

IV. The Essence of Sin Is to Fail to Give God His Due; Sin Is Robbing God of the Glory that is Rightfully Due to Him (Rom. 3.23).

We Can Rob God of Glory in at Least Four Respects.

A. First, we can *take for ourselves the glory* that is reserved for God alone.

    1. *Satan*, Isa. 14.13-20

    2. *Herod*, Acts 12.20-23

    3. Illustrations and Principles

        a. One of the hardest things in life is for us to know that God does things for his own sake, and not for our sake, Isa. 48.11.

        b. The credit for all things belongs to God and not to us, Ps. 115.1.

Giving Glory to God (continued)

      c. The tendency to take the credit usually occurs when we segment God off to a little part of our lives, rather than seeing everything we do as capable of honoring or dishonoring God—everything!

The well-known Christian author, Keith Miller, makes this point well: "It has never ceased to amaze me that we Christians have developed a kind of selective vision which allows us to be deeply and sincerely involved in worship and church activities and yet almost totally pagan [oblivious to God] in the day-in, day-out guts of our business lives and never realize it."

B. Second, we can rob God of *the praise and adoration he deserves by ascribing the glory we owe to him alone to someone or something else*, Isa. 42.8.

The threefold power grid of sin and substitute for God: money, sex, and power (greed, lust, and pride), 1 John 2.15-17; Exod. 20.2-3.

It is possible to practice unconscious idolatry, even as a Christian, that is, to temporarily worship something else by giving it our love and allegiance.

1. You may worship the god of pleasure.

2. Many people today worship at the altar of greed and possession. (We live in a culture that glorifies acquisition, buying, selling, getting, as the most significant thing in our lives.)

Between 1983 and 1988, Americans bought 62 million microwave ovens, 88 million cars and light trucks, 105 million color television sets, 63 million VCR's, 31 million cordless phones, and 30 million telephone answering machines.

~ Newsweek

3. Do not worship the god of sport.

4. Offer no sacrifices to the god of marriage and family.

5. Do not seek to glorify the god of ethnicity and country.

Giving Glory to God (continued)

    6. You many not worship the god of work.

    7. Do not bow down to the god of possessions

    8. The god of Religion

    9. Illustrations

        a. We as a society are more psyched over *Michael Jordan and Michael Jackson* than the Lord Jesus.

        b. The four C's: people are more committed to *country, color, culture, and clan* than Christ.

        c. What *John Lennon said about the Beatles*

C. Third, we can rob God of the glory that is due him by *being indifferent to his praise*—not really caring about it one way or another.

    1. We can be *unconcerned and even nonchalant about what we give to God*, Mal. 1.7.

    2. We can *find giving glory to God contemptible* (this is a fault and a problem of many young people who feel forced to believe in God because of their parent's faith), Mal. 1.7.

What do you suppose is the central task of one of the devil's tempters of human beings, what do they seek to do most?

C.S. Lewis, the author of **The Screwtape Letters**, *suggests that it is to keep you indifferent to the things of God. In this book the devil counsels his nephew, Wormwood, on the subtleties and techniques of tempting people. The goal, he counsels, is not wickedness but indifference. Satan cautions his nephew to keep us, his prospect and patient, comfortable at all costs. If he should become concerned about anything of importance, encourage him to think about other little plans; not to worry, it could induce indigestion. Then the devil counsels his nephew to this eery job description: "I, the devil, will always see to it that there are bad people. Your job, my dear Wormwood, is to provide me with the people who do not care."*

See Philippians 2.21 in the New King James Version and The Living Bible.

Giving Glory to God (continued)

    D. Fourth, we can *rob God of the glory that is due him by giving God less than he deserves*, Mal. 1.6-8, 12-14.

        1. We can be *stingy our offerings to God, giving him the crumbs of our harvest and of our hearts*, Mal. 3.8-10.

        2. We can *give God sacrifices that are imperfect and filled with blemishes*, Mal. 1.8, 13.

        3. We can *give to God offerings that are polluted, stained by the unconfessed sin and wrong in our lives, (it is possible to come to church when things are a total mess in the rest of our lives)*, Mal. 1.7.

        4. Illustrations

            a. "Any old thing will do" syndrome

            b. God doesn't mind

            c. There are three kinds of people who live for the Lord.

There are three kinds of Christians who live for the Lord — the *flint*, the *sponge* and the *honeycomb*. To get anything out of a flint you must hammer it. *Flint Christians* give God a little, and only after a lot of hammering. And then you get only chips and sparks. To get water out of a sponge you must squeeze it, and the more you use pressure, the more you will get. *Sponge Christians* give God his due, but you have to constantly squeeze them in order to get them to participate. But the honeycomb just overflows with its own sweetness. A *honeycomb Christian* is full of God's heart and simply gives out of her abundant love and commitment to him. Which kind of Christian lifestyle do you lead right now?

V. The High Calling of Every Christian Is to Glorify God in All that We Are, All We Say, and All We Do, 1 Cor. 10.31.

    A. We are to glorify God *in our bodies*, 1 Cor. 3.16,17; 6.19-20.

        1. Sexual Purity

        2. Physical health

Giving Glory to God (continued)

B. We are to glorify God *in our thoughts*, Rom. 8.5-8; 2 Cor. 10.3-5.

   1. More than 19,000 thoughts per day, think four to five times as fast as a person can talk.

   2. The last battleground of your life is your thought life; be careful what you think about.

   3. Prov. 23.7

C. We are to glorify God *in the words of our conversation*, 1 Cor. 10.31; Eph. 4.29, James 3.2.

   1. Attitude makes all the difference; more Christians dishonor God in their attitudes probably more than in any other single way.

   2. Attitudes are contagious and infectious, whether good or bad.

   3. Your tongue is connected to your heart.

   4. Not just profanity and cussing

   5. Negativism and sarcasm

   6. Complaining and murmuring

   7. Backbiting and gossip

D. We are to glorify God *in our conduct and our character*, Matt. 5.16; Eph. 2.8-10.

   1. God can receive glory from the kind of things you do, just your everyday actions.

   2. Your character, your reputation is stitched to the reputation of Christ.

   3. No matter what you say, you can never go beyond the kind of conduct and life you are living.

E. We are to glorify God *in all of our relationships*, 1 Pet. 2.11-12.

   1. In our marriages

   2. In our parenting

   3. In our extended family

Giving Glory to God (continued)

4. With our brothers and sisters in the body of Christ
5. In our friendships
6. In our work relationships
7. In our neighborhood relationships

2 Thess. 1.11-12 (ESV) - To this end we always pray for you, that our God may make you worthy of his calling and may fulfill every resolve for good and every work of faith by his power, [12] so that the name of our Lord Jesus may be glorified in you, and you in him, according to the grace of our God and the Lord Jesus Christ.

APPENDIX 33

Your Kingdom Come: "The Story of God's Glory"
Living Under His Reign and Doing Missions in an Unchurched World
Rev. Dr. Don L. Davis

I. The Significance of Story, the Importance of Myth, and the Kingdom of God

   A. Human beings operate according to their interpretive frameworks: human beings exist as "walking worldviews."

      1. Every human existence is basically a "story-ordered world."

      2. Myth-making as a primary act of human beings

      3. The role of culture: enabling us to compose our realities from scratch

   B. Integrating the details: story and the need to live purposefully

      1. Purposeful mindset: relating all details to the whole

      2. Provisional mindset: relating to details as wholes

   C. The problem of a reductionistic faith

      1. Reductionism–substituting a comprehensive religious vision of Christian faith for an alternative, smaller, usually culturally-oriented substitute notion, activity, relationship, or element

      2. Rationalism–spending the majority of time using modern scientific proofs and arguments to underwrite faith in Jesus, reducing Christian faith to holding of particular, contextualized doctrinal positions over against other contrary views

      3. Moralism–reducing the Christian vision to personal and communal decency and ethics, e.g., living well in a nuclear family context, holding certain views on selected socially controversial moral issues

   D. Elements of a comprehensive biblical worldview

      1. The recovery of "Christian myth"

      2. *The Picture and the Drama*: From Before to Beyond Time

Your Kingdom Come: "The Story of God's Glory" (continued)

       3. Living in the upside-down Kingdom of God: the *Principle of Reversal*

       4. Philosophical big picture: the *Presence of the Future*

  E. Components of a guiding worldview (Arthur Holmes)

       1. It has a *wholistic* goal. (Where did we come from and where are we going?)

       2. It is a *perspectival* approach. (From what vantage point do we see things?)

       3. It is an *exploratory* process. (How do we continue to understand our lives?)

       4. It is *pluralistic*. (What other views are suggested by our collective vision?)

       5. It has *action outcomes*. (What ought we to do in light of our mythic vision?)

  F. The wonder of story

       1. The centrality of human experience

       2. The richness of human affections

       3. The use of sanctified imagination

       4. The power of concrete image, action, and symbol

       5. The immediacy of heightened reality

       6. The enjoyment of artistic craftsmanship

  G. Key propositions of story theology

William J. Bausch lists ten propositions related to story theology that help us understand the significance and importance of the study of stories and the understanding of Bible and theology. (William J. Bausch, *Storytelling and Faith*. Mystic, Connecticut: Twenty-Third Publications, 1984.)

       1. Stories introduce us to *sacramental presences*.

       2. Stories are always more important than *facts*.

Your Kingdom Come: "The Story of God's Glory" (continued)

3. Stories remain *normative (authoritative)* for the Christian community of faith.

4. *Christian traditions* evolve and define themselves through and around stories.

5. The stories of God precede, produce, and empower the *community of God's people*.

6. Community story implies *censure, rebuke, and accountability*.

7. Stories produce *theology*.

8. Stories produce *many theologies*.

9. Stories produce *ritual and sacrament*.

10. Stories are *history*.

H. The importance of the biblical framework of the Kingdom

1. Kingdom teaching is the ultimate point of reference.

2. Teaching on the kingdom story was the heart of Jesus' teaching.

3. The kingdom story is the central focus of biblical theology.

4. The kingdom story is final criterion for judging truth and value.

5. The kingdom story provides an indispensable key to understanding human history.

6. The kingdom story is the basic biblical concept that enables us to coordinate and fulfill our destinies under God's reign today, where we live and work.

II. *Tua Da Gloriam: "The Story of God's Glory"*

Ps. 115.1-3 - Not to us, O Lord, not to us, but to your name give glory, for the sake of your steadfast love and your faithfulness! [2] Why should the nations say, "Where is their God?" [3] Our God is in the heavens; he does all that he pleases.

Your Kingdom Come: "The Story of God's Glory" (continued)

From Before to Beyond Time (Adapted from Suzanne de Dietrich, *God's Unfolding Purpose*. Philadelphia: Westminster Press, 1976.)

A. *Before Time* (Eternity Past), Ps. 90.1-3

    1. The eternal triune God, Ps. 102.24-27

    2. God's eternal purpose, 2 Tim. 1.9; Isa. 14.26-27

        a. To glorify his name in creation, Prov. 16.4; Ps. 135.6; Isa. 48.11

        b. To display his perfections in the universe, Ps. 19.1

        c. To draw out a people for himself, Isa. 43.7, 21

    3. The mystery of iniquity: the rebellion of the Dawn of the Morning (*Lucifer*), Isa. 14.12-20; Ezek. 28.13-17

    4. The principalities and powers, Col. 2.15

B. *The Beginning of Time* (The Creation), Gen. 1-2

    1. The creative Word of the triune God, Gen. 1.3; Pss. 33.6, 9; 148.1-5

    2. The creation of humanity: the Imago Dei, Gen. 1.26-27

C. *The Tragedy of Time* (the Fall and the Curse), Gen. 3

    1. The Fall and the Curse, Gen. 3.1-9

    2. The *protoevangelium*: the promised Seed; Gen. 3.15

    3. The end of Eden and the reign of death, Gen. 3.22-24

    4. First signs of grace; Gen. 3.15, 21

D. *The Unfolding of Time* (God's plan revealed through the people Israel)

    1. The Abrahamic promise and the covenant of Yahweh (Patriarchs); Gen. 12.1-3; 15; 17; 18.18; 28.4

    2. The Exodus and the covenant at Sinai, Exodus

    3. The conquest of the inhabitants and the Promised Land, Joshua through 2 Chronicles

Your Kingdom Come: "The Story of God's Glory" (continued)

4. The city, the temple, and the throne, Ps. 48.1-3; 2 Chron. 7.14; 2 Sam. 7.8ff.

    a. The role of the prophet, *to declare the word of the Lord*, Deut. 18.15

    b. The role of the priest, *to represent God and the people*, Heb. 5.1

    c. The role of the king, *to rule with righteousness and justice in God's stead*, Ps. 72

5. The Captivity and the Exile, Daniel, Ezekiel, Lamentations

6. The return of the remnant, Ezra, Nehemiah

E. *The Fullness of Time* (Incarnation of the Messiah Yeshua [Christ Jesus]), Gal. 4.4-6

1. The Word becomes flesh, John 1.14-18; 1 John 1.1-4

2. The testimony of John the Baptist, Matt. 3.1-3

3. The Kingdom has come in the person of Jesus of Nazareth, Mark 1.14-15; Luke 10.9-11; 10.11; 17.20-21

    a. Revealed in his person, John 1.18

    b. Exhibited in his works, John 5.36; 3.2; 9.30-33; 10.37-38; Acts 2.22; 10.38-39

    c. Interpreted in his testimony, Matt. 5-7

4. The secret of the Kingdom revealed, Mark 1.14-15

    a. The Kingdom is already present, Matt. 12.25-29

    b. The Kingdom is not yet consummated, Matt. 25.31-46

5. The passion and death of the crucified King, Matt. 26.36-46; Mark 14.32-42; Luke 22.39-46; John 18.1ff.

    a. To destroy the devil's work: *Christus Victor*, 1 John 3.8; Gen. 3.15; Col. 2.15; Rom. 16.20; Heb. 2.14-15

    b. To make atonement for sin: *Christus Victum*, 1 John 2.1-2; Rom. 5.8-9; 1 John 4.9-10; 1 John 3.16

Your Kingdom Come: "The Story of God's Glory" (continued)

- c. To reveal the Father's heart, John 3.16; Titus 2.11-15

6. *Christus Victor*: the resurrection of the glorious Lord of life, Matt. 28.1-15; Mark 16.1-11; Luke 24.1-12

F. *The Last Times* (the descent and age of the Holy Spirit)

1. The *arrabon* of God: the Spirit as Pledge and Sign of the Kingdom's presence, Eph. 1.13-14; 4.30; Acts 2.1-47

2. "This is that:" Peter, Pentecost, and the presence of the future

   a. The Church as foretaste and agent of the Kingdom of God, Phil. 2.14-16; 2 Cor. 5.20

   b. The present reign of Messiah Jesus, 1 Cor. 15.24-28; Acts 2.34; Eph. 1.20-23; Heb. 1.13

   c. The ushering in of God's kingdom community "in-between the times"; Rom. 14.7

3. The Church of Messiah Jesus: sojourners in the Already and the Not Yet Kingdom

   a. The Great Confession: Jesus is Lord, Phil. 2.9-11

   b. The Great Commission: go and make disciples among all nations, Matt. 28.18-20; Acts 1.8

   c. The Great Commandment: love God and people, Matt. 22.37-39

4. The Announcement of the Mystery: Gentiles as fellow-heirs of Promise, Rom. 16.25-27; Col. 1.26-28; Eph. 3.3-11

   a. Jesus as the Last Adam, the head of a new human race, 1 Cor. 15.45-49

   b. God drawing out of the world a new humanity, Eph. 2.12-22

5. In-between the times: tokens of *Age of Sabbath and of Jubilee*, Acts 2.17ff., cf. Joel 2; Amos 9; Ezek. 36.25-27

Your Kingdom Come: "The Story of God's Glory" (continued)

G. *The Fulfillment of Time* (The *Parousia* of Christ), 1 Thess. 4.13-17

1. Completion of world mission: the evangelization of the world's *ethnoi*, Matt. 24.14; Mark 16.15-16; Rom. 10.18

2. The apostasy of the Church, 1 Tim. 4.1-3; 2 Tim. 4.3; 2 Thess. 2.3-12

3. The Great Tribulation, Matt. 24.21ff; Luke 21.24

4. The *Parousia*: the Second Coming of Jesus, 1 Thess. 4.13-17; 1 Cor. 15.50-58; Luke 21.25-27; Dan. 7.13

5. The reign of Jesus Christ on earth, Rev. 20.1-4

6. The Great White Throne and Lake of Fire, Rev. 20.11-15

7. "For he must reign": the final placement of all enemies under Christ's feet, 1 Cor. 15.24-28

H. *Beyond Time* (Eternity Future)

1. The creation of the new heavens and earth, Rev. 21.1; Isa. 65.17-19; 66.22; 2 Pet. 3.13

2. The descent of the New Jerusalem: the abode of God comes to earth, Rev. 21.2-4

3. The times of refreshing: the glorious freedom of the children of God, Rom. 8.18-23

4. The Lord Christ gives over the Kingdom to God the Father, 1 Cor. 15.24-28

5. The Age to Come: the triune God as all-in-all – Zech. 14.9; 2.10; Jer. 23.6; Matt. 1.23; Ps. 72.8-11; Mic. 4.1-3

III. **Implications of the *Drama of All Time***

A. God's sovereign purpose underwrites all human history.

1. Whatever he pleases, he does, Ps. 135.6.

2. God's counsels and plans stand forever, to all generations, Ps. 33.11; Ps. 115.3.

Your Kingdom Come: "The Story of God's Glory" (continued)

      3. God declares the end of all things from the beginning, Isa. 46.10.

      4. Nothing and no one can withstand the plan of God for salvation and redemption, Dan. 4.35.

  B. God is the central character in the unfolding of the divine drama, Eph. 1.9-11.

  C. Missions is the *recovery of that which was lost* at the beginning of time.

      1. God's sovereign rule, Mark 1.14-15

      2. Satan's infernal rebellion, Gen. 3.15 with Col. 2.15; 1 John 3.8

      3. Humankind's tragic fall, Gen. 3.1-8 cf. Rom. 5.5-8

  D. Making disciples among all nations is *fulfilling our role in the script of Almighty God!*

IV. "Thy Kingdom Come": Living Under God's Reign

  A. The distinctiveness of Jesus' gospel: "The Kingdom is at hand," Mark 1.14-15.

  B. Jesus and the inauguration of the Age to Come into this present age

      1. The coming of John the Baptist, Matt. 11.2-6

      2. The inauguration of Jesus's ministry, Luke 4.16-21

      3. The confrontation of Jesus with demonic forces, Luke 10.18ff.; 11.20

      4. The teaching of Jesus and his claim of absolute authority on earth, Mark 2.1-12; Matt. 21.27; 28.18

  C. "The Kingdom has come and the strong man is bound": Matt. 12.28, 29

      1. The Kingdom of God "has come" – *pleroo*

      2. The meaning of the Greek verb: "to fulfill, to complete, to be fulfilled, as in prophecy"

      3. The invasion, entrance, manifestation of God's kingly power

---

Christ's death for our sins — His payment of the penalty declared against us — was His legal victory whereby He erased Satan's legal claim to the human race. But Christ also won dynamic victory. That is, when He was justified and made alive, adjudged and declared righteous in the Supreme Court of the universe, Satan, the arch foe of God and man, was completely disarmed and dethroned. Christ burst forth triumphantly from that age-old prison of the dead. Paul says that He "spoiled principalities and powers" and "made a show of them openly, triumphing over them in it." (Colossians 2.15).
~ Paul Billheimer. *Destined for the Throne*. Minneapolis: Bethany House Publishers, 1996. p. 87.

Your Kingdom Come: "The Story of God's Glory" (continued)

4. Jesus as the binder of the strong man: Matt. 12.25-30 (ESV) - Knowing their thoughts, he said to them, "Every kingdom divided against itself is laid waste, and no city or house divided against itself will stand. [26] And if Satan casts out Satan, he is divided against himself. How then will his kingdom stand? [27] And if I cast out demons by Beelzebul, by whom do your sons cast them out? Therefore they will be your judges. [28] But if it is by the Spirit of God that I cast out demons, then the kingdom of God has come upon you. [29] Or how can someone enter a strong man's house and plunder his goods, unless he first binds the strong man? Then indeed he may plunder his house. [30] Whoever is not with me is against me, and whoever does not gather with me scatters."

D. Two manifestations of the Kingdom of God: The Already/Not Yet Kingdom (Oscar Cullman, *Christ and Time*; George Ladd, *The Gospel of the Kingdom*)

1. The *first advent*: the rebellious prince bound and his house looted and God's reign has come

2. The *second advent*: the rebellious prince destroyed and his rule confounded with the full manifestation of God's kingly power in a recreated heaven and earth

V. The Christo-centric Order: Messiah Yeshua of Nazareth as Centerpiece in Both God's Revelation and Rule

A. Messiah's *mission*: to destroy the works of the devil, 1 John 3.8

B. Messiah's *birth*: the invasion of God into Satan's dominion, Luke 1.31-33

C. Messiah's *message*: the Kingdom's proclamation and inauguration, Mark 1.14-15

D. Messiah's *teaching*: kingdom ethics, Matt. 5-7

E. Messiah's *miracles*: his kingly authority and power, Mark 2.8-12

F. Messiah's *exorcisms*: his defeat of the devil and his angels, Luke 11.14-20

G. Messiah's *life and deeds*: the majesty of the Kingdom, John 1.14-18

Jesus' message was the Kingdom of God. It was the center and circumference of all He taught and did. . . . The Kingdom of God is the master-conception, the master-plan, the master-purpose, the master-will that gathers everything up into itself and gives it redemption, coherence, purpose, goal.

~ E. Stanley Jones

Your Kingdom Come: "The Story of God's Glory" (continued)

    H. Messiah's *resurrection*: the victory and vindication of the King, Rom.1.1-4

    I. Messiah's *commission*: the call to proclaim his Kingdom worldwide, Matt 28.18-20

    J. Messiah's *ascension*: his coronation, Heb. 1.2-4

    K. Messiah's *Spirit*: the *arrabon* (surety, pledge) of the Kingdom, 2 Cor. 1.20

    L. Messiah's *Church*: the foretaste and agent of the Kingdom, 2 Cor. 5.18-21

    M. Messiah's *session in heaven*: the generalship of God's forces, 1 Cor. 15.24-28

    N. Messiah's *Parousia (coming)*: the final consummation of the Kingdom, Rev. 19

VI. The Kingdom of God as Present and Offered in the Midst of the Church

    A. The *Shekinah* has reappeared in our midst as his temple, Eph. 2.19-22.

    B. The people (*ecclesia*) of the living God congregate here: Christ's own from every kindred, people, nation, tribe, status, and culture, 1 Pet. 2.8-9.

    C. God's *Sabbath* is enjoyed and celebrated here, freedom, wholeness, and the justice of God, Heb. 4.3-10.

    D. The *Year of Jubilee* has come: forgiveness, renewal, and restitution, Col. 1.13; Matt. 6.33; Eph. 1.3; 2 Pet. 1.3-4.

    E. The Spirit (*arrabon*) indwells us: God lives here and walks among us here, 2 Cor. 1.20.

    F. We taste the powers of the Age to Come: Satan is bound in our midst, the Curse has been broken here, deliverance is experienced in Jesus' name, Gal. 3.10-14.

    G. We experience the *shalom* of God's eternal Kingdom: the freedom, wholeness, and justice of the new order are present here, Rom. 5.1; Eph. 2.13-22.

    H. We herald the good news of God's reign (*evanggelion*): we invite all to join us as we journey to the full manifestation of the Age to Come, Mark 1.14-15.

Your Kingdom Come: "The Story of God's Glory" (continued)

I. Here we cry *Maranantha*!: our lives are structured by the living hope of God's future and the consummation, Rev. 22.17-21.

VII. The Already/Not Yet Kingdom (See *A Schematic for a Theology of the Kingdom and the Church* and *Living in the Already and the Not Yet Kingdom* appendices)

> When Christ took his seat in the heavens, He proved conclusively that Satan's devastation was complete, that he was utterly undone. Hell was thrown into total bankruptcy. Satan was not only stripped of his legal authority and dominion, but by an infinitely superior force he was stripped of his weapons also. But this is not all. When Jesus burst forth from that dark prison and "ascended up on high," all believers were raised and seated together with Him "But God . . . brought us to life with Christ. . . . And in union with Christ Jesus he raised us up and enthroned us with him in the heavenly realms" (Ephesians 2.4-6 NEB).
> ~ Paul Billheimer. *Destined for the Throne*. Minneapolis: Bethany House Publishers, 1996. p. 87.

A. Through the Incarnation and the Passion of Christ, Satan was bound.

1. Jesus has triumphed over the devil, 1 John 3.8.
2. Jesus is crowned as Lord of all, Heb. 1.4; Phil. 2.5-11.
3. Satan is now judged, Luke 10.17-21.
4. Satan's power has been severely curtailed, James 4.8.
5. His authority has been broken, 1 Pet. 5.8.
6. His minions are being routed, Col. 2.15.
7. His system is fading away, 1 John 2.15-17.
8. Those he enslaved are being set free, Col. 13-14.
9. His eventual doom has been secured, Rom. 16.20.

B. Although Satan has been defeated, he is still lethal and awaits his own utter destruction.

1. "Bound, but with a long rope," 2 Cor. 10.3-5; Eph. 2.2
2. "A roaring lion, but sick, hungry, and mad," 1 Pet. 5.8
3. Satan continues to be God's active enemy of the Kingdom
4. Blinds the minds of those who do not believe, 2 Cor. 4.4
5. Functions through deception, lying, and accusation, John 8.44
6. Animates the affairs of nations, 1 John 5.19
7. Distracts human beings from their proper ends, cf. Gen. 3.1.ff.

Your Kingdom Come: "The Story of God's Glory" (continued)

8. Oppresses human beings through harassment, slander, fear, accusation, and death, Heb. 2.14-15

9. Resists and persecutes God's people, Eph. 6.10-18

C. Satan's final doom is certain and future.

1. He has been both spoiled and utterly humiliated in the Cross, Col. 2.15.

2. His final demise will come by Christ at the end of the age, Rev. 20.

3. Missions is the announcement and demonstration of the defeat of Satan through Christ.

    a. The ministry of reconciliation, 2 Cor. 5.18-21

    b. The ministry of disciple-making, Matt. 28.18-20

VIII. The Call to Adventure: Embracing the Story of God as Your Story

A. God's call to salvation and ministry involves participation by faith in the kingdom promise of God.

1. Salvation by grace through faith, Eph. 2.8-10

2. Repentance: metanoia and conversion, Acts 2.38

3. Regeneration by the Holy Spirit of God, John 3.3-8; Titus 3.5

4. Affirm our need for a biblical framework, a disciplined study of the Kingdom of God

Have I experienced the freedom, wholeness, and justice of the Kingdom that I am preaching to others?

B. God's call to salvation and ministry involves demonstration of the life of the Kingdom in one's personal life and faith.

1. As a faithful servant and steward of God's mysteries, 1 Cor. 4.1-2

2. As a godly Christian in one's character, personal life, and family responsibilities, 1 Tim. 3; 1 Pet. 5.1-3; Titus 1

3. As a beloved brother or sister in the midst of the assembly, 2 Cor. 8.22

Your Kingdom Come: "The Story of God's Glory" (continued)

4. As a compelling testimony in the presence of unbelievers and outsiders, Col. 4.5; Matt. 5.14-16

Do I demonstrate in my own personal and family life, and my walk in the body and with my neighbors and associates a compelling testimony of what it means to be Christ's disciple where I live?

C. God's call to salvation and ministry involves separation of one's life and goods to testify and demonstrate the freedom, wholeness, and justice of the Kingdom of God.

1. A willingness to become all things to all men in order to save some, 1 Cor. 9.22-27

2. A readiness to suffer and even die in order for Christ's reign to be proclaimed and extended, Acts 20.24-32

3. A commitment to make oneself unconditionally available to Christ in order to be used to testify solemnly of the grace and gospel as the Spirit leads, John 12.24; Acts 1.8; Matt. 28.18-20

4. Celebrate our Father's gracious intent and action to defeat our mortal enemy, the devil

Have I made myself unconditionally available to Jesus Christ to be used as his bondservant and instrument whenever and wherever he may lead in order for the kingdom message to be proclaimed and demonstrated?

D. God's call to salvation and ministry involves preparation to steward God's mysteries of the Kingdom, the Sacred Scriptures, and the Apostolic doctrine.

1. To rightly divide the Word of truth as God's workman, 2 Tim. 2.15

2. To hear and obey the sacred Scriptures which equip for every good work, 2 Tim. 3.16

3. To defend and guard the apostolic testimony regarding Christ and his Kingdom, 2 Tim. 1.14 with Gal. 1.8-9 and 1 Cor. 15.1-4

Have I spent the requisite time in the Word and in training to be equipped even as I equip others for the work of the ministry?

Your Kingdom Come: "The Story of God's Glory" (continued)

E. God's call to salvation and ministry involves proclamation of the message of the Kingdom through preaching, teaching, and discipling in order that others may enter and make disciples of the Kingdom.

1. To preach the good news of the Kingdom with those who do not know God, its inauguration in the Son of God and its enjoyment and demonstration in the Church, Acts 2.1-18

2. To teach and disciple the faithful in the words of Jesus so that they may be his disciples and mature as members of his body, John 8.31-32; 1 Pet. 2.2; 2 Tim. 3.16-17

3. To equip those who are members of Christ's body to do the work of the ministry in order that the Church may grow numerically and spiritually, Eph. 4.9-15

4. Offer unending praise and worship to our Lord Jesus, who invaded Satan's dominion and crushed his malicious insurrection in God's universe

5. Resolve to embody, express, and proclaim Christ's present and coming reign until he comes

Am I ready and willing to preach the Word of the Kingdom in and out of season in order that the lost may be saved, the saved may mature, and the mature may multiply the fruit of the Kingdom of God?

The Bottom Line: Are you willing to suffer for the message of the Kingdom regarding Messiah Yeshua? (See *Suffering, the Cost of Discipleship and Servant-Leadership* Appendix)

APPENDIX 34
God's Three-In-Oneness: The Trinity
Rev. Dr. Don L. Davis

The Church has not hesitated to teach the doctrine of the Trinity. Without pretending to understand, she has given her witness, she has repeated what the Holy Scriptures teach. Some deny that the Scriptures teach the Trinity of the Godhead on the ground that the whole idea of trinity in unity is a contradiction in terms; but since we cannot understand the fall of a leaf by the roadside or the hatching of a robin's egg in the nest yonder, why should the Trinity be a problem to us? "We think more loftily of God," says Michael de Molinos, "by knowing that He is incomprehensible, and above our understanding, than by conceiving Him under any image, and creature beauty, according to our rude understanding."

~ A. W. Tozer. **The Knowledge of the Holy**.
New York: Harper Collins, 1961 pp. 18-19.

"Glory be to the Father," sings the church, "and to the Son, and to the Holy Ghost." What is this? we ask—praise to three gods? No; praise to one God in three persons. As the hymn puts it, "Jehovah! Father, Spirit, Son! Mysterious Godhead! Three in One! This is the God whom Christians worship — the triune Jehovah. The heart of Christian faith in God is the revealed mystery of the Trinity. Trinitas is a Latin word meaning threeness. Christianity rests on the doctrine of the trinitas, the threeness, the tripersonality, of God.

~ J. I. Packer. **Knowing God**.
Downers Grove: InterVarsity Press, 1993. p. 65.

Questions to Ponder

- What is the relationship between understanding something and giving witness to something?

- Why do you suppose the Church's best testimony of the Trinity is captured in its hymns and worship as well as its doctrines and teachings?

- In what ways is a keen understanding of the nature of mystery so important in studying the doctrine of the Trinity?

- Why is understanding God as Trinity so important for both our own spiritual growth as well as our ministry to others?

God's Three-In-Oneness: The Trinity (continued)

Some Initial Difficulties in Pondering God as Trinity

- Beyond our ability to understand
- No earthly analogies exist
- Modernity, post-modernity, and the dominance of science: the character of our age
- Biblical illiteracy, theological novices, and no sermons

The Need for Wonder

- God is utterly incomprehensible as he is in himself.
- We must take off our sandals in the presence of such a being.
- Worship, not calculation, is the end of such reflection.

The Need for Submission

- The Scriptures are infallible as our rule of faith and practice.
- The Church's teaching must guide us true.
- Our wills, not our intellects must finally overcome our human inability to grasp that which cannot be fully grasped.

The doctrine of the Trinity is truth for the heart. The spirit of man alone can enter through the veil and penetrate into that Holy of Holies. "Let me seek Thee in longing," pleaded Anselm, "let me long for Thee in seeking; let me find Thee in love, and love Thee in finding." Love and faith are at home in the mystery of the Godhead. Let reason kneel in reverence outside.

~ A. W. Tozer. **The Knowledge of the Holy.** p. 20.

God's Three-In-Oneness: The Trinity (continued)

*All references to Erickson in this outline refer to: Millard J. Erickson, **Introducing Christian Doctrine**. Grand Rapids: Baker Books, 1992.*

I. The Biblical Basis for the Trinity (Erickson, p. 97)

A. God is ONE.

1. The unity of God is witnessed to in the Decalogue (i.e., the Ten Commandments), Exod. 20.2-4.

    a. The first commandment, Exod. 20.2-3.

    b. The second commandment, Exod. 20.4.

2. The unity of God is testified in the *Shema* of Deuteronomy 6, (the Great Commandment of Jesus), Deut. 6.4.

3. The OT witness

    a. Neh. 9.6

    b. Isa. 42.8

    c. Isa. 43.10

    d. Isa. 44.6,8

    e. Isa. 45.6,21-22

    f. Isa. 46.9

    g. Zech. 14.9

4. The NT Witness

    a. James 2.19

    b. Mark 12.29-32

    c. John 5.44

    d. John 17.3

    e. 1 Cor. 8.4,6

    f. Eph. 4.5-6

    g. 1 Tim. 2.5

God's Three-In-Oneness: The Trinity (continued)

    B. The Deity of Three is asserted (Erickson, p. 98).

    Each person of the Godhead, (Father, Son, and Holy Spirit) is described as possessing the attributes which are affirmed of God alone.

      1. The Father is God (universally asserted).

      2. The Son is God (Phil. 2.5-11; John 1.1-18; Heb. 1.1-12; John 8.58, etc.).

      3. The Holy Spirit is God (Acts 5.3-4; John 16.8-11; 1 Cor. 12.4-11; 3.16-17; Matt. 28.19; 2 Cor. 13.14).

      4. All three of these biblical personages share the same attributes together.

        a. Eternal, Rom. 16.26 with Rev. 22.13; Heb. 9.14

        b. Holy, Rev. 4.8, 15.4, Acts 3.14, 1 John 9.14

        c. True, John 7.28, John 17.3, Rev. 3.7

        d. Omnipresent, Jer. 23.24, Eph. 1.23; Ps. 139.7

        e. Omnipotent, Gen. 17.1 with Rev. 1.8; Rom.15.19; Jer. 32.17

        f. Omniscient, Acts 15.18; John 21.17; 1 Cor. 2.10-11

        g. Creator, Gen. 1.1 with Col. 1.16; Job 33.4; Ps. 148.5 with John 1.3, and Job 26.13

        h. Source of eternal life, Rom. 6.23; John 10.28; Gal. 6.8

        i. Raising Christ from the dead, 1 Cor. 6.14 with John 2.19 and 1 Pet. 3.18

    C. God as THREE?: logical inference or biblical teaching (Erickson, p. 99)

      1. Textual clues: the problem of 1 John 5.7

      2. The plural form of the noun for God: Elohim, Gen. 1.26, Isa. 6.8

      3. The Imago Dei in humankind, Gen. 1.27 with 2.24

      4. Equal naming: unity and plurality, Matt. 3.16-17; 28.19; 2 Cor. 13.14

      5. John the Apostle's threefold formula

        a. John 1.33-34

God's Three-In-Oneness: The Trinity (continued)

        b. John 14.16,26

        c. John 16.13-15

        d. John 20.21-22

    6. The assertion of Jesus' oneness with the Father

        a. John 1.1-18

        b. John 10.30

        c. John 14.9

        d. John 17.21

II. Historical Models and Arguments for the Trinity (Erickson, p. 101)

  A. The "Economic" View of the Trinity (Hippolytus and Tertullian)

    1. No attempt to explore the eternal relations among the three members of the Trinity

    2. Focus on creation and redemption: Son and Spirit are not the Father, but are inseparably with him in his eternal being

    3. Analogy: the mental functions of a human being

  B. Dynamic Monarchianism (Late 2nd and 3rd centuries)

  Monarchianism = "sole sovereignty" (stress both the uniqueness and unity of God); both views of monarchianism are seeking to preserve the idea of God's oneness and unity

    1. Originator: Theodotus

    2. God was present *in* the life of the man, Jesus of Nazareth.

    3. A working force *upon, in, or through Jesus*, but no real presence of God *within* Jesus

    4. Before his baptism, Jesus was simply an ordinary (albeit virtuous) man, cf. Matt. 3.16-17.

God's Three-In-Oneness: The Trinity (continued)

       5. At the baptism, the Spirit descended on Jesus and God's power flowed through him.

       6. This view never became popular.

  C. Modalistic Monarchianism

       1. There is one Godhead which may be designated as Father, Son, or Spirit.

       2. These terms do not stand for real distinctions of different personalities or members, but names appropriate for God's one working at different times.

       3. Father, Son, and Spirit are the identical, ongoing revelations of the same, single person.

       4. One person with three different names, activities, or roles

       5. This view insufficient to take full biblical data seriously

  D. The Orthodox Formulation (Erickson, pp.102-103)

       1. The Council of Constantinople (381) and the view of Athanasius (293-373) and the "Cappadocian fathers" (Basil, Gregory of Nazianzus, and Gregory of Nyssa)

       2. One *ousia* [substance] in three *hypostases* [persons] (a common substance but multiple, separate persons)

          a. The Godhead exists of only one essence

          b. The Godhead exists at one and the same time in three modes or beings or *hypostases* (persons)

       3. The Cappadocian focus

          a. Individual *hypostases* is the *ousia* of Godhead.

          b. Each of the persons are distinguished by the characteristics or properties unique to him (like individual humans are to universal humanity).

God's Three-In-Oneness: The Trinity (continued)

4. Not tri-theism: belief in three gods. Why?

    a. "If we can find a single activity of the Father, Son, and Holy Spirit which is in no way different in any of the three persons, we must conclude that there is but one identical substance involved" (Erickson, p.102).

    b. The persons of the Trinity may be distinguished numerically as persons, but cannot be distinguished in their essence or substance (different in persons, one in being).

III. Essential Elements, Analogies, and Implications of the Trinity (Erickson, 103)

A. Essential elements

1. God is one, not several.

2. The Father, Son, and Holy Spirit are each one divine. (Each possesses the attributes and qualities of the one true God.)

3. God's oneness and God's threeness are not, in reality, contradictory.

4. The Trinity is eternal.

5. Subordination among the persons does not suggest inferiority in their essence.

    a. The Son is subject to the Father.

    b. The Spirit is subject to the Father.

    c. The Spirit is subject to the Son as well as to the Father.

    d. This subordination is functional only; the subjection never speaks of inferiority.

6. The Trinity is incomprehensible.

God's Three-In-Oneness: The Trinity (continued)

- B. The search for analogies of the Trinity
    1. Analogies from physical nature
        a. The egg: yolk, white, and shell
        b. Water: solid, liquid, and vaporous form
        c. Suggestive not persuasive
    2. Analogies from human personality: Augustine and *De trinitate*
        a. The analogy of the individual human self-conscious personality: self-referential thinking
        b. The analogy of interpersonal human relations: twins
- C. Implications of the Doctrine of the Trinity
    1. Know God: Father, Son, and Holy Spirit
    2. Worship God: Father, Son, and Holy Spirit
    3. Pray to God: Father, Son, and Holy Spirit
    4. Obey God: Father, Son, and Holy Spirit
    5. Imitate God: Live in love, affection, and community

APPENDIX 35

God's Sovereignty and Universal Revelation
Conflicting Theories of God and the Universe
Rev. Dr. Don L. Davis

I am not trying, Lord, to penetrate your sublimity, for my understanding is not up to that. But I long in some measure to understand your truth, which my heart believes and loves. For I am not seeking to understand in order to believe, but I believe in order that I may understand. For this too I believe: that unless I believe, I shall not understand.

~ Anselm. **Proslogion** 1.
**Anselm of Canterbury, Volume 1:
Monologion, Proslogion, Debate with Gaunilo, and a Meditation on Human Redemption.**
Edited and translated by Jasper Hopkins and Herbert W. Richardson.
New York: The Edwin Mellen Press, 1975. p. 93.

The correct order is to believe the deep things of the Christian faith before undertaking to discuss them by reason. But we are negligent if, having come to a firm faith, we do not seek to understand what we believe. By God's prevenient grace, I consider myself to hold the faith of our redemption, so that even were I totally unable to understand it, nothing could shake the constancy of my belief. Please show me what, as you know, many others as well all seek to know: Why should God, who is omnipotent, have assumed the smallness and frailty of human nature in order to renew it?

~ Anselm. **Cur Deus Homo** (Boso to Anselm) 1:2.
Why God Became Man and The Virgin Conception and Original Sin,
by Anselm of Canterbury. Albany, NY: Magi Books, 1969. p. 65.

Questions to Ponder

- According to Anselm, what is the relationship between believing and understanding the truths of the Christian faith?

- Why does Anselm believe it to be wrong not to engage the truths of our Christian belief at the deepest levels of reason and argument?

- What is more critical for theological understanding: our reflection on the truth we understand or our commitment to understand the truth we do not? Explain your answer.

God's Sovereignty and Universal Revelation (continued)

I. God's Sovereignty and Revelation

    A. The definition of revelation (Erickson, p. 33)

        1. God cannot be known unless he reveals himself to us, John 6.44.

            a. We are finite, whereas God is infinite.

            b. We are sinful, whereas God is holy.

            c. We are human, whereas God is divine.

        2. General revelation

        3. Special revelation

    B. What are the "*modes*" (i.e., *the means by which*) God makes himself known to humankind in general revelation? (Erickson, p. 34)

        1. The created physical order (cf. Erickson, pp. 38-39)

            a. Ps. 19

            b. Rom. 1-2

            c. Acts 14.15-17

            d. Acts 17.22-31

        2. History

            a. Acts 2.22-24

            b. Historical preservation of Israel

        3. Human beings (capacities and qualities) *Imago Dei*

            a. Personhood: personality

            b. Intellect: reason

            c. Morality: conscience

            d. Spirituality: religious natures

---

*All references to Erickson in this outline refer to: Millard J. Erickson, **Introducing Christian Doctrine**. Grand Rapids: Baker Books, 1992.*

God's Sovereignty and Universal Revelation (continued)

C. Questions concerning general revelation

1. Is it accessible to everyone?

2. Can we all understand the implications of it?

3. Does its content actually reveal God's purposes to us?

4. Can we respond to it in saving faith?

II. **The Reality and Efficacy of General Revelation: Is it Legitimate and Effective?**

A. "Natural Theology"

1. Basic assumption #1: God has made himself known in nature.

   a. It is objectively verifiable.

   b. It is basically intact.

2. Basic assumption #2: The effects of the fall or the natural human limitations of human beings prevent them from perceiving this revelation.

3. Basic assumption #3: The order of the human mind corresponds to the order of the universe.

   a. Congruity of the mind and the world

   b. The sufficiency of the laws of logic

   c. The basic adequacy of reason alone

B. *Thomas Aquinas*: Natural Theology's theologian par excellence (Erickson, p. 35)

1. *Cosmological* argument (Erickson, p. 35)

2. *Teleological* argument (Erickson, p. 35)

3. *Anthropological* argument, (Immanuel Kant) (Erickson, p. 36)

4. *Ontological* argument, (Anselm) (Erickson, p. 36)

God's Sovereignty and Universal Revelation (continued)

C. Problems with Natural Theology

1. The proofs *may work against us*: they have leaks and cracks (Erickson, p. 37).

2. The assumptions they contain may be *unprovable* (Erickson, p. 37).

3. Some contain *logical flaws*: can you argue effectively from the observable to that which cannot be (or has not been) experienced? (Erickson, p. 37)

4. Other alternative explanations deal with the same evidence in a different way: teleology versus mutation (Erickson, p. 38).

5. Do the proofs demonstrate what kind of God that God is? (What about the existence of evil, "theodicy"?) (Erickson, p. 38)

D. John Calvin: General Revelation without Natural Theology (Erickson, p. 39)

1. The revelation of God in nature is *objective and valid*.

2. Due to human sin and limitations due to that sin, *humankind cannot adequately perceive God* in that general revelation (Erickson, p. 39).

3. *Human fallibility*, therefore, restricts the efficacy (i.e., adequateness, effectiveness) of general revelation for unregenerated humanity (Erickson, p. 40).

4. We require the "*spectacles of faith*" (Erickson, p. 40).

E. Can general revelation provide enough content for someone to be saved?

1. The case against

   a. What of personal faith in Jesus Christ?

   b. What of the Romans 10 necessity?

   c. What of the impulse to "go into all the world?" (Cf. Matt 28.18-20)

Basically, this is the view that God has given us an objective, valid, rational revelation of himself in nature, history, and human personality. It is there for anyone who wants to observe it. General revelation is not something read into nature by those who know God on other grounds; it is already present by the creation and continuing providence of God.
~ Erickson, p. 39.

God's Sovereignty and Universal Revelation (continued)

    2. The case in favor

        a. Throwing ourselves on the mercy of God

        b. The analogy with Old Testament believers

        c. Must you be conscious of the provision that has been made for your salvation to be saved?

        d. The single ground of salvation for Old Testament and the New: Christ's deliverance from the Law (Galatians 3-4)

III. The Implications of General Revelation

  A. Because of God's general revelation, all human beings share access to God's revelation of himself.

    1. We share common capacities.

    2. We share God's glorious creation.

  B. Truth about God is accessible outside of special revelation (Erickson, p. 41).

    1. This truth is objective.

    2. This truth is supplemental to special revelation from God, not a substitute for it.

  C. General revelation eliminates the claim of innocence for anyone who refuses to seek God.

    1. God's power and Godhead is known to all.

    2. Our suppression of that truth makes us all susceptible to condemnation.

  D. The reality of religion in human experience arises from general revelation.

    1. Every human community has a knowledge of God.

    2. The religious impulse is an attempt to make sense of our suppressed, unclear knowledge of God in general revelation.

God's Sovereignty and Universal Revelation (continued)

E. Biblical truth and the created order are both revelations of God, and correspond and reinforce one another (Erickson, p. 42).

1. God is the source for both kinds of revelation.

2. As sources of truth about God, they complement and supplement each other.

F. Human knowledge and human morality, to the extent that they are truth, all arise from God (Erickson, p. 42).

1. All truth everywhere in every domain is God's truth.

2. All right in every sphere mirrors God's own righteousness.

3. Human knowledge and ethical right is a "spark" from the flame of the Almighty.

APPENDIX 36
Substitution
Don L. Davis

The Principle of Substitution

Myth
Story
Narrative
Parable
Allegory
Re-enactment
Ritual
Liturgy
Remembrance
Festival

Resemblance Analogy Comparison

Metaphor
Personification
Imagery
Symbol
Representation
Type
Archetype
Simile

$$\frac{A}{B} :: \frac{C}{D}$$

"As a *shepherd* is to *sheep* so *the Lord* is to *his people*."

The Lord is my Shepherd, I shall not want for anything. ~ Psalm 23.1

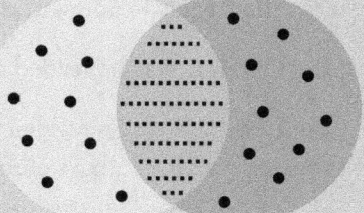

The Lord   A Shepherd

Analysis of Imagistic and Narratival Substitution

1. Main subject of discourse or religious idea
2. A concrete image or narrative derived from a cultural fund or reservoir of images and stories
3. Analogy-resemblance-comparison of selected elements or characteristics of (2) to illumine the nature of (1)
4. Implicit or explicit association, comparison, and identification of the two together
5. New understanding and experience of (1) through its association and identification with (2) representing new knowledge

Levels of Association

1. The Holy Spirit's inspiration of associations
2. The cultural fund of associations for societal meaning
3. The missiological association to communicate truth

Rules of Association

1. No analogy is perfect
2. Selection of elements to compare is critical
3. Theology explores connections and possible connections
4. Creative connection demands mastery of core images and stories

APPENDIX 37
Suffering: The Cost of Discipleship and Servant-Leadership

Don L. Davis

To be a disciple is to bear the stigma and reproach of the One who called you into service (2 Tim. 3.12). Practically, this may mean the loss of comfort, convenience, and even life itself (John 12.24-25).

All of Christ's Apostles endured insults, rebukes, lashes, and rejections by the enemies of their Master. Each of them sealed their doctrines with their blood in exile, torture, and martyrdom. Listed below are the fates of the Apostles according to traditional accounts.

- Matthew suffered martyrdom by being slain with a sword at a distant city of Ethiopia.

- Mark expired at Alexandria, after being cruelly dragged through the streets of that city.

- Luke was hanged upon an olive tree in the classic land of Greece.

- John was put in a caldron of boiling oil, but escaped death in a miraculous manner, and was afterward branded at Patmos.

- Peter was crucified at Rome with his head downward.

- James, the Greater, was beheaded at Jerusalem.

- James, the Less, was thrown from a lofty pinnacle of the temple, and then beaten to death with a fuller's club.

- Bartholomew was flayed alive.

- Andrew was bound to a cross, whence he preached to his persecutors until he died.

- Thomas was run through the body with a lance at Coromandel in the East Indies.

- Jude was shot to death with arrows.

- Matthias was first stoned and then beheaded.

- Barnabas of the Gentiles was stoned to death at Salonica.

- Paul, after various tortures and persecutions, was at length beheaded at Rome by the Emperor Nero.

APPENDIX 38
Documenting Your Work
A Guide to Help You Give Credit Where Credit Is Due
The Urban Ministry Institute

Avoiding Plagiarism

Plagiarism is using another person's ideas as if they belonged to you without giving them proper credit. In academic work it is just as wrong to steal a person's ideas as it is to steal a person's property. These ideas may come from the author of a book, an article you have read, or from a fellow student. The way to avoid plagiarism is to carefully use "notes" (textnotes, footnotes, endnotes, etc.) and a "Works Cited" section to help people who read your work know when an idea is one you thought of, and when you are borrowing an idea from another person.

Using Citation References

A citation reference is required in a paper whenever you use ideas or information that came from another person's work.

All citation references involve two parts:

- Notes in the body of your paper placed next to each quotation which came from an outside source.

- A "Works Cited" page at the end of your paper or project which gives information about the sources you have used

Using Notes in Your Paper

There are three basic kinds of notes: parenthetical notes, footnotes, and endnotes. At The Urban Ministry Institute, we recommend that students use parenthetical notes. These notes give the author's last name(s), the date the book was published, and the page number(s) on which you found the information. Example:

> In trying to understand the meaning of Genesis 14.1-24, it is important to recognize that in biblical stories "the place where dialogue is first introduced will be an important moment in revealing the character of the speaker . . ." (Kaiser and Silva 1994, 73). This is certainly true of the character of Melchizedek who speaks words of blessing. This identification of Melchizedek as a positive spiritual influence is reinforced by the fact that he is the King of Salem, since Salem means "safe, at peace" (Wiseman 1996, 1045).

Documenting Your Work (continued)

A "Works Cited" page should be placed at the end of your paper. This page:

- lists every source you quoted in your paper
- is in alphabetical order by author's last name
- includes the date of publication and information about the publisher

Creating a Works Cited Page

The following formatting rules should be followed:

1. Title

The title "Works Cited" should be used and centered on the first line of the page following the top margin.

2. Content

Each reference should list:

- the author's full name (last name first)
- the date of publication
- the title and any special information (Revised edition, 2nd edition, reprint) taken from the cover or title page should be noted
- the city where the publisher is headquartered followed by a colon and the name of the publisher

3. Basic form

- Each piece of information should be separated by a period.
- The second line of a reference (and all following lines) should be indented.
- Book titles should be underlined (or italicized).
- Article titles should be placed in quotes.

Example:

> Fee, Gordon D. 1991. *Gospel and Spirit: Issues in New Testament Hermeneutics.* Peabody, MA: Hendrickson Publishers.

Documenting Your Work (continued)

4. Special Forms

A book with multiple authors:

> Kaiser, Walter C., and Moisés Silva. 1994. *An Introduction to Biblical Hermeneutics: The Search for Meaning.* Grand Rapids: Zondervan Publishing House.

An edited book:

> Greenway, Roger S., ed. 1992. *Discipling the City: A Comprehensive Approach to Urban Mission.* 2nd ed. Grand Rapids: Baker Book House.

A book that is part of a series:

> Morris, Leon. 1971. *The Gospel According to John.* Grand Rapids: Wm. B. Eerdmans Publishing Co. The New International Commentary on the New Testament. Gen. ed. F. F. Bruce.

An article in a reference book:

> Wiseman, D. J. "Salem." 1982. In *New Bible Dictionary.* Leicester, England - Downers Grove, IL: InterVarsity Press. Eds. I. H. Marshall and others.

(An example of a "Works Cited" page is located on the next page.)

For Further Research

Standard guides to documenting academic work in the areas of philosophy, religion, theology, and ethics include:

> Atchert, Walter S., and Joseph Gibaldi. 1985. *The MLA Style Manual.* New York: Modern Language Association.

> *The Chicago Manual of Style.* 1993. 14th ed. Chicago: The University of Chicago Press.

> Turabian, Kate L. 1987. *A Manual for Writers of Term Papers, Theses, and Dissertations.* 5th edition. Bonnie Bertwistle Honigsblum, ed. Chicago: The University of Chicago Press.

Documenting Your Work (continued)

Works Cited

Fee, Gordon D. 1991. *Gospel and Spirit: Issues in New Testament Hermeneutics*. Peabody, MA: Hendrickson Publishers.

Greenway, Roger S., ed. 1992. *Discipling the City: A Comprehensive Approach to Urban Mission*. 2nd ed. Grand Rapids: Baker Book House.

Kaiser, Walter C., and Moisés Silva. 1994. *An Introduction to Biblical Hermeneutics: The Search for Meaning*. Grand Rapids: Zondervan Publishing House.

Morris, Leon. 1971. *The Gospel According to John*. Grand Rapids: Wm. B. Eerdmans Publishing Co. *The New International Commentary on the New Testament*. Gen. ed. F. F. Bruce.

Wiseman, D. J. "Salem." 1982. In *New Bible Dictionary*. Leicester, England-Downers Grove, IL: InterVarsity Press. Eds. I. H. Marshall and others.

Mentoring
The Capstone Curriculum

Before the Course Begins

- First, read carefully the Introduction of the Module found on page 5, and browse through the Mentor's Guide in order to gain an understanding of the content that will be covered in the course. The Student's Workbook is identical to your Mentor's Guide. Your guide, however, also contains a section of additional material and resources for each lesson, called *Mentor's Notes*. References to these instructions are indicated by a symbol in the margin: 📖. The Quizzes, Final Exam, and Answer Keys can all be found on the TUMI Satellite Gateway. (This is available to all approved satellites.)

- Second, you are strongly encouraged to view the teaching on both DVDs prior to the beginning of the course.

- Third, you should read any assigned readings associated with the curriculum, whether textbooks, articles or appendices.

- Fourth, it may be helpful to review the key theological themes associated with the course by using Bible dictionaries, theological dictionaries, and commentaries to refresh your familiarity with major topics covered in the curriculum.

- Fifth, please know that the students *are not tested on the reading assignments*. These are given to help the students get a fuller understanding of what the module is teaching, but it is not required that your students be excellent readers to understand what is being taught. For those of you who are receiving this module in any translation other than English, the required reading might not be available in your language. Please select a book or two that is available in your language - one that you think best represents what is being taught in this module - and assign that to your students instead.

- Finally, begin to think about key questions and areas of ministry training that you would like to explore with students in light of the content that is being covered.

Before Each Lesson

Prior to each lesson, you should once again watch the teaching content that is found on the DVD for that class session, and then create a *Contact* and *Connection* section for this lesson.

Review the Mentor's Guide to understand the lesson objectives and gather ideas for possible Contact activities. (Two to three Contacts are provided which you may use, or feel free to create your own, if that is more appropriate.)

Then, create a Contact section that introduces the students to the lesson content and captures their interest. As a rule, Contact methods fall into three general categories.

Attention Focusers capture student attention and introduce them to the lesson topic. Attention focusers can be used by themselves with motivated learners or combined with one of the other methods described below. Examples:

- Singing an opening song related to the lesson theme.

- Showing a cartoon or telling a joke that relates to an issue addressed by the lesson.

- Asking students to stand on the left side of the room if they believe that it is easier to teach people how to be saved from the Gospels and to stand on the right side if they believe it is easier to teach people from the Epistles.

Story-telling methods either have the instructor tell a story that illustrates the importance of the lesson content or ask students to share their experiences (stories) about the topic that will be discussed. Examples:

- In a lesson on the role of the pastor, a Mentor may tell the story of conducting a funeral and share the questions and challenges that were part of the experience.

- In a lesson about evangelism, the Mentor may ask students to describe an experience they have had of sharing the Gospel.

Problem-posing activities raise challenging questions for students to answer and lead them toward the lesson content as a source for answering those questions, or they may ask students to list the unanswered questions that they have about the topic that will be discussed. Examples:

- Presenting case studies from ministry situations that call for a leadership decision and having students discuss what the best response would be.

Preparing the Contact Section

- Problems framed as questions such as "When preaching at a funeral, is it more important for a minister to be truthful or compassionate? Why?"

Regardless of what method is chosen, the key to a successful Contact section is making a transition from the Contact to the Content of the lesson. When planning the Contact section, Mentors should write out a transition statement that builds a bridge from the Contact to the lesson content. For example, if the lesson content was on the truth that the Holy Spirit is a divine Person who is a full member of the Godhead, the Contact activity might be to have students quickly draw a symbol that best represents the Holy Spirit to them. After having them share their drawings and discuss why they chose what they did, the Mentor might make a transition statement along the following lines:

> *Because the Holy Spirit is often represented by symbols like fire or oil in Scripture rather than with a human image like the Father or the Son, it is sometimes difficult to help people understand that the Spirit is a full person within the Godhead who thinks, acts, and speaks as personally as God the Father or Jesus Christ. In this lesson, we want to establish the scriptural basis for understanding that the Spirit is more than just a symbol for "God's power" and think about ways that we can make this plain to people in our congregations.*

This is a helpful transition statement because it directs the students to what they can expect from the lesson content and also prepares them for some of the things that might be discussed in the Connection section that comes later. Although you may adapt your transition statement based on student responses during the Contact section, it is important, during the planning time, to think about what will be said.

Three useful questions for evaluating the Contact section you have created are:

- Is it creative and interesting?

- Does it take into account the needs and interests of this particular group?

- Does it focus people toward the lesson content and arouse their interest in it?

Again, review the Mentor's Guide to understand the lesson objectives and gather ideas for possible Connection activities.

Preparing the Connection Section

Then, create a Connection section that helps students form new associations between truth and their lives (implications) and discuss specific changes in their beliefs, attitudes, or actions that should occur as a result (applications). As you plan, be a little wary of making the Connection section overly specific. Generally this lesson section should come to students as an invitation to discover, rather than as a finished product with all the specific outcomes predetermined.

At the heart of every good Connection section is a question (or series of questions) that asks students how knowing the truth will change their thinking, attitudes, and behaviors. (We have included some Connection questions in order to "prime the pump" of your students, to spur their thinking, and help them generate their own questions arising from their life experience.) Because this is theological and ministry training, the changes we are most concerned with are those associated with the way in which the students train and lead others in their ministry context. Try and focus in on helping students think about this area of application in the questions you develop.

The Connection section can utilize a number of different formats. Students can discuss the implications and applications together in a large Mentor-led group or in small groups with other students (either open discussion or following a pre-written set of questions). Case studies, also, are often good discussion starters. Regardless of the method, in this section both the Mentor and the learning group itself should be seen as a source of wisdom. Since your students are themselves already Christian leaders, there is often a wealth of experience and knowledge that can be drawn on from the students themselves. Students should be encouraged to learn from each other as well as from the Mentor.

Several principles should guide the Connection discussions that you lead:

- First, the primary goal in this section is to bring to the surface the questions that students have. In other words, the questions that occur to students during the lesson take priority over any questions that the Mentor prepares in advance–although the questions raised by an experienced Mentor will still be a useful learning tool. A corollary to this is to assume that the question raised by one student is very often the unspoken question present among the entire group.

- Second, try and focus the discussion on the concrete and the specific rather than the purely theoretical or hypothetical. This part of the lesson is meant to focus on the actual situations that are being faced by the specific students in your classroom.

- Third, do not be afraid to share the wisdom that you have gained through your own ministry experience. You are a key resource to students and they should expect that you will make lessons you have learned available to them. However, always keep in mind that variables of culture, context, and personality may mean that what has worked for you may not always work for everyone. Make suggestions, but dialogue with students about whether your experience seems workable in their context, and if not, what adaptations might be made to make it so.

Three useful questions for evaluating the Connection section you have created are:

- Have I anticipated in advance what the general areas of implication and application are likely to be for the teaching that is given in the lesson?

- Have I created a way to bring student questions to the surface and give them priority?

- Will this help a student leave the classroom knowing what to do with the truth they have learned?

Finally, because the Ministry Project is the structured application project for the entire course, it will be helpful to set aside part of the Connection section to have students discuss what they might choose for their project and to evaluate progress and/or report to the class following completion of the assignment.

Steps in Leading a Lesson

- Take attendance.
- Lead the devotion.
- Say or sing the Nicene Creed and pray.
- Administer the quiz.
- Check Scripture memorization assignment.
- Collect any assignments that are due.

[Opening Activities]

- Use a Contact provided in the Mentor's Guide, or create your own.

[Teach the Contact Section]

- Present the Content of the lesson using the video teaching.

[Oversee the Content Section]

  Using the Video Segments
  Each lesson has two video teaching segments, each approximately 25 minutes in length. After teaching the Contact section (including the transition statement), play the first video segment for the students. Students can follow this presentation using their Student Workbook which contains a general outline of the material presented and Scripture references and other supplementary materials referenced by the speaker. Once the first segment is viewed, work with the students to confirm that the content was understood.

  Ensuring that the Content is Understood
  Segue
  Using the Mentor's Guide, check for comprehension by asking the questions listed in the "Student Questions and Response" section. Clarify any incomplete understandings that students may demonstrate in their answers.

  Ask students if there are any questions that they have about the content and discuss them together as a class. NOTE - The questions here should focus on understanding the content itself rather than on how to apply the learning. Application questions will be the focus of the upcoming Connection section.

Take a short class break and then repeat this process with the second video segment.

Teach the Connection Section

- Summary of Key Concepts
- Student Application and Implications
- Case Studies
- Restatement of Lesson's Thesis
- Resources and Bibliographies
- Ministry Connections
- Counseling and Prayer

Remind Students of Upcoming Assignments

- Scripture Memorization
- Assigned Readings
- Other Assignments

Close Lesson

- Close with prayer
- Be available for any individual student's questions or needs following the class

Please see the next page for an actual "Module Lesson Outline."

The quizzes, the final exam, and their answer keys are located at the back of this book.

Module Lesson Outline

Lesson Title — Introduction
Lesson Objectives
Devotion
Nicene Creed and Prayer
Quiz
Scripture Memorization Review
Assignments Due

Contact (1-3) — Contact

Video Segment 1 Outline — Content
Segue 1 (Student Questions and Response)
Video Segment 2 Outline
Segue 2 (Student Questions and Response)

Summary of Key Concepts — Connection
Student Application and Implications
Case Studies
Restatement of Lesson's Thesis
Resources and Bibliographies
Ministry Connections
Counseling and Prayer

Scripture Memorization — Assignments
Reading Assignment
Other Assignments
Looking Forward to the Next Lesson

Prolegomena
The Doctrine of God and the Advance of the Kingdom

MENTOR'S NOTES 1

📖 **1**
Page 13
Lesson Introduction

Welcome to the Mentor's Guide for Lesson 1, *Prolegomena: The Doctrine of God and the Advance of the Kingdom*. The overall focus of the God the Father module is to help your students come to grips with the critical ideas associated with the doctrine of God, and specifically the doctrine of God the Father Almighty. The intent of this study is not academic primarily, but to encourage your students to seek the Lord according to the truth of the Scriptures. Please try throughout this module to distinguish between knowledge about God, and the knowledge of the Lord by faith in Jesus Christ. The academic study of the Lord has its place, but it can and should never supersede or overshadow the fact that the knowledge of Scripture is to so enrich the life of the seeker that they can walk with God, and then, through that walk, become a chosen vessel through whom the Lord can work. What a wonderful blessing it is to engage in rigorous intellectual study regarding the Lord and his person! This warning is not to suggest that we ought not love the Lord with all our mind (cf. Deut. 6.4-6), but simply to warn that knowledge puffs up but love builds up (1 Cor. 8.1). May the Lord bless you as you lead these students into an exciting adventure of pondering the infinite glory of our Lord God Almighty!

📖 **2**
Page 13
Lesson Objectives

Please pay careful attention to the "Lesson Objectives" within each lesson. In some ways, this is the most significant part of the *pedagogy* of the class time. The objectives shape and give meaning to all of the various activities, and focus attention during all of the sharing, study, discussion, and even times of prayer. Hopefully you will find that the objectives are clearly stated and accessible. These aims must shape all that you as a mentor do within the class time. Make certain that you emphasize these lesson aims throughout every phase of your discussions and presentations, and bring them to your student's attentions during the quizzes, dialogues, debates, and your interactions with them. The more you can highlight the objectives throughout the class period, the better the chances are that they will understand and grasp the magnitude of these objectives.

📖 **3**
Page 13
Lesson Objectives

Again, this section summarizes the objectives for both segments, represents a snapshot of the key concepts of the lesson, and gives a plank-by-plank overview of the lesson's thesis. In everything you do, try to find ways to make these objectives come alive for the students and gauge your effectiveness by your ability to emphasize them from beginning to the end of your class period. Press these ideas strongly for, in a very real sense, these concepts lie at the center of your learning sessions for this lesson. Everything you discuss, suggest, and do ought to, in some way, point back to these objectives. Find ways to highlight these at every turn, to reinforce them and reiterate them as you go.

This devotion reaffirms the biblical testimony that the existence of the heavens and earth serve as sure evidence of God the Father Almighty's existence. Creation also serves as notice to those who pretend that no evidence exists for the reality of God in the universe. The idea of God refusing to bicker and banter around with people about his existence is a clear emphasis throughout this module. We do not study the knowledge of God in order to put God on trial, but rather to acknowledge our need of him who is both our Maker and our Lord. The idea that God needs to defend himself to his creation is a ludicrous idea in the Bible, and this devotion seeks, right from the beginning, to make plain that in the study of God, the Lord is never on trial. As Lord and Creator, all things are his, and we belong to him. Humility must govern every phase and part of what we are doing in our study of the Lord.

> Ps. 24.1-2 - The earth is the Lord's and the fullness thereof, the world and those who dwell therein, [2] for he has founded it upon the seas and established it upon the rivers.
>
> Deut. 10.14 - Behold, to the Lord your God belong heaven and the heaven of heavens, the earth with all that is in it.
>
> 1 Chron. 29.11 - Yours, O Lord, is the greatness and the power and the glory and the victory and the majesty, for all that is in the heavens and in the earth is yours. Yours is the kingdom, O Lord, and you are exalted as head above all.
>
> Job 41.11 - Who has first given to me, that I should repay him? Whatever is under the whole heaven is mine.

 4
Page 13
Devotion

📖 **5**
Page 15
Contact

All of the contacts for this lesson hone in on the notion that God is challenged in every place. He is denied as the Lord who is the first and foremost being in the universe, challenged by idols whose worshipers deny the glory of the God and Father of the Lord Jesus. Even more so, his very justice and righteousness is called into question by those who are prone to blame him for all the things that take place in this fallen world. Perhaps the greatest ministry for those called by the Lord is their need to make plain to modern people precisely what the Scriptures declare about God, who he is, what he is doing in the world, what his intentions are, how he works, and what his ultimate intention is for his creation.

📖 **6**
Page 16
Summary of Segment 1

The title of this lesson and segment, "The Doctrine of God and the Advance of the Kingdom" is explicitly seeking to connect the relationship between God as one who is revealing his rule and glory in the world and his person. In other words, seek to make the connection that the Kingdom of God (God's righteous rulership over the universe) is directly tied both to his person, and to what he reveals to us regarding his will. Without him revealing himself to humankind we would not know any of his will, and would not therefore be able to respond to his will. Being ignorant of his purposes and motives, we would simply generate, as the world does today, false foundations upon which to build life and pursue "success." In one sense, this is a wonderful way to understand the world, as one big false worldview factory that is cranking out little, unimportant, unbiblical alternative styles of life other than the one designed for us by the Lord.

> 1 John 2.15-17 - Do not love the world or the things in the world. If anyone loves the world, the love of the Father is not in him. [16] For all that is in the world—the desires of the flesh and the desires of the eyes and pride in possessions—is not from the Father but is from the world. [17] And the world is passing away along with its desires, but whoever does the will of God abides forever.

📖 **7**
Page 18
Outline Point I-B

In helping your students understand the relationship of studying the person of God and the intellectual life, you might want to use these quotes from two of the early

Christian fathers who warned about over reliance on philosophy, the intellectual life, and reason and logic to make sense of the Christian faith.

> *I both boast and strive with all my strength to be found a Christian. Not because the teachings of Plato are different from those of Christ, but because they are not totally identical. The same applies to the Stoics, poets, and historians. For each man spoke well, in proportion to the share that he had of the seminal Word, seeing what was related to it. . . . Whatever things were rightly said by any man, belong to us Christians. For next to God we worship and love the Word, who is from the unbegotten and ineffable God, since he also became man for our sakes, that by sharing in our sufferings he might also bring us healing. For all those writers were able to see reality darkly, through the seed of the implanted Word within them.*
>
> ~ Justin Martyr, 2nd century. **2 Apology 13**

> *What indeed has Athens to do with Jerusalem? What concord is there between the Academy and the Church? What have heretics to do with Christians? Our instruction comes from the porch of Solomon, who himself taught that the Lord should be sought in simplicity of heart. Away with all attempts to produce a Stoic, Platonic, and dialectic Christianity. We want no curious disputation after possessing Christ Jesus, no speculation after enjoying the Gospel. With our faith we desire no further belief. For this is our prime belief: that there is nothing more that we should believe besides.*
>
> - Tertullian, 2nd century. **Prescription of Heretics 7**

These questions are designed to ensure that your students have grasped the critical concepts covered in the first video segment. Again, a focus upon the objectives is invaluable here, since they can serve as sheep dogs to keep the herd of idle comments and thoughts in line! However you have organized your class, you will want to gauge your time carefully, making certain that you steward your time well, allowing for the necessary time to engage your students and ensure that they have a good understanding of the basic concepts. Be careful especially if your students are

📖 8
*Page 23
Student Questions
and Response*

intrigued with certain ideas and want to go on God-ordained tangents in their discussions. Allow for the proper time to focus in on the main points, and still have enough time for a break before the next video segment is started.

Page 24 Summary of Segment 2

Helping your students understand the limits of the intellect to find God is one of the most important tasks for the mentor during this module. In this we can learn from those great theologians of history. Below are two quotes from Anselm, an early bishop of the Church in the 11th century, whose opinion about God's transcendence helped him set realistic goals in his study of God the Father Almighty. Both of these quotations emphasize the need for the student of the Word of God to be humble; it is not *seeking to understand in order to believe*, but rather *believing in order to understand*.

> *I am not trying, Lord, to penetrate your sublimity, for my understanding is not up to that. But I long in some measure to understand your truth, which my heart believes and loves. For I am not seeking to understand in order to believe, but I believe in order that I may understand. For this too I believe: that unless I believe, I shall not understand.*
>
> ~ Anselm. **Proslogion** 1

> *The correct order is to believe the deep things of the Christian faith before undertaking to discuss them by reason. But we are negligent if, having come to a firm faith, we do not seek to understand what we believe. By God's prevenient grace, I consider myself to hold the faith of our redemption, so that even were I totally unable to understand it, nothing could shake the constancy of my belief. Please show me what, as you know, many others as well all seek to know: Why should God, who is omnipotent, have assumed the smallness and frailty of human nature in order to renew it?*
>
> ~ Anselm. **Cur Deus Homo (Boso to Anselm)** 1:2

This section is critical for a "snapshot" of all the key concepts covered in the video teaching segments. These truths represent the fundamental truths that the students should have mastered as they have discussed, studied, read their textbooks and materials, and gleaned from other sources for this lesson. If you want to rehearse quickly with the students the critical ideas for the lesson, this is the section that you ought to take them through. This list then becomes a handy ready-reference of the big ideas for each lesson. Make sure that these concepts are clearly defined and carefully considered, for their quiz work and exams will be taken from these items directly.

📖 **10**
Page 33
Summary of
Key Concepts

One of the most important habits to cultivate in your students is the ability to not only master the contents of various material, but to discover new contexts in which the truths just found may be applied and appropriated. Creative application of the truth demands a willingness to explore connections, to make suggested applications, to think through their own situations in order that they might engage the text with a new level of seriousness and commitment. The rule of thumb for this section is simple: *the best questions are the ones that are important to the students where they are*. What is significant here is not the questions written below, but for you, in conversation with your students, to settle on a cadre of issues, concerns, questions, and ideas that flow directly from their experience and relate to their lives and ministries. Do not hesitate to spend the majority of time on some question that arose from the video, or some special concern that is especially relevant in their ministry context right now. The goal of this section is for you to help them think critically and theologically in regards to their own lives and ministry contexts. Again, the questions below are provided as guides and primers, and ought not to be seen as absolute necessities. Pick and choose among them, or come up with your own. The key is relevance now, to their context and to their questions.

📖 **11**
Page 34
Student Application
and Implications

These case studies have been informed by experiences in real ministry situations, and reflect the kinds of applications that your students will likely encounter as they minister in the city. What is significant about them is that they are not *academically*

📖 **12**
Page 35
Case Studies

oriented. Although they include a number of questions and issues that have to do with the way in which people come to view and understand their life situation, the heart of these studies require *wisdom* in applying the truth of the Gospel to a particular situation in a specific context. Your job as mentor with the case studies is to help the students *explore the ways in which the truths they are learning can be appropriated and applied within a particular situation*. Allow them to create scenarios, and to think of the consequences of different solutions they might suggest. The goal here is to help the students begin to *think like leaders think*. Most of the application of the Word demands an openness to the Lord and an awareness of the situation so the Spirit can equip you to apply the truth well.

> 13
> Page 38
> Assignments

Your job as mentor is not necessarily to become the expert on every question that the students have, but rather to ensure that the students continue to move through the materials and the assignments. Make sure that you know ahead of time what is demanded of the students for the next week, and always have available the appropriate information and materials they will need to complete their assignments for next week. This is highly important work for their learning experience, and, thankfully, it is not difficult to do.

In regards to their reading assignments, remind your students that the goal is that they read the material as best as they can, and then write a few sentences on what they believe the author was trying to communicate. While we do not base the learning of the module on the texts, it is nevertheless a critical intellectual skill for your students to learn to process the thoughts of others. So, spend good time encouraging their efforts in this process. Of course, for those students who might find it difficult or impossible to finish the assignments, assure them of *the intent behind this assignment*, and emphasize their participation in the class as the key to their learning, not their reading or writing skills *per se*. While we are praying for and will work hard to help each student improve these skills, we want to emphasize the interactions among the students and the Scriptures as the heart of the course. Even in light of this, let's not sell our students short. Strike to find the midpoint between challenge and encouragement here.

God as the Creator
The Providence of God

MENTOR'S NOTES 2

📖 1
Page 43
Lesson Introduction

Welcome to the Mentor's Guide for Lesson 2, *God as the Creator: The Providence of God*. In this important lesson your aim will be to help your students comprehend some of the ways in which God the Father Almighty exercises his sovereign rulership over his creation. An abundance of biblical texts speak to God's oversight, his protection, preservation, and governance of the world by his power and wisdom.

Just a few texts of Scripture are enough to whet our appetites regarding the remarkable oversight of our sovereign God over his creation.

> Ps. 135.5-7 - For I know that the Lord is great, and that our Lord is above all gods. [6] Whatever the Lord pleases, he does, in heaven and on earth, in the seas and all deeps. [7] He it is who makes the clouds rise at the end of the earth, who makes lightnings for the rain and brings forth the wind from his storehouses.

> 1 Chron. 16.31 - Let the heavens be glad, and let the earth rejoice, and let them say among the nations, "The Lord reigns!"

> Ps. 33.14-15 - . . . from where he sits enthroned he looks out on all the inhabitants of the earth, [15] he who fashions the hearts of them all and observes all their deeds.

> Ps. 47.7 - For God is the King of all the earth; sing praises with a psalm!

As you lead the students through these and other related truths, make certain that you enable them to see that these truths should lead them to marvel at the person of God, to worship him, to acknowledge in their lives that the God and Father of our Lord Jesus is God, deserving of praise and honor.

This lesson especially is critical for those serving the Lord in the midst of difficult situations and circumstances, who live in times where it seems as if evil is winning, God's power is absent and the forces of evil are large and crushing. As you emphasize your objectives in this lesson, try to keep a mental tally of how you might guide the discussions to enable your students to apply the truths of God's providence during times and periods of suffering and loss. This has special applications for us in urban ministry and in urban neighborhoods.

W.B. Pope puts the importance of providence in the study of religion when he says:

> *Providence is the most comprehensive term in the language of theology. It is the background of all the several departments of religious truth, a background mysterious in its commingled brightness and darkness. It penetrates and fills the whole compass of the relations of man with his Maker. It connects the unseen God with the visible creation, and the visible creation with the work of redemption, and redemption with personal salvation, and personal salvation with the end of all things. It carries our thoughts back to the supreme purpose which was in the beginning with God, and forward to the foreseen end and consummation of all things, while it includes between these the whole infinite variety of the dealings of God with man.*
>
> ~ W. B. Pope. **Compendium of Christian Theology**, I. p. 456.

Such a comprehensive subject demands both our hard work, and our humility.

This devotion focuses on the greatness of our God in his unlimited rulership and ownership of all things. God's oversight of the world includes all beings and things, it encompasses the tiniest flea to the largest sperm whale, and touches the whiskers on our face to the furthest galaxy trillions and trillions of trillions of miles away. The care of God is like his nature–infinite and remarkable. Psalm 145 offers a good synopsis and summary of the extraordinary providence of God over all things in the universe:

> Ps. 145.9-13 - The Lord is good to all, and his mercy is over all that he has made. [10] All your works shall give thanks to you, O Lord, and all your saints shall bless you! [11] They shall speak of the glory of your kingdom and tell of your power, [12] to make known to the children of man your mighty deeds, and the glorious splendor of your kingdom. [13] Your kingdom is an everlasting kingdom, and your dominion endures throughout all generations. [The Lord is faithful in all his words and kind in all his works.]

📖 **2**
Page 43
Devotion

There can only be one God, one true and living Creator of the ends of the earth. The God and Father of our Lord Jesus Christ, YHWH, the Father Almighty is this true Lord. Singular, unique, and magnificent, and now, our God by faith in Jesus Christ.

📖 **3**
Page 45
Quiz

In reviewing the quizzes with the students always focus on the main concepts that the questions were aiming to uncover. Beware of the tendency for students to want to rehash the quiz, arguing for their points or calling into question the validity of the very question itself. What is critical to know is that the quizzes are an *instrument of review*. The truths are the issue, and if they master the truths they will certainly know the answers. As simple as this may seem, it is an idea that is oftentimes lost on students.

📖 **4**
Page 46
Contact

These contacts focus on the idea of God's presence and control of situations and issues that fly out of control. If there is one constancy about the nature of urban life and ministry it is that *there is no such thing as constancy*. Many urbanites live in situations where they are constantly in danger, experiencing unjust and oftentimes horrendous things, with no sign that anyone cares or is even aware of their pain. To study the subject of the providence of God among urban people is to ask the questions of *theodicy*, an idea of why do horrific things happen to good people. Explore with the students the ideas of God's providence as a lead in to investigating some of the biblical evidence on the subject.

📖 **5**
Page 53
Student Questions and Response

Your intent during this section is to ensure that the students understand the general outline of the teaching of Scripture regarding the providence of God as was covered in the first video segment. In some ways the difficulty to comprehend the sovereign providence of the Father is normal for us; how can any mind come to understand God's ultimate intention to bring the entire creation under his sway, to fulfill his own high purpose for creation, which is nothing less than the establishment of his kingdom rule throughout the entire universe (Eph. 1.9-11; Col. 1.19-20).

Help the students review the teaching of the video in order that they may have a mastery of the foundational concepts covered within it. Concentrate on ensuring that the students understand the answers in light of the lesson aims of the first segment. This kind of review is critical for them to build on their understanding of these truths as they go. As always, be careful in your use of time, giving attention to the key ideas and watching out for any side roads or ditches which may lead you from rehearsing the critical facts and main points of the providence of God.

In reviewing with the students the truths for this segment, make sure to review with them a quick overview of the some of the alternative theories surrounding the existence of a God of providence in the world.

The atheistic or materialistic view holds that no God exists, and that the material universe is eternal. This is the popular view of atheistic evolution which would say that the material universe possessed within itself the needed properties that produced the heavens and the earth through the long process of evolution.

The pantheistic view says that God is everything and everything is God. This view holds that the universe is like the very "living garment" of God, who is the soul of the universe, which is the physical creation of his form. In this view God is equated with the universe itself, and differs little with the basic materialistic views of the universe.

The deistic view holds that God does exist, that he made all things, but that he created them so they need neither his involvement nor oversight in their continuance. God made the material world subject to certain unchanging laws which they obey, but humankind maintains their personal freedom as a "rational and morally free agent." The clock maker analogy is used often to explain this view: God is to creation as a clock-maker is to his timepiece. God made the clock, wound it up, and left it alone. God is the Great Uninvolved in human affairs; true religion by this view is only natural religion. Nature's laws and processes are the highest we can go to understand the person and influence of this absentee God.

📖 **6**
*Page 63
Student Questions
and Response*

As you explore the meanings of the second segment, make sure that you help the students wrestle with the way in which a biblical understanding of the providence of God provides insight into how we may engage and refute the many alternatives to the simple Bible declaration that the Father Almighty oversees his universe.

Page 66
Case Studies

All of these case studies seek to unearth some of the objections to the biblical doctrine of the providence of God. In an age of mass violence, run amok science, and brash sensualism, it is hard to assert sometimes that "our God reigns." The natural result of making this assumption in the face of such naked aggression and terrible cruelty is to ask precisely *how does God reign*. To discuss these ideas is critical, for without having at least a context in which to discuss them, there can be no way of answering the objections. Students today must learn to obey 1 Peter 3.15 and be ready always to give an answer to those who ask them about the hope that they have within themselves.

Again, the goal for your students is the ability to grapple with the truth of God and to make clear how the objections and rebuttals of those who reject the biblical worldview can be answered. The desire here is not to *argue down* our enemies but rather to *make the truth so plain that the naysayer must at least acknowledge the validity of the truth of Scripture*. Frankly, conversion is God's responsibility, articulating the truth so others can understand its claims clearly is ours:

> Ps. 119.46 - I will also speak of your testimonies before kings and shall not be put to shame.

> Col. 4.6 - Let your speech always be gracious, seasoned with salt, so that you may know how you ought to answer each person.

> 2 Tim. 2.25 - . . . correcting his opponents with gentleness. God may perhaps grant them repentance leading to a knowledge of the truth.

At the core of this module is the need to grapple with the difference between what the Scriptures assert on behalf of God's people and *what appears to be taking place in their lives*. This issue, this struggle, animates much of the discussion and activity of those who share the Good News with urban dwellers, many of whose lives are a constant burden and pain. What are urban ministers to say to those whose lives appear to be ravaged and hurting, exposed to every kind of pain and destruction imaginable?

As ministers of the grace of God in Christ, they must learn to so understand the providence of God that they can testify of God's love, and yet, also speak of the existence of the world, the flesh, and the devil, and their ability to interfere and resist the good will of God. This struggle and conflict is at the heart of any valid urban theology, making plain how the good providence of God can answer the challenges and needs faced by those who live in the dangerous cities of the world. Keep this cardinal duty in mind as you seek to lead the students into open dialogue about the Word of God.

Pray for your students every chance you have, during the week or during the class session. Never take prayer for granted; in every way, prayer can dramatically impact your students. The Word of God is clear that the Holy Spirit can teach them and lead them into the truth:

> 1 John 2.20 - But you have been anointed by the Holy One, and you all have knowledge.

> 1 John 2.27 - But the anointing that you received from him abides in you, and you have no need that anyone should teach you. But as his anointing teaches you about everything—and is true and is no lie, just as it has taught you—abide in him.

> 1 John 4.13 - By this we know that we abide in him and he in us, because he has given us of his Spirit.

> 1 Cor. 2.13 - And we impart this in words not taught by human wisdom but taught by the Spirit, interpreting spiritual truths to those who are spiritual.

*8
Page 67
Restatement of the Lesson's Thesis*

*9
Page 68
Counseling and Prayer*

1 Thess. 2.13 - And we also thank God constantly for this, that when you received the word of God, which you heard from us, you accepted it not as the word of men but as what it really is, the word of God, which is at work in you believers.

Expect the Holy Spirit to lead the students into all truth as they discuss and explore the Word of God together. Never consider it overly familiar or an unnecessary thing to ask the students if they need prayer for someone or something connected to the ideas and truths presented in the lesson. Prayer is a wonderfully practical and helpful way to apply truth; by taking specific needs to God in light of a truth, the students can solidify those ideas in their soul, and receive back from the Lord the answers they need in order to be sustained in the midst of their ministries.

Of course, everything is somehow dependent on the amount of time you have in your session, and how you have organized it. Still, prayer is a forceful and potent part of any spiritual encounter and teaching, and if you can, it should always have its place, even if it is a short summary prayer of what God has taught us, and a determination to live out its implications as the Holy Spirit teaches us.

The Triune God
The Greatness of God

Page 73
Lesson Introduction

Welcome to the Mentor's Guide for Lesson 3, *The Triune God: The Greatness of God*. The overall focus of this lesson is twofold. In the first segment, we will introduce to the students the idea of the Trinity, the biblical concept relating to the triune nature of God as Father, Son, and Holy Spirit. The second segment concentrates on the *greatness* of the first person of the Trinity, God the Father Almighty. In it we explore the various attributes associated with the eternal glory and splendor of God the Father. Both of these topics are comprehensive, and cannot possibly be covered fully in the time frames allotted to us by the video teaching. What is possible, however, is that we provide a skeleton outline of the major issues associated with both of these interrelated doctrines which will allow the students to continue their study of these important subjects in the months and years to come.

As you lead your students to engage the teaching of the Trinity, seek to keep in mind four simple ideas that can guide you as you discuss this important doctrine with them.

First, *remember that God is one God*. There are not two Gods in the Bible, one in the Old Testament and the other in the New Testament. The same God is in both testaments, and the nature of God receives a fuller and more comprehensive display in the New Testament through Jesus Christ, who provides a complete and comprehensive knowledge of the Father to us (cf. John 1.14-18).

Second, God *reveals himself to us in three distinct personalities all involved in the salvation event, and yet God remains one undivided unity*. As you will see as you explore the texts in this lesson, that the Father reveals himself in the Son and Spirit without in any way ever melding personality with them, or they as persons with the Father's person. The Godhead is diverse yet unified.

Third, *we can grasp the Trinity best as we understand the role of each person in the plan of salvation*. The Father purposes, the Son executes, and the Spirit applies the blessing of redemption in the believer and in the Church. The New Testament doesn't speculate about the essence of the Godhead, but rather reveals what each person does in regards to the salvation won for us through Christ.

Fourth, *the scriptural doctrine of the Trinity cannot be plumbed by an appeal to logic and analysis alone; it remains for us an absolute mystery*. While there have been numerous attempts to make plain the meaning of the biblical teaching of the Trinity, it simply ought not surprise us that no human explanation can fully comprehend the glory and splendor of the nature of the persons of the Godhead, Father, Son, and Holy Spirit. As you and your students explore the Word of God in this lesson, I trust that you will allow both your humility and your diligence to express themselves in this study. Undoubtedly, both will be needed!

This devotion focuses on the *absolute mystery* in seeking to comprehend the Lord as a tri-unity.

Although the term *trinity* is not found in the Bible, it has become the term coined to make plain the teaching of Scripture of God's unity subsisting in three distinct Persons. This term comes from the Greek word *trias*, and was first used by Theophilus (A.D. 168-183). Another use came from the Christian apologist and advocate Tertullian (A.D. 220), who was the first to use the Latin term *trinitas* to lay out this doctrine.

While in the immediate post-biblical era believers in the Church sought to explain the doctrine of God's tri-unity in terms and language that was compelling and coherent philosophically, the use of various Greek ideas helped only some to make sense of God's nature. It appears that the Church has tended to shift from the plain confessions of the New Testament on how the Father, Son, and Holy Spirit act in salvation to more abstract discussions about the precise nature of the Godhead's very inner working. While such efforts are valiant, they cannot possibly provide final understandings of the Trinity.

I believe that there is another way, a simpler way. We can appeal to mystery and faith. The Trinity as a doctrine is not the result of trying to use Greek ideas to explain the God of Abraham. Rather, it comes from wrestling with the meaning of the Old and New Testament Scriptures which speak of a God who manifests himself in three persons, Father, Son, and Holy Spirit, and yet does not in any way assert himself as three gods, or as one God who takes three different forms for various purposes. This great God of Scripture reveals himself in Christ, who by the Holy Spirit fulfilled the purposes of his Father for the sake of saving the world.

2
Page 73
Devotion

David's testimony in the little Psalm 131 is a veritable gold mine of insight for us as we seek to delve into the depths of the Lord's own person:

> Ps. 131.1-3 - O Lord, my heart is not lifted up; my eyes are not raised too high; I do not occupy myself with things too great and too marvelous for me. [2] But I have calmed and quieted my soul, like a weaned child with its mother; like a weaned child is my soul within me. [3] O Israel, hope in the Lord from this time forth and forevermore.

Let us then assert the plain language of the Bible: God is one.

> Deut. 6.4 - Hear, O Israel: The Lord our God, the Lord is one.

> 1 Kings 8.60 - . . . that all the peoples of the earth may know that the Lord is God; there is no other.

> Isa. 44.6 - Thus says the Lord, the King of Israel and his Redeemer, the Lord of hosts: "I am the first and I am the last; besides me there is no god."

But let us also assert that Jesus is the Word made flesh (John 1.14), and affirm the Holy Spirit as Lord and life-giver to the Church (2 Cor. 3.17-18).

Let's allow the authors of our textbooks to have the last word here:

> *The Church has not hesitated to teach the doctrine of the Trinity. Without pretending to understand, she has given her witness, she has repeated what the Holy Scriptures teach. Some deny that the Scriptures teach the Trinity of the Godhead on the ground that the whole idea of trinity in unity is a contradiction in terms; but since we cannot understand the fall of a leaf by the roadside or the hatching of a robin's egg in the nest yonder, why should the Trinity be a problem to us? "We think more loftily of God," says Michael de Molinos, "by knowing that he is incomprehensible, and above our understanding, than by conceiving him under any image, and creature beauty, according to our rude understanding."*

> ~ A.W. Tozer. **The Knowledge of the Holy.** New York: Harper San Francisco, 1961. p. 18-19.

"Glory be to the Father," sings the Church, "and to the Son, and to the Holy Ghost." What is this? we ask—praise to three gods? No; praise to one God in three persons. As the hymn puts it, "Jehovah! Father, Spirit, Son! Mysterious Godhead! Three in One!" This is the God whom Christians worship — the triune Jehovah. The heart of Christian faith in God is the revealed mystery of the Trinity. Trinitas is a Latin word meaning threeness. Christianity rests on the doctrine of the trinitas, the threeness, the tripersonality, of God.

~ J.I.Packer. **Knowing God**.
Downers Grove: InterVarsity Press, 1993. p. 65.

In a time where formal teaching of God's revelation concerning himself is considered "theological baggage," it is important to remind the students of what is at stake in right belief about God. Both of their texts affirm the importance of seeing and understanding God aright, in sync with what he has revealed himself to be to us. Our responsibility is to discover God as he is, and not as we think him to be, and want him to be.

That our idea of God correspond as nearly as possible to the true being of God is of immense importance to us. Compared with our actual thoughts about him, our creedal statements are of little consequence. Our real idea of God may lie buried under the rubbish of conventional religious notions and may require an intelligent and vigorous search before it is finally unearthed and exposed for what it is. Only after an ordeal of painful self-absorbing are we likely to discover what we actually believe about God.

~ A.W. Tozer. **The Knowledge of the Holy**.
New York: Harper San Francisco, 1961. p.2.

One can know a great deal about God without much knowledge of him. I am sure that many of us have never really grasped this. We find in ourselves a deep interest in theology (which is, of course, a most fascinating and intriguing subject — in the seventeenth century it was every gentleman's hobby). We read books of theological exposition and apologetics. We dip into Christian history, and study the Christian *creed. We learn to find our way around in the Scriptures. Others appreciate our interest in these things, and we find ourselves asked to give our opinion in public on this or that question, to lead study groups, to give papers, to write articles, and generally to accept responsibility, informal if not formal, for acting as teachers and arbiters of orthodoxy in our own Christian circle. Our friends tell us how much they value our contribution, and this spurs us to further explorations of God's truth, so that we may be equal to the demands made upon us. All very fine — yet interest in theology, and knowledge about God, and the capacity to think clearly and talk well on Christian themes, is not at all the same thing as knowing him. We may know as much about God as Calvin knew — indeed, if we study his works diligently, sooner or later we shall — and yet all the time (unlike Calvin, may I say) we hardly know God at all.*

~ J. I. Packer. **Knowing God.**
Downers Grove: InterVarsity Press, 1993. p. 26.

Remind the students that what is at stake in trinitarian study is quite literally *our very knowledge of God as he has revealed himself to us*. It means that everything is at stake in studying God as he is.

📖 4
*Page 88
Student Questions
and Response*

Tozer's claims regarding the trinity are as true today as the first moment he thought and penned the following words:

The doctrine of the Trinity is truth for the heart. The spirit of man alone can enter through the veil and penetrate into that Holy of Holies. "Let me seek Thee in longing," pleaded Anselm, "let me long for Thee in seeking; let me find Thee in love, and love Thee in finding." Love and faith are at home in the mystery of the Godhead. Let reason kneel in reverence outside.

- A.W. Tozer. **The Knowledge of the Holy.**
New York: Harper San Francisco, 1961. p. 20.

Your discussion of the truths regarding the Trinity should concentrate not on trying to solve the mystery of the Godhead, but understanding the "lay of the land" so to speak in biblical and theological studies concerning the Trinity. Focus on the major points of trinitarian doctrine: the unity of God, three persons sharing the same substance in the Godhead, the distinctiveness of the members of the Trinity. By focusing on the main points you can set a framework in which we not only help the students to master this data, but will also give them a way to study this important subject in the future.

To cover the *greatness* of God the Father Almighty in a session is either revolutionary or fool-hardy, or both! There is no way that the second video segment, which sought in thirty minutes to cover a skeleton outline of the great attributes of our God, could possibly go in-depth and feed upon these great truths. The purpose of this segment is to show the greatness of our Father, and through that, to be moved to praise and worship him with our very lives. The greatness of the Lord is to be answered by our worship and our obedience and awe.

> Ps. 145.3 - "Great is the Lord, and greatly to be praised, and his greatness is unsearchable."

> Ps. 48.1 - "Great is the Lord and greatly to be praised in the city of our God! His holy mountain."

> Ps. 96.4 - "For great is the Lord, and greatly to be praised; he is to be feared above all gods."

> Ps. 147.5 - "Great is our Lord, and abundant in power; his understanding is beyond measure."

> Rev. 15.3 - "And they sing the song of Moses, the servant of God, and the song of the Lamb, saying, 'Great and amazing are your deeds, O Lord God the Almighty! Just and true are your ways, O King of the nations!'"

> Ps. 147.5 - "Great is our Lord, and abundant in power; his understanding is beyond measure."

As you discuss the concept of God's greatness with the students, covering the critical ideas, be sure to emphasize this notion of greatness. Also, refer the students to the appendix on the *Names of God* as it highlights in a different way the glorious nature of the infinitely lovely and glorious Father. Make sure that the students

□ 5
*Page 99
Student Questions
and Response*

understand the various attributes and can provide common language explanations for these qualities of God.

📖 **6**
Page 103
Case Studies

These case studies seek to explore the significance of belief in God as Trinity for both life and ministry. Help the students consider what is at stake in someone denying the truth of the Scriptures regarding the person of God, and help them define the boundaries of what is considered acceptable in terms of different beliefs regarding the Trinity.

📖 **7**
Page 106
Assignments

By the end of the second class session, you ought to have mentioned to the students the need for them to have given some thought and spadework to their Ministry Project. Now, by the end of the third lesson, you should also have emphasized their need to select a passage for their Exegetical Project. Both of these assignments tend to "creep up on" the students at the end of the course, so make sure that you emphasize with them the work to be done, the standards for doing it, and the dates when the work will be due. Give them proper notice on the final and any other assignments, and exhort them to be organized and ready for the work ahead.

Do not fail to emphasize these matters to your students for, as in all study, the end of the course is hectic, with many things becoming due and the students feeling the pressure to do many things at once to meet due dates. Any way that you can remind them of the need for advanced planning will be wonderfully helpful for them, whether they realize it immediately or not.

Because of this, we advocate that you consider docking a modest amount of points for late papers, exams, and projects. While the amount may be nominal, your enforcement of your rules will help them to learn to be efficient and on time as they continue in their studies.

God as Father
The Goodness of God

Page 109
Lesson Introduction

Welcome to the Mentor's Guide for Lesson 4, *God as Father: The Goodness of God*. The overall focus of the God the Father module is to understand in the first segment the manifold wonder and blessing of God's goodness to us. In a way completely opposite the definition of the Greek notion of "the good" as a kind of ethical ideal, the biblical view grows out of a sense of the personal self-revelation of God as one who is kind and gracious, and who concretely demonstrates that goodness to all creation. Scripture wholeheartedly affirms that YHWH is both good and does good to all his universe, (1 Chron. 16.34; Ps. 119.68). The goodness of the Lord is associated with his very name (Ps. 52.9), all his promises (Jos. 21.45), his gracious commands and gifts (Ps. 119.39; Rom. 7.12; James 1.17), and all of his works as he shapes and oversees all of history for his own purposes (Gen. 50.20; Rom. 8.28). The very creation itself was fashioned in light of his goodness (Gen. 1.31), and in all of his great acts of redemption and salvation he proves himself to be good to his people. For instance, he was good in his liberation of Israel from Egypt (Exod. 18.9), and good in his drawing them back to himself after the return of a remnant from captivity (Ezra 7.9).

Furthermore, God's goodness is intrinsic to himself, being demonstrated in his deliverance of his saints (Ps. 34.8), to the very salvation he provides to those who believe in Christ (Phil. 1.6). In a very real sense, God alone can be designated as truly good (Ps. 14.1, 3; Mark 10.18). In this segment our intent is to give the students a working outline of the biblical understanding of God's marvelous goodness expressed in his moral attributes of his perfect moral purity, absolute integrity, and unbounded love. The goodness of God's perfect moral purity is expressed through his holiness, righteousness, and justice, while the goodness of his integrity is displayed in his genuineness, veracity, and faithfulness. Finally, we will see how the goodness of God's eternal love is seen in his benevolence, grace, mercy, and persistence.

In the second segment we will look at the severity of God against the backdrop of his goodness. We will explore the wrath of God against all ungodliness and evil. In the Old Testament, God's wrath is manifested against sin and injustice (Num. 11.10), against idolatry (Ps. 78.56-66), and against those who reject and resist his good, perfect, and acceptable will (Deut. 1.26-46; Josh. 7.1; Ps. 2.1-6). A day is yet to come where the Lord will display in apocalyptic fashion his wrath unleashed on the world, called "the great day of the Lord (cf. Zeph. 1.14-15; Isa. 13.9). In the New Testament, Jesus reaffirms the prospect of God the Father Almighty pouring out his wrath on those who reject his will (cf. Luke 16.19-31). The consequences of rejecting God's knowledge is terrifying and drastic (Luke 13.3, 5; John 15.1-11; Matt. 3.7). Faith in Jesus Christ averts the believer from the sure and certain prospect of suffering God's wrath for those who reject God's offer in him (1 Thess. 1.10; Rom. 1.18-32; Eph. 2.2).

The only conceivable way to understand God's goodness and severity is together. In other words, any attempt to describe or depict God as either one or the other is a kind of dialectical thinking that the Bible itself rejects. In the first segment we will explore God's goodness, and in the next segment we will ponder the wrath of God. If there be any confusion or tension in our study, rest assured it will be in our inability to *comprehend them together and simultaneously*, and not in the actual demonstration of God's perfections as our God and king.

Again, please notice the objectives. As usual, your responsibility as Mentor is to emphasize these concepts throughout the lesson, especially during the discussions and interaction with the students. The more you can highlight the objectives throughout the class period, the better the chances are that they will understand and grasp their magnitude.

There appears to be a malady in those who study the attributes of God, one which tends to infect virtually every exegete of Scripture unless they are particularly careful to notice it. What is it? Most interpreters of the attributes of God tend to emphasize one attribute of God to the exclusion or underemphasis of another. This kind of study is, in my mind, built into the idea of looking at the infinitely beautiful character of God as *elements* or as *parts*. While we may, for the sake of study and analysis, speak of God's attributes like a list or collection of perfections, the truth is that God cannot be spliced up into elements. When God acts, he acts in unity with his own perfections and without any confusion or conflict between and among his own qualities. His being is like the seamless garment of our Lord; there are no parts,

📖 2
Page 109
Devotion

sections, elements, or divisions in his mighty character. When God works, his works are in perfect harmony with his will and his being. He is Lord.

Not able to conceive of God as a unity, we tend to isolate parts and then speak authoritatively on the parts without reference to the other great qualities which make up his being. The result oftentimes is a skewed and unbiblical view of God which creates false and unnecessary tensions in our thinking about God, which in fact do not exist.

The challenge for every true student of God is to cultivate an awareness that, when it comes to the study of the Father (or, for that matter, any member of the Trinity) *the analysis is not the person*. While we may analyze God through the attributes, we ought not think that God can be spliced and analyzed like a novel or a car engine. As the living Lord of all, filled with numberless attributes expressing his greatness and goodness, he acts as a unity, subsisting in three persons, working out his will for his own purposes with perfect wisdom and patience. Let us never in our arrogance think that God must conform to our analysis. Rather, may God give us the grace not to be fooled, not to deceive ourselves in pretending that God must conform to our mind. The nature of the wicked mind is to pretend that God acts and thinks just like them (cf. Ps. 50.21 - "These things you have done, and I have been silent; you thought that I was one like yourself. But now I rebuke you and lay the charge before you."

Give God room to surprise you by his fresh revelations of his whole being, and not just the part you tend to gravitate to. He is Lord!

3
Page 113
Summary of
Segment 1

Your procedure for covering these attributes associated with the goodness of God should correspond to what you did in covering the attributes on the greatness of God. In other words, the goal of this segment is to provide an outline that the students can use to get a "bird's eye view" of the scholarly understanding of God's goodness. The richness and depth that each of the attributes demands, the care and rigor, cannot be given here. What can be done, however, is to seek to enable the students to comprehend the overall picture of theological discussion regarding God's moral attributes, and script out a direction for their future studies. Please make certain that you alert your students to the goal of the segment, and the intent of the material in this segment.

Make sure as you approach these questions that you 1) keep in mind that the goal here is to help them review the main points associated with the first video segment and its defining of the outline of God's moral attributes, and 2) ensure that the students are inoculated against the reductive malady of isolating God to a core of attributes to the exclusion or underemphasis of others. Remind them of the need to know that while intellectually we can consider the elements separately, in real time our glorious God is one.

> Deut. 6.4 - "Hear, O Israel: The Lord our God, the Lord is one."

> Isa. 45.5-6 - "I am the Lord, and there is no other, besides me there is no God; I equip you, though you do not know me, [6] that people may know, from the rising of the sun and from the west, that there is none besides me; I am the Lord, and there is no other."

Exhort the students to remember that God is one, and acts in perfect harmony with all of his attributes simultaneously.

*4
Page 128
Student Questions and Response*

The challenge to entertain the idea of God's wrath as we consider his goodness is not something that is encouraged in many church settings today. The absence of this tendency has produced a generation of Christians who are theologically and ethically out of sync, wobbling through life because they focus only on those attributes which seem to resonate with their own experience and interests, and systematically turn their backs on those that don't.

The key in discussing this with the students is challenging directly their right to pick and choose what characteristics of the Godhead they wish to focus upon and emphasize. No Christian has the right to parse through the Bible, skipping and dipping around to the texts that suit their fancy, while racing over or deliberately ignoring the "hard sayings" of the Bible.

*5
Page 138
Student Questions and Response*

As you review these last questions, make sure that you remind the students of this ever-present need to receive the revelation of God as he gives it, and not as we want to hear it.

Remember Jesus' rebuke of Peter at Caesarea Philippi:

> Matt. 16.21-23 - "From that time Jesus began to show his disciples that he must go to Jerusalem and suffer many things from the elders and chief priests and scribes, and be killed, and on the third day be raised. [22] And Peter took him aside and began to rebuke him, saying, 'Far be it from you, Lord! This shall never happen to you.' [23] But he turned and said to Peter, 'Get behind me, Satan! You are a hindrance to me. For you are not setting your mind on the things of God, but on the things of man.'"

📖 **6**
Page 140
Case Studies

Through the case studies in this lesson, attempt to help the students grapple with the notion of God's wrath and the various ways that people in the world and the Church today are conceiving it. As they learn more and more what the Scriptures teach in regard to the person of God the Father Almighty, they will have to grow in their ability to engage and refute the different ideas of God which are out of sync with his own self revelation in the Scriptures.

While the tendency is present for many to think that the doctrine of God is not practical, nothing could be further from the truth. These cases were designed to help your students come to terms with contemporary perspectives about God and his wrath, and the way in which they process the questions and the answers they give will have great impact on the effect of their ministries in the future.

📖 **7**
Page 143
Assignments

Congratulations, you have mentored the module on God the Father, but you haven't completed your task just yet! Your work as an instructor and grader begins in earnest now.

Make sure that you have communicated all the necessary information about due dates and assignments to the students, and that you have secured from them commitments for the ministry projects, exegetical projects, and any other data that will be important for you to determine the student's overall grade. Again, your discretion regarding late work can easily determine whether you dock students of points, resulting in letter grade changes, or give students an "Incomplete" until the work is finished. However you adopt your standard regarding their work, remember that our courses are not primarily about the grades that students receive, but the spiritual nourishment and training these courses provide. Also, however, remember that helping our students strive for excellence is an integral part of our instruction.

On behalf of your students and the Lord, we congratulate you on your efforts. May the Lord deeply bless your investment in these dear sisters and brothers, to the honor and glory of the great and good God, the Father Almighty.

Amen!

www.ingramcontent.com/pod-product-compliance
Lightning Source LLC
Chambersburg PA
CBHW080730300426
44114CB00019B/2538